D1189584

A Theatre of Disguise

A Theatre of Disguise

Studies in French Baroque Drama

(1630 – 1660)

by

John D. Lyons

French Literature Publications Company
Columbia, South Carolina
1978

173896

Et affin qu'on ne se mocque pas de moy, si dans
cette application je compare la Poésie aux
songes, qu'est elle après tout que la resverie
d'un esprit tranquille, une chose douce, vaine,
diverse et chimérique, comme la pluspart des
songes, et qui s'attribuë je ne sçay quoy de
divin aussi bien qu'eux?

—Vion D'Alibray, Au lecteur
de Torrismon (1636)

Acknowledgments

I owe much to the work of many scholars who have led me through the labyrinths of the seventeenth century, but I have a special debt to teachers and colleagues who have encouraged and advised me at different stages of my work. Jean Boorsch, Jacques Guicharnaud, André Winandy, Paul Newman, David Sices, and Lawrence E. Harvey have read all or part of the manuscript and made many useful criticisms. Victor Brombert gave invaluable advice about the general form of the study, and Stephen G. Nichols, Jr. provided the encouragement that got me through the last stages of the work.

The editors of *Neophilologus* kindly consent to the publication of those portions of Chapter I which appeared in that review. Dartmouth College generously furnished financial support for this work.

I have an immense gratitude to Mary E. Lyons for all that she has done to help me along the path that led to this publication. Most of all I thank my wife and best reader, Patricia Stuart Lyons, for her understanding, her patience, and her gentleness.

Contents

Introduction

Because disguise and mistaken identity have so often played an important part in narrative and drama—from *Genesis* to Balzac and from Plautus to Beckett—they have become almost invisible themes. They seem such basic elements of plot construction, banalities of perfect simplicity, that they merit perhaps little more than the smile accorded to a child's question. But for those whom the Demon of Repetition has not dulled the question beckons, "Why are there so many disguises? Why is the hero so often unknown?"

Attentive readers and spectators of baroque theatre can call to mind scores of disguises, lost children, amnesiac heroes, unknown kings, heroines disguised as pages, and princes become shepherds. The present brief study is an attempt to see how these problems of identity in the theatre organize themselves into patterns, patterns which could be the components of a baroque myth of identity.

The baroque theatre of France is to be the field of this study and within the theatre disguise our object. At once a certain circularity appears, a troubling redundancy. All theatre, after all, is based on disguise of identity, and conversely any meditation on disguise is bound to lead eventually to thoughts of people playing roles, hiding behind masks, putting on costumes. The analogies between any apparent change of identity and the role-playing of the theatre are striking. Is the theme of disguise in the theatre a form of the theme of the play-within-a-play, the theatre about theatre? This too is an important baroque theme but one which attains a higher level of formalization or reflexivity. The presence of a physically present stage on the stage is a kind of third degree of theatricality, a nesting of levels or *mise en abîme* of the theatre. Disguise in the theatre more frequently remains in a second degree, one in which the players are presenting a performance within a performance, but an unframed, unacknowledged one. The pretense remains within the fictive reality posited for the activity on stage. The disguise is shown as disrupting a life like our own.

Confusion is not easily described with clarity and grace.
Terminology for dramatic confusions of identity straddles with
difficulty two concepts. At times a character hides his name, face, and
rank from others voluntarily. This is what is generally known as
"disguise." In other cases the individual character is, as much as
anyone, ignorant of his own name. Voluntary disguise seems at first
glance a more accessible concept. Not only is it easier to allude
to—disguise is much handier a term than "ignorance of identity"—
but voluntary concealment makes possible direct examination of given
motivation. Yet in most other ways disruption of identity communication functions within the play in the same way whether the disruption
be brought about voluntarily or involuntarily on the part of the
subject, that is, the disguised character. In either case this disruption
causes a *quiproquo* of identity. Whether a king disguises himself as a
peasant or a prince sincerely believes that he is a fisherman's son, the
basic distortion of identity patterns is the same.

The disruption of ordinary identity patterns in drama is, in its
essence, a complex and troubling thing. Few human activities are
more shocking than the performance of dramatic roles. In the theatre
men and women strip themselves of their everyday, recognized selves
and take on the comportment, the speech, the dress, of others. Several
contrasting attitudes towards this act have prevailed.

Plato described this playing of roles as not only unworthy of the
Guardians of his Republic but as undesirable of anyone in this ideal
realm where "one man does one job and does not play a multiplicity of
roles"[1] (III, 397) and from which he banishes "someone who has the
skill to transform himself into all sorts of characters and represent all
sorts of things" (III, 398). Clearly the assignment of more than one
pattern of human activity to a single real person is for Plato a
subversion of the necessary specialization and hierarchical organization of human society. While the philosopher of the *Republic* excoriates
and ridicules all literary fiction, the idea of a *multiplicity* of roles or
characters in the behavior of a single human individual is evidently for
him the most distressing and immoral element in literature.

This multiplicity of characters and comportments marks not only
the player's relation to his scenic and professional life but also the
fictive life of the characters he impersonates. For characters within
dramatic spectacles can be assigned more than one role (or identity) to
impersonate simultaneously. When this happens the actor is presented

to the spectators as embodying one character who is viewed in the course of the play as having radically different social roles—different names, social rank, kinship, sex, or other criteria by which the "role" is determined. There are many ways in which the one character played by an actor, as distinguished from several different and distinct individuals represented alternately by a single actor, is subjected to a multiplicity of roles. When people think about the drama and its use of multiple roles, they usually start from the end of the play. Most attention is drawn to the device known as dramatic (or tragic) *recognition* in which the different characters of a play discover that the social role assigned to one of them is not based on the reality of the play. In other words, one of the actors has been impersonating a character with multiple roles, of which only one is finally considered appropriate and true. In this moment of the play, usually near the end of the action, attention is focused on the unraveling of the threads and on the disposal of the untrue roles previously attributed to the character.

Aristotle's discussion of the use of this *anagoresis* is the basis for most of our thinking about the multiplicity of roles within the dramatic work. For him, recognition or discovery is a plot element on the same level as peripety. The best recognition is one which leads to a sudden change in fortune although recognition can exist separately from this change. Aristotle links the concepts of recognition and the categories of human kinship closely, for the recognition of persons is the most productive of peripety:

> And "recognition" is, as indeed the name indicates, a shift from ignorance to awareness, pointing in the direction either of close blood ties or of hostility, or people who have previously been in a clearly marked state of happiness or unhappiness. The finest recognition is one that happens at the same time as a peripety, as is the case with *Oedipus*. Naturally, there are also other kinds of recognition: it is possible for one to take place in the prescribed manner in relation to inanimate objects and chance occurrences, and it is possible to recognize whether a person has acted or not acted. But the form that is most integrally a part of the plot, the action, is the one aforesaid; for that kind of recognition combined with peripety will excite either pity or fear . . . .[2]

Aristotle returns to the effect of recognition by stressing the emotional content of the passage from ignorance to knowledge of identity:

> when the tragic acts come within the limits of close blood relationship, as when brother kills or intends to kill brother or do something else of that kind to him, or son to father or mother—those are the situations one should look for.
>
> (14536)

Aristotle is clearly not talking here of the more abstract dramatic effects of surprise and irony but of the emotion produced by the discovery of kinship itself, in a way that could happen outside fiction as well. And this emotional effect seems to Aristotle to be so much a part of the human imagination that he does not hesitate to install it in the very center of his thinking about tragedy. In doing so he propounds a mimetic view, but one that goes beyond the imitation of human actions which he specifically discusses. This use of kinship and the fears associated with its temporary ignorance is imitative, on the deeper level, of human phantasies more than of observed human activities. After all, the kind of action imitated in tragedy is of a rare sort: "the poet's job is not to report what has happened but what is likely to happen: that is, what is capable of happening according to the rule of probability or necessity" (14516). This action must also excite terror and pity and "these come about contrary to one's expectation yet logically, one following from the other" (1452a). What does this signify if not that the events of tragedy must have a closer connection to the human mind and its fears than to the everyday world from which it borrows its framework of what is possible? Belonging both to the world of our deep emotions—both of hostility and of desire—and to the structure of societies in which family and class are intertwined, kinship has a privileged position in literary fiction.[3] If Aristotle's comments on comedy had also been handed down to us, we might find a discussion of other forms of identity recognition. As it is, sudden discovery that a character's rank or sex is different from what it seemed to be is covered in both genres by Aristotle's remarks. For such discovery would lead to changes in the relationships between characters and thus create a peripety.

At first glance the aspects of drama discussed by Plato and Aristotle may seem to be quite separate. One writer is concerned with the social function of the actor in real life and the other refers to a totally fictive sort of role, that which occurs within an already illusionary society. Yet both are concerned with the assignment of more than one role to a single, physically present individual, whose relationship to others, in the social and economic structure of the group, in their emotions, is somehow transformed by this multiplicity of fictive identities. Both critics are basing their comments on the assumption that society, either the real one in which we live or the fictive dramatic one which mirrors it somehow, is composed of individuals each having a "place" defined by certain divisions—the specialization of work, the activity and importance in government, the wealth, and, especially, the kinship of those who are related by marriage or birth—and that this place or role is used or manipulated to produce drama. While the differences in the use they make of this observation are great, both Plato and Aristotle pinpoint the importance of social identity and its fictive transformation in the first degree, when the actor transforms himself into a "character," and in the second degree, when the character discovers or reveals that his role is not the one he has appeared to be playing.

Taken together these two attitudes toward the temporary fictive change of identity point to the real effect and power of identity, the sanctity of kinship and rank, which can lead either to tragic guilt or comic laughter. Plato's comments, which seem simply a condemnation of drama, may lead, on the contrary, to an appreciation of the upheaval caused by identity changes. If the philosopher's purpose in banishing players from his republic was to assure a stable social order and hierarchy, then surely one of the worst types of play, from this point of view, would be the play within which identities or social roles are shown to be uncertain, subject to constant revision or verification. And surely there is, even for the spectator who has succeeded in putting himself into the frame of mind necessary for the acceptance of the fictive spectacle, something rather disquieting about the repeated discovery that a protagonist is a king rather than the commoner he was believed to be, the brother or son, rather than a stranger, a girl in disguise rather than the young man and lover.

There is a tendency in seventeenth-century literary theory to unite these two points of view and to apply them to multiplicity of identity within the drama itself. The theory of the verisimilar as expounded, among others, by Jules de La Mesnardière in his *Poétique* (1639) represents the severe and classical reading of Aristotle in reaction against what La Mesnardière himself saw as Castelvetro's populist

version. In the *Discours* which opens the text La Mesnardière berates
his Italian predecessor for designating poetry as the "passetemps du
public,"[4] "et non seulement [du] peuple, mais [de] la vile populace,
grossière, ignorante et stupide" (p. H). Given this supposition, it is
understandable that La Mesnardière insists that the theatre should
portray things not as would give pleasure to the people but as the
people should be made to see them, in such a way that everything be
fitting, logical, decorous, and *vraisemblable*. Furthermore verisimilitude for La Mesnardière implies certain ideas about the structure of
society which he appears to share with the Plato of the *Republic*.   At
least half of La Mesnardière's text is occupied by the description or
prescription of the appropriate *Moeurs* (or decorum) and the
corresponding *Sentiments*. The criterion for judging these two qualities
of the dramatic text is the *vraisemblance* attached to the qualities and
sentiments of individual characters. La Mesnardière's approach to
decorum is highly categorical; each type of individual fits into a role
which can be defined and listed for the use of authors. Each *condition*
has certain unvarying qualities as do certain historical characters, like
Alexander. La Mesnardière lists, for instance, countries with the
qualities appropriate to the inhabitants of each. Within each society
the various classes and the sexes also have fixed qualities which the
author must not alter. An interdiction weighs on deformations of the
natural image of the woman and of the lower class: "Pour la Propriété
des Moeurs, le Poëte doit considérer qu'il ne faut jamais introduire
sans nécessité absoluë, ni une Fille vaillante, ni une Femme sçavante,
ni un Valet judicieux" (p. 137). The playwright is enjoined on the
other hand to portray each character in his proper qualities:

> faire les Héros généreux, les Philosophes prudens, les Femmes
> douces et modestes, les Filles pleines de pudeur, les
> Ambassadeurs hardis, les Espions téméraires et peu soucieux
> de la vie, les Valets grossiers et fidelles; et ainsi des autres
> personnes, chacune selon sa fortune, son age, et sa condition
> (p. 140).

This insistence on a rigid and conventional verisimilitude is linked to
La Mesnardière's rejection of *divertissement* as the end of poetry. The
poet must strive to show the ideal character of each condition of
mankind in an exemplary and stable typology. To play havoc with

this classification is to fall into the vulgarity of writing to give pleasure, to amuse the people, and to betray reality. La Mesnardière could be described, without too much exaggeration, as opposing the pleasure of the people and the poets on the grounds of reality and duty. He criticizes a number of contemporary authors for their violation of these principles, their depiction of the exceptional rather than the typical, and their exaggeration:

> Un Amant de leur manière ne paroîtra généreux qu'en accomplissant en un jour cent Avantures de Romans, qui surpassent toute créance. Un Roy n'est point Politique, s'il ne renonce à la conscience, et aux sentimens humains, comme à ceux de la Religion; ni une femme amoureuse, si elle n'est effrontée, et si elle ne fait cent choses qui chocquent égallement et les coûtumes de son séxe, et la pudeur mesme des hommes (p. 243).

At the moment La Mesnardière's *Poétique* appeared, it confronted an increasing tendency to choose this world of the antireal, the nonverisimilar, which is not a renunciation of typologies and categories but rather, as La Mesnardière indicates so correctly, an opposite or contrary typology. In this other system a woman in love does, as often as not, transgress the "coûtumes de son séxe." The critic pretends not to recognize that this other way of writing is a form of art with differing principles, based on pleasure rather than idealized reality. Instead he prefers to attribute it either to the author's failure to observe reality or to his lack of skill in writing:

> Or il est aisé de voir que des manquemens si grossiers viennent de l'un de ces rincipes; ou bien de ce que le Poëte ne sçait pas comment les hommes se comportent dans les affaires; ou de ce qu'il n'a pas l'addresse d'appliquer différemment aux diverses conditions, les Sentimens différens que la raison et l'usage leur inspirent égallement (p. 245).

The third principle from which the phenomenon could arise, namely a systematic deformation or transformation of identity and its attendant qualities, is left aside.

La Poétique's rejection of variations in characteristics of identity in literary works on the grounds of verisimilitude has a corollary concerning disguise itself. Here La Mesnardière is indeed closer to more naïve conceptions of what constitutes the real and the probable. The striking efficacy of disguises in the plays of the period did not escape him, and appeared to him as a convention violating all credibility. He observes correctly,

> ces grossiéretéz d'esprit que quelques Poëtes Dramatiques attachent à leurs Personnages; soit quand ils font que les Amans méconnoissent leurs Maîtresses; ou quand ils veulent que les Pères ne reconnoissent plus leurs enfans, sous ombre qu'ils sont travestis. Comme si la connoissance que nous avons des personnes, étoit simplement attachée à ces endroits de leurs corps, que les habits cachent aux yeux et qu'elle ne dépendit point du visage, de la taille, de la démarche, de la voix, et de ces autres façons qui sont exposées à la veuë, et que l'on ne peut détruire par des changemens si légers (pp. 264-65).

The reader may agree with La Mesnardière that these situations are slightly "au delà de la Vrai-semblance."

La Mesnardière, by his categorization of identities, by his remarkably long and explicit description of the proper and totally unchanging qualities of each nation, each class, each profession, and each sex, typifies the conception of identity against which the theatre of disguise defines itself. There is, between a La Mesnardière and a Rotrou, no profound disagreement about the social realities implied in the concepts of class and sexual roles. In the final scene of all of these plays the characters reenter the order from which they may have departed during the preceding action. The difference in the aesthetic use of identity, nonetheless, is considerable.

If then the theatre of disguise violates the ordinary vision of human society and its norms of conduct what are the implications of this theme for the function of drama in society? Since the whole tradition of mimetic drama depends on some relationship between society and theatre how does the deliberate confusion of identity define the drama which uses this theme? Because the heroes of these plays, as we shall see, are often unconscious of their socially defined relationship to others and to the group, their actions are necessarily given different values. The murder of a stranger, as Aristotle points out, gives rise to very different feelings from a parricide. Similarly a man's love for a woman is viewed with much different emotion from a man's love for his mother or sister in societies where incest taboos apply. When a character in disguise provokes an emotion from another character, it is not without significance that the emotion provoked is socially incompatible with the real identity of the disguised character. For example, that a man should fall in love with a woman, then find that his passion is incestuous, and then discover again that it is not (as in Rotrou's *La Soeur*) constitutes a theme which obviously invests identity confusion with a certain meaning. Or, when a woman falls in love with another woman disguised as a man only to learn, finally, her beloved's true identity (the case in Rotrou's *Célimène*), this distortion of normal social conduct seems to call for some elucidation. Perhaps the explanation lies precisely in the scandal which these disguises provoke.

The emotive effect of the theatre, indeed of fiction in general, is usually supposed to derive from a certain identification with the imaginary being whose activities we witness.[5] Even if those actions are contrary to the normal comportment expected of man in society, we still continue to take some pleasure in these adventures. Plato and Bossuet denounce this effect.[6] Yet more recent observers have been less harsh. Ernst Kris defines such participation, and its advantage over social misbehavior: "This maintenance of the aesthetic illusion promises the safety to which we were aspiring and guarantees freedom from guilt, since it is not our own fantasy we follow."[7] Charles Mauron, describing three sources of the comic, observes this same vicarious freedom: "Le génie comique, à sa guise, jouera donc . . . satirique, soit de l'abandon à la régression, soit de la raillerie satirique, soit enfin de l'ivresse goutée à se libérer de la double servitude des tendances instinctives et des normes sociales."[8]

However, few spectators would find the spectacle of an incest, a parricide, a homosexual relationship comic. The release of repressed desires presupposed by psychoanalysis demands a more complex representational mechanism than what is usually considered erotic literature. Disguise or ignorance of identity could function as such a mechanism for the maintenance of aesthetic distance. Identity confusion makes it seem that the character himself is not responsible for his actions. He does not know what he is doing, and the guilt of the act is somehow removed. In the case of parricide, the guilt generally falls on the hero at the end of the play, as may happen with the incest theme as well. In this way the spectator is left free from any personal guilt. But the guilt may also simply vanish and not fall on anyone. With incest this exorcism of guilt is brought about by a series of complex alternations between guilty desire and discovery of final innocence and other formulas described below. Perhaps the best example of possible guilt vanishing is Célimène's reaction (in Rotrou's *Célimène*) upon discovering that the "man" she loved was a woman. Her anger at her faithless lover disappears; she simply laughs.

During the time in which an incongruity is created between a character's actions and the true vision of identity possessed by the spectator, there is often also a comic effect. Georges Blin observes of this moment: "Quant à l'hilarité qui se rapporte à la soudaine vue d'une inconvenance, elle demeure nécessairement compromise avec l'accident obscène ou incongru qu'elle sanctionne."[9] We might experience such a reaction by perceiving, for instance, that a character is unwittingly violating an incest prohibition.

The emphasis in the examples given of the kind of abnormal conduct permitted by identity confusion is probably too narrowly sexual. Taking root as they may in the basic conflicts which psychoanalysis defines, the actions permitted in this theatre go beyond the simple liberation of sexual drives. Identity confusion, the combination in one man of several roles, is, as Plato understood, a potential upheaval of society in its entirety. The social disorganization caused by the loss of a name can be so great that even incest is only a kind of symptom of a broader disruption of the norm. Recalling the position of the actor in Christian and many other cultures as a pariah, excommunicated and damned, Duvignaud attributes this male-diction to the subversive power of the actor, "sa capacité indéfinie à représenter n'importe quel rôle et à actualiser, c'est-à-dire à socialiser, n'importe quelle conduite."[10] In the violence of Elizabethan drama Duvignaud finds an extreme example of this power of the theatre to combat the constraints of the social order. "Le théâtre," he writes, "comme la littérature, est une révolte contre la 'culture' . . . ."[11]

The play is not simply a representation of life in society, not a direct account of the daily life of the period which produced it. Hence the weakness of certain "sociological" studies which attempt to use literature as a mere account of everyday life.[12] How naïve it would be to assume that sibling incest was commonplace in Jacobean England, that women habitually disguised themselves as men in the France of Louis XIII and Anne d'Autriche, or that princes were often adopted by fishermen! As an expression of the imagination's revenge on culture, theatre appeals to its public by providing people with what they lack. One may suppose that the most successful spectacle owes its popularity to its contrast with limited, day-to-day existence.[13] In contrast to the limitations on conduct and desire, theatre, as Artaud passionately declared, "libère l'inconscient comprimé, pousse à une sorte de révolte virtuelle et qui d'ailleurs ne peut avoir tout son prix que si elle demeure virtuelle . . . ."[14]

This sort of disruption, which confines itself to the stage, can result from a deliberate confusion of identity, an unknown or misappropriated name. Elsewhere the name has a similar compelling and even magic significance. The ancient fear of telling a name and thus giving dominion over the bearer of that name is not too distant from some of the almost obsessive themes of the drama. In antiquity, Frazer observes, "every Egyptian received two names, which were known respectively as the true name and the good name, or the great name and the little name; and while the good or little name was made public, the true or great name appears to have been carefully concealed."[15] Even in modern times this reticence has been detected among non-Europeans:

> . . . the savage commonly fancies that the link between a name and the person or thing denominated by it is not a mere arbitrary and ideal association, but a real and substantial bond which unites the two in such a way that magic may be wrought on a man just as easily through his name as through his hair . . . or any other material part of his person. In fact, primitive man regards his name as a vital portion of himself and takes care of it accordingly (p. 2845).

There is then an apparently ageless concern with the magic of the individual human identity. Yet there are periods and traditions in which the problem of identity and its concealment acquire a special prominence. French theatre of the years 1630-1660, the period of Rotrou and Corneille, is haunted by perpetual disguises, the loss of names, the recognition of long-lost children or brothers. It is a time when disguise became almost a constitutive element of the prevalent genre, the tragicomedy.[16]

In two hundred forty-four French plays of the period the author forces the spectator to take special notice of character identity through a *quiproquo* of identity.[17] In doing so the playwright strikes at the very center of all nonallegorical drama: the depiction of a group of recognizable beings who have a concept of themselves and of others with whom they interact. Not only is the error of identification important because it affects the essence of the dramatic *persona* but also because of its frequency. It is the most widespread of the Baroque *quiproquos*.[18] There remain extant four hundred sixty-two plays first performed or published during this period and more than half of them involve disguise or mistaken identity.[19] Is this explosive proliferation of identity confusion simply an aspect of the Baroque? Or can this theme be seen as more than another indication of a taste for illusion, doubt, and metamorphosis?

Surprisingly little attention has been paid to a theme that stands close to the core of the literary imagination of a period so much discussed. Jean Rousset devotes fewer than ten pages of his major study of the Baroque to an analysis of disguise (pp. 51-57). Yet the phenomenon is so important that it figures in the title of the first part of Rousset's book, "De la métamorphose au déguisement." Other critics and historians have been less conscious of the importance of this characteristic theme. True to his Lansonian heritage and typical of readers of his generation, Lancaster dismisses plays based on disguise as superficial and conventional. The defect of Rotrou's *La Soeur* is that "it is almost entirely a comedy of intrigue, based on a substitution of children, extraordinarily opportune meetings, a series of recognitions, and very superficial psychology."[20] Of Bazire d'Amblainville's *Lycoris* Lancaster notes that "it contains the conventional chain of lovers . . . the reappearance of a shepherd, supposed dead, who turns out to be the lost brother of his would-be murderess, an attempted suicide, a satyr, etc. [sic] The chief interest lies, not in these *banalités*, but in the style" (I, 209). While conceding the popularity of the play during Corneille's lifetime, Lancaster remarks dryly of *Héraclius* that "the intrigue is overemphasized at the cost of ideas and the study of character" (II, 498). Disguise and mistaken identity seem to some readers cheap and superficial tricks, unworthy of great drama. For this reason certain critics are afflicted with a sort of peripheral astigmatism—they notice characteristics in minor authors which they refuse to see in major ones. A critic who had no taste for the *romanesque* asserted of Corneille that he eliminated "quiproquos qu'un seul mot dit à propos suffirait à dissiper; mystérieux personnages dont tout le monde ignore l'origine ou les desseins; reconnaissances; 'la croix de ma mère' quand ce n'est pas 'le sabre de mon père'. Ces petits moyens, romanesques et enfantins, sont rares chez Corneille et ceux que nous rencontrons sont en général susceptibles d'une explication entièrement rationnelle."[21] The same critic goes on to assure us that *Don Sanche* is not romanesque, and that the *quiproquos* in *OEdipe* spring from the legend itself. On the other hand *Héraclius* "n'est qu'invention et invention romanesque."[22] The same unevenness in appreciating Corneille's identity plays appears in Emile Faguet's judgments. Of *Héraclius* he writes "les Paul *crus* Jean et les Pierre *crus* Paul et tout cet arsenal du mélodrame vulgaire et *la difficulté même*, pour le public, de comprendre et de suivre *l'intrigue*, devaient lui paraître des beautés hors du commun." Yet Faguet inconsistently finds *OEdipe* "un excellent mélodrame dans le goût du XVII e siècle" and *Don Sanche* "une comédie romanesque qui est tout à fait charmante."[23] Octave Nadal comments that in *Héraclius* and *Pertharite* "Le merveilleux, le conventionnel, l'arbitraire, reviennent peupler la scène de leurs artifices, de leurs ficelles, de leurs lieux communs les plus significatifs . . ."[24]

However difficult critics find reconciling his taste for identity confusion with his popularity and reputation, Corneille clearly favored this theme and did not abandon it quickly. His interest in disguise lasts from his early tragicomedy *Clitandre* (1630) to his much later tragedy *OEdipe* (1659). These disguises are not simply inherent in Corneille's subject. In *Pertharite*, as Corneille points out in the *Examen*, he added to historical material suspicions of imposture and the problem of recognition of identity.[25] Corneille added to *Rodogune* the uncertainty of the order of birth of Séleucus and Antiochus, a problem of seniority which becomes a real identity problem (II, 320). The historical Nicomedes, as known through Justin's account, did have two brothers raised in Rome and Rotrou's *Cosroès*, which may have influenced Corneille, does have a character like Attale (II, 678). Yet Corneille alone seems responsible for the meeting and recognition of kinship at the end of the play. Sophocles' *Oedipus the King* is based on an identity question, but to this Corneille added a second very significant *quiproquo* of name and kinship in his *OEdipe*. *Don Sanche*, according to the author, is the combination of a Spanish play, *El Palacio confuso*, and a French novel, *Don Pélage*, which contributed "la double reconnaissance qui finit le cinquième [acte]" (II, 612-13). Theodore's disguise, in the tragedy to which that heroine gives its title, derives from the legend, but Corneille changes the point of view in order to surprise the spectator and draw the maximum effect from the disguise.

In choosing to make plays of his own from subjects staged by Alarcon (in *Le Menteur*) and by Du Ryer (*Héraclius* resembles his *Bérénice*) Corneille indulged his own evident taste for disguise.

Corneille's plays of disguise and mistaken identity, mostly from the period 1643-1651 (from *Le Menteur* to *Pertharite*) are often masterpieces of dramatic suspense and irony. Yet his works are only the tip of a large mass of similar texts lying forgotten now but obviously much appreciated by the public of their day.

The theatre is not alone in its use of confusions and metamorphoses. The novel, deriving its themes from the Italian dramatic pastoral, carried disguise and illusion to their apogee. The atmosphere of the baroque novel, as Bruce Morrissette observes, is marked by "le déguisement, qui trouve aussi dans l'oeuvre de d'Urfé son épanouissement et sa plénitude baroque. Le doublement et le dédoublement des êtres, les personnages ambigus, le travestissement, la feinte: tout y parait, dans un échange perpétuel d'identités qui fait de l'intrigue presque tout entière un système de personnalités fausses, un jeu de miroirs, où les caractères se substituent les uns aux autres, pénètrent par le déguisement et la feinte dans les milieux défendus, triomphant de la réalité par l'illusion et le change."[26] Some years later the ferment of these apparent metamorphoses, known especially through the *Astrée*, yielded in the narrative to different preoccupations. The disguises became less numerous, replaced by simpler love stories and novels of psychological analysis.[27] In the drama, however, it was different. Characters restlessly searched for lost identities on the stage even after d'Urfé's last page was completed after the author's death by his secretary Baro. While the themes of disguise disappeared from the novel, harbinger of new preoccupations, they continued to thrive in the theatre. There were more plays concerning identity in the 1650's than in the preceding decade.[28] The baroque novel seems to have given rise to this theatrical ferment which outlived its early source. Immediately before 1630 there were surprisingly few plays involving disguise. In Hardy, for instance, the themes of disguise and recognition appear five times, a much smaller proportion of the whole work than in Rotrou.[29] Yet once the wave of *romanesque* began to be felt in the theatre, disguise did not limit itself to works directly inspired by novels.

The stage became obsessed with the problem of identity which had inspired the narrative. Corneille's contemporaries seem to have felt the magical power which the ancients and the non-Europeans attribute to the name. They often established a direct equivalence between the man and his name. When a character changes, if only by taking on some new virtue, the name which belongs to him changes as well. This happens even in works which are not concerned with disguise. Rodrigue's real transformation into the hero he is at the end of *Le Cid* is reflected precisely, as J.D. Hubert so aptly observes, by his new denomination. Henceforth Rodrigue will be called "le Cid."[30] Any disguise or even change of social state calls for such a transformation of name. In some texts the character's name is so intimately tied to his individual existence that to give it up is the ultimate sacrifice. La Mesnardière, in his tragedy *Alinde* (published in 1642), has the heroine say,

Après avoir quitté ma superbe thiare, Changé mon air natal
pour ce pays barbare, Perdu la Majesté dans ce déguisement,
Quitté jusqu'à mon nom pour suivre mon amant . . . .

Rank, appearance, country—all this is surrendered before those potent syllables. This surrender is not always voluntary. Policandre, in Du Vieuget's *Policandre et Basolie* (1632), becomes amnesiac and calls himself Nivelle. When asked his name he replies,

Monsieur, excusez-moy, je ne le sçaurois faire,
En ce que je pourray je vous veux satisfaire;
Mais non pas au désir qui vous faict informer
De mon nom, qu'ignorant je ne sçaurois nommer
Je perdis tout d'un coup, avecque la sagesse,
Mon nom et mes souliers, en perdant ma maistresse.

(IV, ii)

The change in name can be, as for Policandre, the sign of a deep and involuntary disorientation. But it may also be, not only for the savage, a form of protection. Simply by changing names, the dramatic character adds immeasurably to the difficulty others find in identifying him. Alphonse, in Rotrou's *Clarice*, asks Hortense (really Léandre), "Que te dit-elle encore? t'a-t-elle reconnue?" Hortense replies:

Non, car mon nom changé, le poil qui m'est venu,
Et les travaux soufferts pendant ce long servage,
N'ont presque rien laissé de mon premier visage.

(I, ii)

Hortense places the change of name on the same level as the physical transformation. Both are effective elements of disguise. One might even say that the change of name is an especially magic change, since it takes primacy over the others and may suffice to make a character unrecognizable. This use of the name for deliberate concealment, combined with the seemingly automatic change of name resulting from transformations of mental or social state, can turn the whole system of nomenclature and human relations upside down. Du Vieuget, in the *argument* of his *Policandre*, evokes the total identity confusion of his fictive world:

Or après l'exil de ces deux damoiselles, les père & mère, assavoir Pélicare & Méléane, père & mère de Basolie & de Céralide, nommée en l'hermitage Théoparte & Cémire, Méantin & Erymène, père & mère de Policandre, nommé Nivelle en sa frenaisie, s'en allèrent d'un commun accord consulter un devin nommé Astrasore . . . .

This startling preoccupation with the name, which appears in Du Vieuget as a delirium, an oneiric proliferation, belongs to the same imaginative world as Corneille's severe demonstration of the fragility of identity in *Héraclius*. How can we find our way into this maze, share in this delirium with more than surprise, uneasiness, or scorn?

Although ultimately historical and sociological contributions are needed for the resolution of the problems of the collective imagination, the first step towards understanding must be an attentive description of identity confusion as it falls into patterns in a large number of texts. There appears an intertextual system of identity confusion in which a certain number of patterns dominate, specifically the thematics of sexual disguise, of the unknown woman, of the unknown king, and of pastoral disguise or the disguise of rank. The statistical, empirical base, however, only furnishes guidance to the areas of major concern. The content of the problems thus defined requires an effort, to some extent necessarily subjective, of the reader's imagination to give life to the text and to underline its major elements. Such an enterprise resembles that of Jean-Pierre Richard in defining the imaginative world of Mallarmé or perhaps more precisely Georges Poulet's tracing of a theme from work to work. Reconstructing in its complexity the mental and perceptual world of another author or group poses, though, the problem of respecting the work of art. Obviously analysis must dissolve or destructure the text in the hope that a future reading of the text will more nearly reveal the fullness that is the original work. The critical reading must temporarily reduce but also allude constantly to the work in its unity, not only for confirmation of hypotheses but also in order to preserve that which makes the work of art, its aesthetic unity and delimitation.

This study, rather than risk the dissolution of the text as presented in its unity to the spectator-reader in favor of the imaginative background or context in which it was apprehended, will examine each major pattern of identity confusion within a single text. It is only within the sequence of actions which constitute dramatic plot that identity themes have their effect. But in order to confirm the validity or usefulness of the description of one example of identity confusion, the pattern will be verified in a number of other texts.

In the interplay between single works in which the identity theme reaches its coherence and the intertextual background which displays its significance and popularity I hope to illuminate an important aspect of the theatre of the early seventeenth century. Scorned as it has been, or rescued only to be quickly subsumed under the broad category of the Baroque, this pervasive fascination with disguise deserves a serious effort. And such an effort may be rewarded in the breaking down of a barrier to our appreciation of the Baroque aesthetic and to a greater sympathy with the public of Rotrou and Corneille.

Footnotes

1. Plato, The Republic, III, 397 (translated by H.D.P. Lee [Baltimore: Penguin Books, 1955; rpt. 1968), p. 137.

2. Aristotle, *Poetics*, translated by Gerald F. Else (Ann Arbor: University of Michigan Press, 1967), 1452a.

3. Ernest Jones, *Hamlet and Oedipus* (1949; rpt. New York: Anchor Books, 1954). See especially ch. IV, "Tragedy and the Mind of the Infant," pp. 81-103.

4. Jules de La Mesnardière, *La Poétique* (Paris: A. de Sommaville, 1639), p. F.

5. Ernst Kris, *Psychoanalytic Explorations in Art* (New York: International Universities Press, 1952), p. 46.

6. Bossuet, *Maximes et réflexions sur la comédie* (1694).

7. Kris, pp. 45-46.

8. Charles Mauron, *Psychocritique du genre comique* (Paris: Corti, 1964), p. 23.

9. Georges Blin, "Notes pour une Erotique du Rire," *Cahiers de la Pléiade*, Spring, 1950, p. 131.

10. Jean Duvignaud, *L'Acteur, esquisse d'une sociologie du comédien* (Paris: Gallimard, 1965), p. 205.

11. Duvignaud, *Sociologie du théâtre: Essai sur les ombres collectives* (Paris: P.U.F., 1965), p. 205.

12. See Jacques Schérer's "Pour une sociologie des obstacles au mariage dans le théâtre français du XVII e siécle," *Dramaturgie et Société, XVI et XVII¹ siècles*, ed. Jean Jacquot (Paris: Publications du C.N.R.S., 1968), I, 297-302.

13. Duvignaud, *Sociologie du théâtre*, p. 175.

14. Antonin Artaud, *Le Théâtre et son double* (1938; rpt. Paris: Gallimard, "collection des idées," 1964), p. 39.

15. Sir James George Frazer, *The Golden Bough* (1890; abridged edition, 1940; rpt. New York: The Macmillan Company, 1963), p. 285.

16. Jean Rousset, *La Littérature de l'âge baroque en France* (1954; rpt. Paris: José Corti, 1965), p. 54.

17. See bibliography at end of volume, section I.

18. Jacques Schérer, *La Dramaturgie Classique en France* (Paris: Nizet, 1950), p. 77.

19. H. C. Lancaster in his *History of French Dramatic Literature in the Seventeenth Century* (Baltimore: Johns Hopkins Press, 1928-1942) lists these extant texts: I, 760-763; II, 777-781; III, 863-868.

20. *Ibid.*, II, 479.

21. F.-J. Tanquerey, "Le Romanesque dans le théâtre de Corneille," *Revue des cours et Conférences,* 1ᵉʳ ᵉ série (1938-39), p. 373.

22. *Ibid.,* pp. 379, 376, 271.

23. Emile Faguet, *En lisant Corneille* (Paris: Hachette, 1913), pp. 167, 188, 170.

24. Octave Nadal, *Le Sentiment de l'amour dans l'oeuvre de Pierre Corneille* (1948; rpt. Paris: Gallimard, 1967), p. 227.

25. Corneille, *Examen de Pertharite,* in *Théâtre complet,* ed. Maurice Rat (Paris: Classiques Garnier, n.d.), II, 754; all future references will be to this edition of Corneille's theatre. See Lawrence M. Riddle, *The Genesis and Sources of Pierre Corneille's Tragedies from Médée to Pertharite.* Baltimore: The Johns Hopkins Press, 1926.

26. Bruce Morrissette, "Structures de la sensibilité baroque dans le roman pré-classique," *Cahiers de l'Association Internationale des Etudes françaises,* XI (May, 1959), p. 95.

27. *Ibid.,* p. 102.

28. Between 1650 and 1660 there are seventy-four such plays as compared to sixty-two between 1640 and 1650. See bibliography, part I.

29. In *Alcée, Félismène, Procris, Phraarte,* and *La Belle Esclave,* there are disguises or recognitions of long-lost children.

30. J.-D. Hubert, "Le réel et l'illusoire dans le théâtre de Corneille et dans celui de Rotrou," *Revue des Sciences Humaines,* 1958, p. 337.

The Woman as Man: Célimène

At the end of the first act of Rotrou's *Célimène*, the male protagonist, Filandre, and the heroine, Florante, conspire to create an illusion. The action which they prepare is the temporary transformation of Florante into a male. In this guise she will prove to Filandre her superiority to him in the amorous pursuit of another woman, the cold and heartless Célimène.[1] This projected disguise of identity, the creation of an imaginary person within the already imaginary world of the characters, enters the text in striking terms. Filandre, admitting defeat in his quest for Célimène's love, declares to Florante, whom he has abandoned for his new passion:

> Crois que tu pourrois peu sur cette âme inhumaine,
> Qu'en mon lieu tu serois en une même peine.
> Elle n'estime rien que ses propres appas.
> Venus sous mes habits ne la toucheroit pas:
> Tous objets sont communs à ce coeur insensible.
>
> (I, v)

The arresting image, "Vénus sous mes habits," not only renders Filandre's desire, and therefore the theme of *Célimène* as a whole, but also serves as an emblem of a literary myth especially prominent in the French theatre during the second third of the seventeenth century. Filandre's expression and the disguise it provokes are not isolated, frivolous, or meaningless theatrical details. Rotrou's hero touches here upon a major key to the baroque imagination; his words find echoes in a multitude of texts.

Célimène is a key, furthermore, not only to the specially prevalent disguise of sexual identity, but to the whole theme of disguise. Rotrou, as many of his plays testify, was especially conscious of the creation of illusion.[2] This theme becomes, in *Célimène* as in *Saint Genest*, an occasion for the work to turn reflexively on itself, exposing the means by which it generates truth and illusion, the way in which the actor creates his role. Rotrou, with unusual vigor, defines the ways in which identity in general, and sexual identity in particular, are communicated. This delineation of masculinity and femininity in *Célimène* is an essential prelude to the disguise which constitutes the center of the work. A new sensitivity to the signs of identity is generated by the text. A use of certain codes to create meaning and, with it, the possible use of these codes to create illusion emerge also.

With *Célimène* (as with *Astrée* in narrative literature) one enters a world of progressive sexualization of different characteristics, the separation of the traits of men from those of women. Rotrou begins with generally recognized codes of identity before adding certain nuances which affect the behavior of play.

The first of these codes, announced by Filandre's image of Venus "sous mes habits," is that of dress. Seeing on stage a man and woman performer (or actors of either sex thus costumed), the spectator recalls the limited number of possible relationships into which they can enter according to social or literary convention.[3] Authors of Rotrou's day return constantly to this elementary emotive resource. Yet instead of letting it pass unobserved, they bring this reaction into question, forcing the spectators to reflect upon the link between a person and his sexual identity. This occurs in the case of a woman's assumption of the male costume in the course of a play. The prevalence of this highly self-conscious violation of the dress code by a woman character makes it seem almost that the theatrical misuse of the code is in inverse proportion to the social obedience to the code in everyday life. Perhaps the identity codes (and prohibitions of variance from them) most strongly accepted by society are the most productive of emotional and dramatic effect in their violation.

Next in importance to dress in creating the identity of a character are systems of gesture and the linguistic indices of identity. Normally these indications appear after the sign of dress has already been imposed. A character first changes his or her costume before changing comportment in other ways. The change of clothing creates the outline of the character, the habitual response of anticipation, into which fit the other codes of identity. When a character's words indicate a different sex from the one designated by his clothing, the total identity pattern collapses. The resultant confusion, evoked in several plays (e.g., *Célimène*, V, viii; *Hospital des foux*, III, vi) is described as madness.

Rotrou's *Célimène* plays, in its disguise of sexual identity, on the three codes of dress, gesture, and language. The norms of these three codes are not left to the spectator's everyday social habit but are established

systematically within the text itself. Of course, in the act of destroying
a social or literary convention every work creates the shadow picture
of the norm it undermines. But *Célimène* contains, in addition to the
necessary and inevitable irony conveyed in every disguise, a careful
procedure of elaboration of the patterns it later violates, a process of
rendering the spectator sensitive to certain manifestations of identity.
The first act of the work is a form of prologue to Florante's disguise
as Floridan. Florante, newly arrived from Paris, and her aunt, Orante,
discuss the young woman's love for Filandre, who, they discover, is in
love with Célimène, in spite of his earlier promises to Florante. In the
final scene Florante and Orante confront Filandre and taunt him
because of his lack of success with Célimène. When Filandre
challenges Florante to do better, the project of disguise is set in motion.
However, even before the mention of the disguise, the notions of
communication through gesture (including facial expression) and
language are established in specific relation to their connotation of
masculinity and femininity. Each character's gestures are rendered
not only visually but also through the words of the other characters.
Thus there is a sort of instantaneous interpretation of the meaning of
each gesture. In this way we learn that women, as represented by
Florante, are apt to blush or in some way convey embarrassment
without speaking. Orante says to Florante,
                    . . . jusqu'à ce jour,
      On ne vous a parlé ni d'amant ni d'amour:
      Vous ignorez ces noms, et, dans cette innocence,
      Le discours que je fais vous trouble et vous offense.
                                                              (I,i)
The mobile expressiveness of the face is a feminine characteristic in
this play. Male characters may look worn and haggard as does Alidor,
another of Célimène's suitors (II, iii), but this is a slow wearing of the
expression, not a quick flash of feminine sensitivity. Florante's face
changes immediately when she hears words that touch her. "Son
visage à ces mots a changé de couleur," says Orante. Masculine
expressiveness is much less refined and transparent. Filandre is taken
aback to see Florante emerge in place of Célimène, whom he expects,
but his feelings are apparent through his silence alone rather than
through a subtle play of facial expression (I, ii).
      The language of masculine gesture, however, compensates for this
lack. Although Filandre may not blush and betray his feelings facially,
his comportment is described as significant. He can, with gesture,

express his love for a woman and manifest in this way some of the identity signals emitted by a person of his sex. Florante alludes to his assurances of love for her in Paris:

> Ses discours n'étoient pas mon plus sûr témoignage;
> Ses moindres actions m'en disoient davantage.
> Sa peine et ses devoirs m'ont confirmé ce point;
> Ses pleurs m'en assuroient quand je ne riois point . . . .
>
> (I, i)

The *discours* of a male lover here are reduced to a secondary place in communicating sincere passion. Florante stresses as more important another quality, the masculine style as opposed to mere words.

In addition to these evocations of the signs of masculinity, the three characters appearing in the first act mention, as if in passing and without great emphasis, other elements of the identity code which Florante will use to create her new identity during the rest of *Célimène*. When Orante replies to her niece's question of who had found Filandre's love letters, the words call attention to Florante's feminine costume: "moi-même en vos habits quand vous fûtes couchée" (I, i). This innocent designation of one of the attributes of the woman later finds its meaning in Filandre's important mention of the masculie costume. The male name also appears early in the play with great affective power and in a position of grammatical isolation:

> Florante: Comment le nommez-vous?
> Orante: Filandre
> Florante (bas):   Ô le perfide!
>
> (I, i)

This designation of the male name and its emotive power is echoed at the end of the act when Florante has decided to disguise herself and assume a male name.

These evocations of the various comportments (including voice, dress, and proper name for each sex) occur before Filandre's pivotal comment (scene v) leads to open preparation for Florante's disguise. At that moment the codes have been established for their perversion in the heroine's systematic adoption of the dress ("Que Filandre m'envoie un de ses vêtements"), the name (unspecified but linked to masculinity as a nephew of Orante), and the comportment ("sous le titre d'amant . . .") of the male.

The following acts demonstrate the effective use by Florante, or Floridan as she is called, of the elements designated in the first act. No longer does she express herself through the transparent feminine blush or change of countenance; now it is she who provokes and detects the change in others, as when Floridan (Florante in disguise) asks Célimène,

> Que ce teint est changé! quelle douleur vous presse?
> Dieux! qu'est-ce que je vois?

(IV, vi)

Mysteriously exempt from the *trouble* which betrays the emotion of women, Floridan exercises to perfection masculine gestures, defined at one point as a highly conventionalized ritual of pretense. Floridan reassures Félicie of his love by undermining the word (and even the voice) in favor of accompanying gesture:

> . . . si vous y prenez garde,
> Lui parlé-je jamais que je ne vous regarde?
> Si ma voix parle bien, mes regards parlent mieux,
> Ou vous entendez mal le langage des yeux.

(IV, i)

Just as Filandre captured Florante's love through the perfection of his speech and his writing, so Floridan provokes Félicie's admiration ("que sa voix a d'attraits!") and the colder Célimène's approbation: "Votre discours est sain, quoi qu'il nous persuade" (II, iv). For the period of Florante's disguise, Alidor, a masculine suitor more exemplary in his activity than the almost invisible Filandre, emphasizes the male act of capture through poetry, a theme mentioned in the first act. Alidor's explicit development of the doctrine of poetry as a form of seduction through flattery and pretense is a commentary on Floridan's language as it appears in the same act. The active nature of Floridan's male language and its basis in *feinte* is described through Alidor as the male form of courtship, a form which Florante knows she must adopt as a part of her disguise. Alidor describes his skill in poetry by beginning with the boast:

> Il est vrai que j'ai l'art de flatter qui me plaît,
> Je peins quand bon me semble un oeil plus beau qu'il n'est.

(II, ii)

The fact that Floridan is lying in half of what "he" says to the two sisters simply accentuates, in the ironic eyes of the spectator, the maleness of "his" technique. Floridan is in this, as in other ways, a super-male by the very falseness of "his" comportment. As Félicie makes clear, the male's identity as a lover is established through a ritual of imitation and lying in which he mouths a series of conventional compliments and assumes attitudes expected of the despairing suitor. The proper description of such a position, reflecting Alidor's doctrine, is that of a *feinte*:

> Que Floridan sait bien feindre les passions!
> O dieux! comme il contraint toutes ses actions!
> Avec combien d'adresse et combien d'artifice
> Il promet à mes voeux un fidèle service.
>
> (IV, i)

Unlike the quick blush of the woman Florante, the expression of the "man" Floridan is impenetrable, conventional, fixed:

> Oui, quelques passions dessus ce front sont peintes:
> Vous soupirez parfois et vous poussez des plaintes.
> Si je crois vos discours vous êtes tout de feu;
> Enfin vous feignez bien, ou vous aimez un peu.
>
> (IV, i)

Célimène too alludes to the male practice of flattery, "un propos commun que vous tenez à d'autres," and is thus praising Floridan's masculinity in saying "qu'il sait bien feindre," thereby grouping Floridan with the most ordinary of male seducers. "His" masculinity is thus of the most standard sort, containing the common denominator of the male. This is the sense of Célimène's allusion to Parisian flatterers as the normal man (III, iv). Alidor's long scene of poetic and amorous doctrine is thus a link between the earlier discussions of Filandre's male qualities and the two sisters' discussions of masculine character in reference to Floridan.

Through a mastery of the signs of masculine identity Floridan conquers the cold and inaccessible woman as well as the amorously experienced one. In doing so "he" carries the male traits to their exhaustive limits; Floridan pushes the characteristic of *feinte* to a level of irony inaccessible to the real male. However, the nature of disguise in the theatre is to manifest not simply the mastery of identity codes but also the separation of these codes from the real nature of the disguised character. Identity plays exist by virtue of the distance separating the message of a character's identity from the bearer of that message. The signs of maleness have no reflection in the signified male, since there is no real Floridan from the point of view of the spectator. Yet, at the same time, there is no sign of femininity within the character viewed by Célimène and Félicie. In the disguise there is, for the other characters, a signified identity which (as they find later) has no physical reality, no referent or bearer. For the spectator there is a physical reality whose identity is temporarily suppressed and is no

longer expressed by the conventional signs. The two descriptions
overlap however in the designation of the neutral, asexual element of
the character, the traits which remain sufficiently constant in the
heroine for the spectator and the other characters to recognize a
common object of their attention. This element figures within the
language of the play in the syllable "Flor-," unmarked by gender, to
which the variable of sexual identity can be attached. Filandre
underlines this constant in speaking to Célimène:
> Un mot, belle inhumaine: un certain gentilhomme
> Nommé Flor. . .Floridan, c'est ainsi qu'il se nomme . . .
>   (III, iii)

The being of the character Floridan consists partly in the linguistic
and extra-linguistic codes of maleness and partly in the stage presence
of the actress playing Florante. What saves the character Florante
from existing solely as a fictive point of encounter of these different
verbal descriptions is this concrete reality, the aspect which makes
disguise in the theatre different from the theme of disguise in the novel.
In a prose narrative Floridan and Florante would be simply fictive
configurations of words subsumed under the designation Florante/
Floridan or the unmarked "Flor," to which is assigned a real feminine
identity and a fictive masculine one. Floridan is a type of synecdoche,
part of the character "Flor" or Florante in which the feminine form is
the definitive, encompassing whole. In the theatre the visual form
taken by the disguise and the physical presence of the actress raise this
rhetorical level to that of a physical, three-dimensional pun. Instead of
having simply a double meaning (which Floridan's words do have)
this disguised character has a double being. To some characters "he"
is a man, to another a woman.

Célimène does not simply contain an example of disguise with its
technical devices of implementation. The work as a whole exists for the
disguise, for the temporary transformation of the heroine into an
image of the hero. The first act establishes the relationship
Florante-Filandre and, after designating the identity codes and their
use, sets in motion the disguise which appears in the following acts.
Although Filandre's desertion to Célimène could be hastily and
vaguely described as the motivation of the disguise that follows, the
reason for the precise choice of disguise as a tactic remains mysterious.
No explanation is given for this peculiar form of counter-offensive

which Florante takes against her rival. In fact, while the first act prepares the spectator for the play on the masculine identity that follows, the idea of disguise slips into the dialogue in a deceptively casual way, as a trope which is seized on and incarnated by the heroine. Significantly, it is Filandre who uses this figure, as we recall, to describe his own lack of success with Célimène:

Crois que tu pourrois peu sur cette âme inhumaine,
Qu'en mon lieu tu serois en une même peine.
Elle n'estime rien que ses propres appas;
Vénus sous mes habits ne la toucheroit pas:
Tous objets sont communs à ce coeur insensible.

(I, v)

Thus the hero introduces the possibility of an exchange of identity with Florante, or an extension of his own identity to Florante. It is here that the disguise takes its impulsion and general form.

Filandre's words not only introduce the project of disguise but trace the underlying system of sexual desire. His allusion to Venus is especially profound. By joining the image of Venus to the male costume, Filandre invests the goddess's name with several levels of meaning. As a mythological entity, Venus personifies an abstract eternal force provoking desire in both men and women. Secondly, and more pertinently, Venus represents the force which arouses passion in women.[4] When Filandre claims that Venus herself could not arouse Célimène, he is saying figuratively that Desire itself could not waken Célimène's desire. But this mythological hyperbole coexists with a less abstract use of the name Venus. The goddess is drawn back from this purely symbolic realm into the physical world in which she could wear a costume. In this sense, no longer an abstraction, she is a physically present, woman-like being, capable of taking on a human costume. Filandre's allusion to Venus's wearing masculine dress exploits a paradox which is inherent in the traditional symbol of feminine desire. A feminine deity depicted as a woman, Venus not only represents woman's heterosexual desire but also the cause of that desire. By imagining the woman goddess in his own masculine costume, Filandre confronts woman with her own desire as she finds it in man. The circularity which exists in this myth—the woman provoking and representing feminine heterosexual love—constitutes the circle within which the action of the disguise is inscribed.

This rich association of the physical and the purely symbolic senses in the image "Vénus sous mes habits" leads to a complex series of circular or reflexive desires. The woman dressed as a man wakens a woman's love. The man finds in a woman dressed like himself the source of his own contentment. Although the hero's expression seems at first merely rhetorical, the text quickly makes clear that Filandre's words have a deep and serious connection with the dream of disguise. At the hint of setting Florante in his place, "en mon lieu," in relation to Célimène, the heroine asks, "Et si je lui plaisois?" The "joke" or trope is transformed into a dreamlike project in which the normal social and sexual order will be violated. The introduction of the disguise in the form of a joke, which can be seen as a socially acceptable expression of a deeper and unacceptable fantasy, makes the rest of the play a kind of interpreted or deconstructed joke. The following four acts of the work render explicit the fantasy which normally precedes the making of a joke in everyday psychic activity.

When Florante's reply, "Et si je lui plaisois?" transforms the image into a project, Filandre expresses his gratitude for her complicity. In an apparently inexplicable way (were one to apply a single-level or realist criterion of verisimilitude) Filandre accepts this transition to an active level of discourse. He declares in fact that all his happiness depends on the success of the disguise and on Florante's conquest of Célimène's affections:

Ta force en cet effet seroit incomparable,
Tu ne me serois plus qu'un objet adorable;
De tels voeux dependroit tout mon contentement,
Et je mépriserois l'amante pour l'amant.

(I, v)

Filandre's image and desire therefore provide the sole impulsion for the disguise that follows. He is the writer, *metteur-en-scène* and spectator of the scenes that follow in a type of play-within-a-play. Florante promptly begins her disguise by assuming the name Floridan (an assimilation of the names Florante and Filandre) and borrowing some of her ex-lover's clothes.

Beyond its source in what seems to be Filandre's whim, the intrigue that follows finds a justification, though not a cause, in the imbalance of relationships that characterizes *Célimène*. Even before the first act the chain of the loved and unloved, typical of pastoral, has begun. Florante loves Filandre, who loves Célimène, who loves only herself; Alidor loves Célimène; Lysis and Félicie, Célimène's sister, are in love. The disequilibrium springs from Filandre's desertion of Florante and from Célimène's refusal of love and her narcissistic attitude. In working from the original state of disarray to a final satisfactory state of three couples, the author introduces a greater disequilibrium, destined, thanks to the peculiar possibilities of identity disguise, to purge the original imbalance.

One effect of Florante's disguise is to break down all of the ties between couples as they stand at the beginning of the play, thus creating a state of freedom in which the couples can be formed or re-formed. Filandre himself suggests the necessity of breaking the *liens* which tie him to Célimène so that he can reenter his *premiers liens* with Florante (I, v). As the play of disguise gets under way it becomes clear that a general breaking up of relationships must take place in order to accomplish this intention. Alidor's desire to conquer Célimène is necessarily frustrated or adjourned by the creation of an affection for Floridan in Célimène. The destruction of the couple Félicie-Lysis has less apparent motivation. However, Filandre, who is responsible for the course the relationships take, makes it clear that Floridan's conquest of Célimène's sister is desirable to him, thus part of the primary design of disengaging Filandre from Célimène. Filandre manifests this wish by inciting Félicie to feel the same attraction towards Floridan as her sister does. After commenting on Célimène's growing love for Floridan, Filandre says to Félicie,

Adieu; craignez vous-même une pareille peine,
Puisqu'il a bien touché cette belle inhumaine.
                                                                    (III, vi)

Filandre also compliments Florante on her power over Félicie (IV, iii) as an element of her accomplishment of their joint project. Thus the reorganization of all affective relationships is set forth as an inherent part of the play of identity.

The coexistence of two sexual identities in one physical character is an extremely economical dramatic device for the reestablishment of the proper relationships at the end of the play. No complex affective reordering at the last moment is involved. A simple revelation of the ambivalent character's sexual identity forces the duped and amorous victims to seek partners from among the available members of the appropriate or permitted sex. The reduction of the number of male characters from four to three by the reapparition of the woman Florante and the simultaneous increase in female characters from two to three produces the necessary balance for the dénouement. Such a neat numerical balance, however, is much more than the innocent trick utilized by Rotrou to bring to an end the misunderstandings and infidelities of pastoral comedy. From numerical balance of the sexes through imbalance to a new stability lies a path which corrects a deeper disequilibrium, one which exists within the characters themselves.

One cause of the instability of the situation of the beginning of the play is that Célimène in a very real sense refuses to enter into the circle of characters. She refuses to play her part as a woman for the sexual balance of the play. In attracting both Alidor and Filandre, Célimène receives twice the male homage to which she is entitled in the play's distribution, yet she refuses to accept either one of them by granting her love in return. She thus fulfills only half of the functions of a woman character. In order to force Célimène to enter the circle of sexual availability or activity, in other words to complete her sexual nature, Florante becomes a man. After having achieved the goal of provoking Célimène's love, Floridan's manliness has the advantage of being neutralizable. Floridan never fully enters the circle of available male characters, and "he" thus does not present any problem in the final arrangement of marriages. The false male awakens Célimène's love only to make it available to Alidor.

Floridan's ambivalent nature serves then as a transition between Célimène's isolation and the sexual participation necessary for the final balance of the play. While Célimène's original position may seem one of excessive freedom, contrasting with the amorous fixations or *liens* of the other characters, in her case as well there is a *lien* for Floridan to break: the bond attaching her to herself. This narcissism appears in numerous allusions. Filandre, of course, asserts, "Elle n'estime rien que ses propres appas" (I, v). Célimène says to her sister, "Je m'aime aujourd'hui seule . . ." (II, iii). To Alidor she says,

C'est assez, Alidor, que chacun songe a soi;
Je ne conserve point ce qui n'est point à moi.
(III, i)

Célimène explicitly removes herself from the circle of lovers and describes her heart as immovable, destined never to tend outside of herself towards another:

Ce n'est que de mon coeur que leurs plaisirs dépendent,
Je n'en possède qu'un, et tous me le demandent.
Qui le doit obtenir? qui seront les jaloux?
Nul de vous ne l'aura, pour vous accorder tous.
(I, iv)

This attitude of the heroine is far from original in the love poetry of the period. Alidor's verses to "Caliste" and their refrain illustrate the extent to which the chastity of the loved woman can be linked with narcissism in the poetic vocabulary:

> Rien ne peut égaler votre moindre ornement.
> Il n'est point de beautés à la votre pareille:
> Si vous désirez voir d'admirables merveilles,
>   Mirez-vous seulement.
>   (II, ii)

Célimène's attitude is one of feminine narcissism in a universe in which a woman-like goddess incarnates the causes of woman's desire. Is this perhaps one of the senses of Filandre's reference to Venus as the ultimate force which, combined with the male guise, could arouse a woman (if she were not totally heartless)? If so, Floridan's role as a disruptor of early sexual ties finds here a partial explanation. Célimène, as a woman turned inward towards her own being and beauty, could be most highly attracted (though unsuccessfully, according to Filandre) by a being possessing this feminine beauty as well as the appanage of masculinity. Floridan represents an intermediate androgynous step from narcissism towards sexual love for the male Alidor. By breaking the bond to self, Floridan creates in Célimène a new but impossible bond of desire for a creature combining, in a sense, Célimène and Filandre (or Alidor). In the impossibility of a return inward lies the creation of the third and final bond of love for Alidor, accepted as an inferior substitute for the ideal male Floridan.

Where does Filandre enter this dissolution and reattachment of affections? Although Filandre is ubiquitous in *Célimène*, he is not always present as an actor. His position in the last four acts of the play is that of internal spectator (or perhaps a kind of chorus). He either watches secretly the activities of Florante and the others (III, iv; V, viii) or openly interrogates them about their actions and feelings (III, iii; IV, iii). In this way Filandre forces Célimène to reveal her growing affection for Floridan (III, iii) or recapitulates with Florante her success (IV, iii). Admiring and satisfied, Filandre comments on the scenes he witnesses. Having seen Célimène and Floridan together, Filandre exclaims,

> Dieux! avec quelle grâce elle fait le transi!
> Célimène est touchée, et je le suis aussi!
>   (III, v).

As a spectator he appreciates the internal workings of the scene (the effect on Célimène) and its effect on himself as the ultimate intended watcher. No sign of the results of Florante's disguise escapes him. He retains and emphasizes the gestures and words which signify passion on the part of Célimène and Félicie. He avidly seeks such signs and echoes them as the internal representative of the spectators, again as a sort of one-person chorus. To Florante he describes his experience of observing her with Célimène:

> Il est vrai que tout cède à des charmes si beaux,
> Et je me sens atteint de mille traits nouveaux;
> Je sais que ton mérite a touché Célimène;
> L'amour qu'elle a pour toi ne m'est plus incertaine:
> Je la connus hier, et, caché dans ce bois,
> J'entendis clairement ses soupirs et sa voix.
>
> (IV, iii)

Florante clearly plays her part as a man with Filandre constantly in mind and accepts homages like this as the natural outcome of her disguise. She even provokes Filandre's attention to the spectacle of Célimène's passion for Floridan as, for example, when they approach Célimène and Alidor:

> Tu n'en peux plus douter; entends d'ici sa plainte,
> Et loue avecque moi cette agréable feinte.
>
> (V, viii)

Filandre, the male character behind the inner play as motivator and spectator, gradually reduces the other males of *Célimène* to similar roles of spectator. Lysis and Alidor, engaged earlier in the play in the active pursuit of the two sisters, one successfully and the other in vain, find themselves in the first scene of the fourth act hidden behind the decor while Floridan courts Félicie. The contagion of the attitude of spectator spreads to these other male characters through Floridan from Filandre. Ejected from the good graces or the tolerant reception of the women they love, the two suitors wish to attack the "rival" Floridan. In "his" defense the seducer asks them to resign themselves to passive observation of his courtship. Or rather, Floridan tells Lysis that he should collaborate by joining his desire to his "rival's" in a state of active mental adhesion to Floridan's conquest: "Vous dussiez souhaiter la voir dans mes bras" (IV, ii). This claim is surprising since it is addressed to Félicie's previously accepted lover, the male character with the least to gain from Floridan's maneuvers. While Floridan's claim to be helping Alidor by provoking Célimène's love has an objective justification (seen at the end of the play), this allusion to Félicie remains, on the level of sexual distribution of the characters, unjustifiable. Filandre and Alidor profit from the loves of the false Floridan, each gains a final match not guaranteed him at the beginning of the play, but Lysis in no palpable way gains from the detour in Félicie's affections. His only advantage, if any, must lie in the hidden value of spectatorship which gives him such delight. At the very end of the play Alidor, and to some extent Lysis, share the pleasure brought by the spectacle of Félicie's love for Floridan and of Célimène's (by then enlightened) complicity.

Filandre, responsible for this spectacle, gains from it a vicarious achievement of his own sexual aims. This seems to be the sense of his statement (I, v) that his contentment depends on Floridan's pursuit of Célimène, of whom Félicie is simply an adjunct or extension. Having no hope of winning Célimène by himself, Filandre suggests to Florante that she take his place in order to break the chain of passionate desire tying him to Célimène. Thereafter he simply allows his delegate to carry out his own original project. This is why he can withdraw his claim to Célimène with ill-concealed glee (III, iii). But in surrendering Célimène in this way it is not as if he had given her up to a stranger. Florante's disguise as a male offers the advantage of a male alter-ego whom Filandre can repossess sexually under her true female identity. Filandre expresses this process very concisely in a dialogue with Florante. She boasts of her amorous good fortune:

> Ce n'est qu'un en ces lieux que m'aimer et me voir;
> Je fais mille jaloux, et toutes vos maîtresses
> Sont prodigues pour moi de voeux et de caresses . . .

Filandre replies,

> J'ai bien plus fait que toi.

Florante: Comment?
Filandre: Je t'ai domptée.

                                                                              (IV, iii)

Filandre's quip opens the way to a clearer understanding of the hero's motivation for his strange insistence on Florante's disguise (I, v) and reveals complex perspectives in his relationships to Florante and Célimène. In order to possess Célimène through Florante, he must renounce for a time his male characteristics—from an aggressive, importunate suitor he becomes passive, from desirous of attracting Célimène's love he becomes indifferent to her. The masculine rituals of courtship are assumed by Floridan, who accepts the role of masculine *feinte.* Filandre does not take on feminine characteristics. His appearance, gesture, and speech are not perceived by any character as those of a woman. He is not disguised. Yet Filandre's role in the economy of the love intrigue takes on special flexibility and ambivalence. There is a complex turn in his vengeance on Célimène. Not only does he conquer her through a delegate acting totally for him, but he also becomes Célimène's successful rival for the hand of Florante/Floridan. In vesting (in the narrow sense of the verb) Florante with his masculine role, Filandre divests himself of a major portion of his own sexual identity. He is thus implicated in the same adventure of disguise of sexual identity that Florante undertakes. The various functions of

The various functions of the disguise already noted—the breaking up of the characters' original emotional bonds, the position of the male character as spectator, Filandre's delegation of Florante to take his place—seem to unite in a device which one could call *interception.* One of the most common dramatic conventions of the early seventeenth century is the movement of information through interception of messages. Characters for whom a message was not originally intended find and read letters, overhear conversations, discover inscriptions. *Célimène* itself contains numerous incidents of this sort, beginning with the discovery of Filandre's letters by Florante's aunt. Alidor's poem to Célimène is found by its intended receiver but also by Félicie, who reads the poem aloud to her sister (II, iii). Félicie, while clearly understanding the destination of the poem, has intercepted it. She in turn communicates the message to Célimène and receives the latter's command to write a reply to Alidor. Félicie thus intercepts, only to transmit, the message from Célimène to Alidor. It is Félicie's message which Alidor later reads (II, v).

The encouragement that he receives from the message is enough to lead Alidor to misunderstand another communication which he intercepts aurally in the first scene of act III. Hearing Célimène's stances to the power of love, Alidor exclaims,

Dieux! est-il en ma faveur qu'elle tient ce discours?
. . .
Enfin le ciel me rit, mes voeux sont approuvés,
Et sa main favorable a mes vers achevés.

In fact Célimène's soliloquy is an expression of her love for Floridan and of the passage from self-love to the love of another. Alidor does not profit from the love whose expression he has intercepted except to the extent that he receives Célimène's love from Floridan in the last act.

Another letter is transmitted to the wrong receiver in the fifth act when Floridan gives a letter from Félicie to Lysis. Félicie intends Floridan to receive the assignation set in the letter, but "he" voluntarily yields the written invitation as well as the opportunity it represents. In this way a third character, Lysis, intercepts his former mistress's expression of love for another. He was in a similar situation when he overheard the conversation between Floridan and Félicie (IV, i). Towards the end of the play Célimène verbally attacks the "traître, aveugle tyran de mes affections" (V, vii). Alidor takes the insults as addressed to him, only to hear Célimène explain,

Je ne vous parle pas, j'adresse ces injures
Au plus vil des mortels, au pire des parjures

that is, to Floridan. Alidor simply mistakes as destined for himself a message which he has intercepted.

While in the majority of pastoral comedies it is simply a convenient stage device, in *Célimène* the act of interception has a fuller meaning. For the characters' relationships are founded on a system of interception permitted by the disguise of identity. Célimène is the interceptor of Florante's love for Filandre. A close examination of Floridan's speeches shows the extent to which they are intended to remain true to the ultimate receiver while passing through the intervening Célimène. Florante differs from the other senders of amorous messages in that her message must be intercepted by a third party in order to be received by its primary or intended receiver.

Florante's goal in her disguise is to regain the affection of Filandre by pursuing Célimène. The latter is thus called upon to be the prism through which Florante's love must pass if it is to succeed. Célimène must not only convey this love (unwittingly, of course) to Filandre, she must believe that she is herself the object of the affection of Florante/Floridan. To this extent she does not simply conduct but intercepts Floridan's love. Such an interception is Filandre's condition for accepting Florante's love, which he refused when it was offered to him directly (act I). The hero makes this condition for acceptance of Florante's love clear by using the conditional mode in his original declaration. If Florante can provoke Célimène's love, he says, "je mepriserois l'amante pour l'amant" (I, v). Conversely, Florante can obtain Célimène's affections only by becoming herself the interceptor of an emotion destined for another, for the beautiful and charming male Floridan. To Célimène the presence of another feminine character would be neutral, transparent, incapable of attracting and retaining her glance. For this reason Florante takes on a guise which is opaque, through which Célimène cannot see and which she cannot ignore. "Floridan" is such a guise, an opaque intercepting figure which, having broken through Célimène's narcissism, captures the love which is destined for a male.

Célimène occupies the central place in the system of interception, since she stands between the strong positive and active love which is Florante's and the most demanding negative (or receiving) and passive love which is Filandre's. The conquest of Célimène is the central condition for the happy resolution of the play announced in the first act. Rotrou, setting the name of this central but passive interceptor in the title *Célimène*, indicates the center of affective transmission rather than the source or goal of the affection transmitted. The degree to which Célimène is simply an interceptor of the emotional message from Florante to Filandre, simply a point at which their affections cross and bond themselves, is indicated in Floridan's words when "he" speaks of his fidelity. While talking to Félicie, Floridan declares:

Je renonce, Madame, au bien de la clarté,
Si rien est comparable à ma fidélité.
                                        (IV, i)

The words signify, of course, Florante's incomparable fidelity to Filandre and are understood in this way by the public. In the same way Floridan's words to Célimène,

Il faut un autre nom à mon amour extrême,
Et c'est dire trop peu que de dire que j'aime
                                        (IV, vi)

are more than banal flatteries to the woman he is courting. They are an evocation of the bizarre path which Florante's love takes towards its destination in Filandre.

Floridan's true message of love is for Filandre, the spectator, who, by seeing his mistress's conquest of other women, becomes the recipient of that love which is sworn and accepted before his eyes. The women characters affirm repeatedly that only unseen love is true. As Floridan say to Félicie in a kind of maxim, "Alors qu'on aime bien souffre-t-on des témoins?" (IV, i). To Célimène Floridan states, playing on the sense of *témoins*,

J'attesterois en vain les hommes et les dieux.
Je ne désire point de témoins que vos yeux.
                                        (IV, vi)

In the middle of this act in which Florante asserts the unseen and private nature of true love, she meets Filandre and boasts to him of her success. She allows him to tell her his experience of listening secretly to Célimène's amorous complaint. From the contrast in Floridan's statements to the sisters and Florante's acceptance of the hero's hidden presence, the importance of the system of interception becomes even more clear. The truly beloved is he who, while unseen, sees what is supposed to be hidden. Célimène is simply the intercepting screen on which Florante's love plays and becomes visible before passing on to the ultimate invisible spectator.

Before becoming a useful mediating object, Célimène had constituted an obstacle to Filandre's love for Florante. Through the language of irony permitted by the false identity of Floridan, the recollection of this obstacle simply becomes another way in which Florante conveys her love for Filandre:

> Que j'atteste le ciel et toute la nature
> Que vous êtes l'objet du tourment que j'endure.
> Si vous n'avez causé la misère où je suis,
> Si votre occasion ne fait tous mes ennuis,
> Si je connois que vous pour sujet de ma peine . . . .
>   (III, iv)

The pain which Célimène causes Floridan comes from the nature of her role as an interceptor having different qualities, depending on the source and direction of the affection which she receives. Filandre's love is stopped by Célimène even though she doesn't feel any corresponding emotion. Florante's love, on the other hand, both creates love in Célimène and passes through, without touching Floridan reflexively, to attain its goal in Filandre, who responds by loving Florante.

Since Célimène's function as passive channel for the love of Florante and Filandre is echoed by Félicie, what becomes of the other male characters of *Célimène*? Filandre gives them no place in the design of the inner play. He announces only the hope that Florante will be able to break down the resistance of the haughty Célimène and makes no reference to the rivalry of other males. Rotrou could have written a play in which Florante and Filandre would have been reconciled while Félicie and Célimène were left disconsolate. This would have been unsatisfying, however, as a comedy in its historical aesthetic context. Are Lysis and Alidor therefore necessary simply as partners to content Félicie and Célimène in the final balance of the play?

Alidor and Lysis, as the other representatives of masculinity in the play, emphasize Florante's success in disrupting the original relationships of the characters. Defeated by Floridan, they gradually enter the circle of spectators formed by Filandre's wish. Floridan creates for "himself" a monopoly of the available women, leaving the men with only the ambiguous consolation that they should wish to see her seduce both women. Finally it is on Florante whom Alidor and Lysis depend to recover their loved ones (and their masculinity). Célimène and Félicie are Florante's to give away.

Floridan, having captivated the women desired by the men of the play, exerts a strong sexual domination over its population. Filandre, however, as he points out ("je t'ai domptée"), is the captor of Florante and through her of Célimène and Félicie. The pyramidal structure of sexual supremacy in the play manifests Filandre's achievement of control over all the characters, both male and female—a conquest all the more remarkable in that he himself is neither disguised nor seducer.

In taking Filandre's place in the courtship of Célimène, Florante demonstrates a greater mastery of maleness than he. In addition she undermines Filandre's sense of masculinity and masculine skill by direct verbal attacks against his conduct and his methods. Even before assuming her disguise she points out his failure as a male in his tactics of courting Célimène:

Tu lui parlois de pleurs, et c'est honte à Filandre
D'être cru seulement capable d'en répandre.
Est-ce par ces discours, ou par cette action
Qu'un homme doit prouver son inclination?
(I, v)

Later in the play she gives little lessons in technique, indicating the ignorance shown by Filandre about his own role. She comments, for instance,

Cette règle d'amour t'est encore inconnue.
Je trompe l'une et l'autre, et toutes deux m'aiment,
Je dois à toutes deux parler séparément.
(IV, iii)

Filandre avows, without any sign of bitterness, that Floridan surpasses him in the masculine art:

Tu sais mieux mon métier que moi-même;
Tu traites mieux l'amour avec moins de souci.
(IV, iii)

Filandre's complacent acceptance of Floridan's lessons and proofs of superiority hardly surprise; Florante only obeys Filandre's wishes in pointing out his weaknesses and insufficiencies. Filandre enjoys his replacement or displacement from the active erotic center of the play.

In doing so Filandre derives pleasure from a doubling, a *dédoublement*, which is depicted in *Célimène* and in other plays of the period as a source of contentment either during the functioning of the disguise itself, or as preparation for the pleasure of a recognition. The theme of the double, as is well known, is usually the source of anguish and fear rather than pleasure.[5] Even in the plays performed between 1630 and 1660 there are numerous indications that men saw the possibility of finding "another oneself" a source of anxiety.[6] In the plays involving feminine disguise, the male characters are often presented with what would seem to be the painful spectacle of their replacement. An irresistible super-male takes their place in the sexual economy of the play and usurps their other appanages of virility. In these plays, however, even when masculine fear and outrage are most violent (as in Rotrou's *Céliane*, for example) the final recognition gives pleasure. This is not simply the pleasure of a relief after a period of dramatic tension, but a contentment surpassing the happiness awaiting the hero had the disguise not taken place. The passage through the disguise constitutes a new relationship between the hero and the heroine.

Florante/Floridan and her kind in other plays of the period accomplish what the male wished to do himself. In certain plays the hero was not originally incapable of winning the love of the principal mediating woman. In these plays, however, as in *Célimène*, the disguised woman assumes the very place which the male held or coveted. She supplants him and becomes his double, his other self, but a double who is not simply an identical version of himself. Florante takes on some of Filandre's clothing, she takes a name which connotes masculinity and resembles Filandre's name, but it is what Florante adds to Filandre's identity which enables her to take his place. By combining the masculine and the feminine Florante becomes the supermale capable of winning all women. Since Filandre knows that he will possess Florante at the end of the play, it is through her that he will possess symbolically all of the women whom she possesses during the play. This same system underlies the male preference in the other plays for the woman who had become a male and captured other women, captives whom she sacrifices to the male upon her retransformation and submission to him.

Thus the disguised woman is an alter ego for the male and an instrument through which he conquers the sexual monopoly of the play. But Florante and her dramatic cousins are also the *personae* in whom heroes like Filandre find the fictive self-contained embodiment of what they demand for permanent satisfaction of their desires. Floridan is simultaneously Filandre's masculine self and the feminine self which will satisfy him in marriage after the end of the play. In the imaginary being called Floridan, the two principal characters are already joined. Moreover, to the extent that Floridan is the creation of Filandre's wishes, one might almost say that in Floridan Filandre is joined to himself, to a fuller, more beautiful, and more successful version of himself. He can possess this dream being through a concrete, physical marriage at the end of the play. The male character gives away his masculine active self only to find it again and repossess it in a new, feminine form. In this respect there exists a definite element of male narcissism in the male internal spectators of these plays. In the case of Filandre himself this narcissism is made more apparent by the juxtaposition of the femine narcissism of Célimène.

This narcissism is also related to the game-like nature of Florante's acts during her disguise. In a sense Filandre has made of his own being and actions a game which can function without reference to real accomplishment but simply for the pleasure of the activity itself, pursued on a higher level of self-consciousness. Since the activities of the fictive male Floridan are meant to yield finally to the normal order of reality in which Célimène will love a true man, they share with games a certain lack of consequence. In other words, in the last act, when Florante's disguise ends, the practical consequences of Célimène's and Félicie's love for "Floridan" also vanish. The rules of the game of disguise end, and the normal social habits are reimposed. The game-like characteristics of Floridan's activities extend also to the cold, abstract mastery with which Florante accomplishes her imitation of the male lover and her comments to Filandre about the *règle* of love (IV, iii). The concluding comments about a *doux passetemps* apply as well to the analogy between disguise and game and to its resemblance to drama. By establishing the form and goals of Florante's disguise, Filandre can see his own activities reflected in an abstract, gratuitous way. Floridan is, in this game, like a mirror image, a rival without substance. His existence is only the outline of Filandre himself; Floridan's game exists only at Filandre's pleasure to suspend the real. The hero can thus see himself reflected in pure activity, not bound by the contingency or consequences of everyday life. Although this game ends, the new relationship between Florante and Floridan created by the disguise remains. Filandre finds his own identity broadened by Florante's achievement. While the heroine courts Célimène, and through her, Filandre, the hero retreats into his new imaginary stance. He revels in the fiction of a possible passivity and receptiveness which, due to the social definition of the male role, is impossible in fact. The hero wishes simultaneously to conquer the feminine characters in his world and to be conquered by the woman who loves him. But such an achievement of the active male role and the passive female role in his own person is possible only by the creation of the fictive intermediary in the person of the pseudo-male, like Floridan. The play revolves around this fictive being (fictive even within the fiction of the theatre at large). The other characters become the pawns in the game between them. The Célimènes of these plays are simply the temporary interceptors and transmitters of the love of the disguised heroines as it passes on to its destination in the minds and imaginations of their lovers.[7]

The thematic structure of *Célimène* appears with surprising insistence in the French theatre during Rotrou's career. Occasionally it fills the whole play as it does in Rotrou's work; sometimes it forms a smaller episode. The major elements, however, reappear under different names and places, in different variations of plot and motivation, to form a system of relationships common to works based on

a woman's disguise as a man. There are at least sixty-one plays in the period from 1630 to 1660 which include an incident of this kind of disguise.[8] In fact, this is the most frequent identity theme after discovery of a hidden kinship. Rotrou in particular gives the woman's disguise as a man an important place in his work. It appears in a third of his total production. Mairet, Mareschal, Benserade, Boisrobert, Desfontaines, and Pierre Corneille each use the theme in two of their plays, and Quinault and Scudéry in three of theirs. Moreover, the way in which women cross the boundary of sexual roles and modify their relationships with the other characters seems to form a similar recurrent theme, a veritable myth of sexual identity proper to the theatre of this period.

Célimène serves here as a guide to the essential elements of the myth into which the theme organizes itself in these texts. Rotrou's comedy contains a pattern that reappears in other plays either in its entirety or in fragments. As in *Célimène* the disguise in other plays is constituted by a temporary deformation of the codes of dress, gesture, and speech resulting in a disruption of their communication of the sex of the bearer of the codes. Dress remains the primary and becomes occasionally the only means of communicating sexual identity to the other characters. This is the case when disguise becomes involuntary, the accident of a costume not changed when the will of the character to disguise herself ends. The disparity between dress and the other codes results in a failure of identity or madness. For example in Beys' *Hospital des foux* (III, vi), Méliane is still dressed as a man but demonstrates her love for Palamède while insisting that she is a woman. The example from Beys tends to confirm the demonstration in act V of *Célimène* that the identity codes involved in disguise can be separated but only at the risk of falling into this state of incoherence. The character who behaves by mixing the codes and by allying the primary code of dress with the wrong gestures and words is rejected into a neutral territory which is classed as homosexuality, a form of madness.

Occasionally the disguise of sex through temporary transformation of speech is suppressed in favor of gesture and dress alone. This happens in Pierre Corneille's *Théodore, vierge et martyre.* Unlike most plays containing this theme, *Théodore* leaves the public as well as the characters of the play to conclude the heroine's identity on the basis of partial and misleading information. In *Célimène,* as in almost all plays of feminine disguise, the public is given sufficient, even abundant, knowledge of the character's identity before the disguise is undertaken. *Théodore* proceeds in the opposite fashion. The heroine is condemned to a degradation calculated to be the most cruel to a Christian woman. However, she escapes from the brothel to which she was taken by exchanging clothes with Didyme, her lover. Using the perspective of an internal spectator in the play in the person of Placide, another suitor of Théodore, Corneille transfers the erotic content of the situation. Instead of the feelings of the heroine herself inside the brothel, the dialogue traces the effect produced on Placide by the appearance of the person who exits from it. The public remains as ignorant as Placide of the identity of this person. This incident, in the fourth act, is prepared by a subtle play of irony. At the end of the third act, the public knows that Marcelle, wife of the governor of Antioch,

where the action takes place, has threatening rather than favorable
intentions towards Placide and Théodore. Placide believes, however,
that Marcelle is acting in his favor although too slowly. Then he
discovers that the woman he loves is no longer in prison but probably
"dans l'ignominie" (IV, i). In the following scene Placide allows
himself to be persuaded that all is well, only to hear an account which
leads him to believe the worst. He is told that Didyme entered the
place of Théodore's captivity to be the first to violate his mistress.
When he left,

<blockquote>

Il n'était plus, en sortant, ce Didyme
Dont l'orgueil insolent demandait sa victime;
Ses cheveux sur son front s'efforçaient de cacher
La rougeur que son crime y semblait attacher,
Et le remords de sorte abattait son courage,
Que même il n'osait plus nous montrer son visage;
L'oeil bas, le pied timide, et le corps chancelant,
Tel qu'un coupable enfin qui s'échappe en tremblant.

</blockquote>

(1275-82)

This misunderstanding is dispelled by Placide's friend Cléobule (IV,
iv) informing him that this shameful Didyme was none other than
Théodore herself. During the moments in which Placide and
the public are duped by the disguise, however, they jointly participate
as fascinated if horrified spectators of the sexual degradation of
Théodore. Théodore's disguise does more than save the heroine from
the humiliation which, paradoxically, it seems to prove. Through this
temporary appearance as a man, Théodore is, on different levels of
identity, both the victim and the ravisher. She thus combines the roles
of the woman who is disguised to court another and the courted
woman which are separated in *Célimène*.

The use of partial disguise in *Théodore* is much subtler than that in
Célimène and in disguise plays generally because the public is
deliberately excluded from the circle of complicity. The resultant
surprise and other effects (including increased erotic content) are
permitted largely by the full utilization of only one of the identity
codes, that of dress. Gesture is here left neutral from the viewpoint of
sexual identity and free therefore, for numerous interpretations of its
emotional connotation. By eliminating speech the disguise is carefully
left open for retrospective interpretations (characteristic of Corneille's
use of identity themes). Silence itself becomes a conveyor of emotion,
that of shame. *Théodore* remains, however, an exception in its partial

use of the signs of sexual identity. Most plays use the elements of disguise more fully and confirm the primary information of dress with masculine gesture, especially in duels and speech.

Considering the relatively large number of plays with the same major plot element, this similarity must not be obscured by differences in the ways of bringing the woman's disguise about. In other words, various and evidently subordinate reasons are used to introduce the motif of disguise just as different methods are used in novels to eliminate, for example, a character whose presence is no longer necessary. The more plays constructed on disguise one views or reads, the more one feels that disguise was such an appreciated dramatic event that it took precedence over other plot elements. A pretext, a motivation or explicit reason must be given to justify the disguise, but it is often very flimsy.

The awkwardness of the insertion of some disguises makes it appear that the play takes a detour to assimilate the disguise. Perside's behavior in Rotrou's *Hypocondriaque, ou le Mort amoureux* is an example of the insertion of a woman's disguise as a man into a work which seems as a whole to have no connection with the theme of sexual identity. Perside exchanges clothes with her male cousin Aliaste. The reason given for this disguise is Perside's father's objection to her leaving the house to visit her lover, the "mort amoureux." Yet the little importance given to the father's prohibition, mentioned in only four lines (III, iv), hardly seems sufficient to explain the rather extreme strategem adopted. Perside, besides, does not disguise herself until much later (IV, iii). Then she appears disguised during fourteen lines and vanishes to reappear later in her own form. After she leaves, her father is duped by Aliaste's disguise as a woman—an incident that seems to have nothing to do with the general plot.

Many plays, in which motivation for disguise is minimal, show that transvestism often does not simply fit into the plot as a convenient device. Instead authors seem to find excuses to insert the disguise even at the cost of *vraisemblance*.[9] The insistence on such episodes or main plots of disguise seems evidence that temporary transformation of sexual identity is not simply a device but a theme in itself, a mysterious convention of the period, a myth of the baroque imagination which can be seized in its unity.

In this light, setting aside the given details of motivation, one finds broad patterns reappearing in feminine disguise in plays which at first seem fairly distant. One such pattern, the most fundamental perhaps, is the motif or set of two motifs, "a woman disguises herself as a man in order to pursue an unfaithful lover." *Célimène* develops this motif at great length and with many nuances, but the same situation arises in other plays where the given motivation (if any) is quite different. In Rotrou's *Deux Pucelles* Don Antoine courts and deserts Théodose and Léocadie. Both girls disguise themselves as men and take the road after him. The same incidents occur in Quinault's *Les Rivales*. In Benserade's *Gustaphe*, the hero flees his father's court and marries the daughter of the king of Turquestan. Later his mistress Célinte, a Persian princess, arrives disguised as a Turk (male) and insists on following him in that disguise to the Turkish court, where she passes for a man. In *Les Trois Orontes* of Boisrobert, Cassandre, Oronte's mistress, disguises herself as a man and comes from Bordeaux to Paris, where she claims to be Oronte and tries to win Caliste, Oronte's fiancée. The titular heroine of Rotrou's *Diane* leaves her pastoral home in pursuit of her lover Lysimant, who has deserted her for the richer marital opportunities of the city. Diane disguises herself, after other transformations, as her brother in order to claim Lysimant's new fiancée for herself. In Desmarets de Saint-Sorlin's *Scipion*, Hyanisbe, "princesse des Isles fortunées" disguises herself as a soldier in order to follow her unfaithful Garamante during the battles between Romans and Carthaginians in Spain.[10]

Within most works of this sort, numerous practical considerations are either given or assumed (to be sought in the general stock of *vraisemblances* and conventions of the period and genre). Thus it can be argued that women dress as men to avoid the brigands with which the forests are always supposed to be infested, or to escape from parents. While Rotrou usually indicates masculine infidelity as cause of the disguise, occasionally he and other playwrights depict women disguising themselves to make the first approach towards a man or to accompany a faithful lover. In Beys' *Hospital des foux*, Rampale's *Belinde*, and Rotrou's *Amélie, Cléagénor et Doristée*, and *L'Heureux naufrage* a girl disguises herself during an elopment. Chevreau's protagonist in the *Advocat duppé* is the victim of the machinations of two sisters, one of whom disguises herself as a man in order to become his clerk and persuade him to marry the other sister and in the *Feint Alcibiade* of Quinault a girl changes places with her male twin to approach the man she loves. All these plays have in common the notion of the necessity of taking on the characteristics of a male in order to provoke or maintain the man's love.

In still another group of plays the reasons for the woman's disguise are tied more closely to the father and the family than to the lover. This happens when the girl is disguised from her infancy, an additional complication which links sexual disguise with the thematic of kinship. The heroine of Boisrobert's *La Belle invisible* was raised as the male Alexis. The marriage between the "son" of her family and Lucille was arranged, before their births, to obtain for Olympe's family the wealth of Lucille's family. Molière uses the theme in his *Dépit amoureux* in which Dorothée is raised as the male Ascagne.[11]

These disguises of women as men, although undertaken for different reasons in the individual works, have in common that they are undertaken in order to deceive, please, and win the love of a man. Transvestism has a male destination in all the plays and often a male instigator as well. The male is at the origin of the woman's disguise when he, like Filandre, suggests it in situations of rivalry of the *Célimène* type, or for the more usual purposes of elopement as in *Cléagénor et Doristée*. A man is also the immediate motivator of the disguise when he demands a male in the place of a female heir in the last group of plays mentioned. The broader and more profound connection appears, however, in the male destination of the disguises. Whatever the relationsips established in the course of the plot, the effect on a principal male character is the determining factor in the success of the transformation of identity. This is true whatever the range of emotional inpulsion given—from the love of the *Deux pucelles* to the hatred and desire for vengeance in Sallebray's *Amante ennemie*. In the larger number of texts the male character whose demands, infidelity, or crime are the immediate cause of a woman's change of identity, is also the goal of the woman's amorous intentions.

In the course of the plays the woman's disguise leads her to situations designed to prove her maleness—her ability to replace a real male and even to surpass him in activities which define his sexual identity. In *Célimène* the stress of the work as a whole is on the heroine's ability to win the love of another woman and replace a male in the most plainly sexual way. Floridan also shows some military prowess against Lysis in a fight. Plays of feminine disguise generally include episodes of a woman's falling in love with the disguised heroine, a number contain also the demonstration of surprising strength, and a few contain only the proof of this last quality. Given the fact that the majority of these plays are comedies in which the love intrigue dominates and in which military exploits enter only marginally as proof of masculinity, it seems proper to designate the motif of "the love of one woman for another woman disguised as a man" as the major characteristic episode of the woman's assumption of male identity. Occasionally two women organize the spectacle of their (pretended) love with the explicit intention of being seen by a man, who, like Filandre, will be drawn back to one of the women by this inner spectacle within the dramatic work. This is an episode especially prevalent in Rotrou. In his *Céliane* the heroine of the title disguises herself as a gardener in order to spy on her unfaithful lover (IV, iii), an act numbered by the characters as amount the "étranges moyens" of regaining a lover. She contents herself with passive observation until Julie conceives a stratagem to revive Florimant's love, a project "Où ce déguisement me servira beaucoup" (IV, vii). In act V Julie informs Florimant, who has deserted Céliane in order to pursue Nise, that Nise has given herself to a peasant. He witnesses, or rather hears (one wonders why such an elaborate visual disguise is created for an aural proof) a tryst between the disguised Céliane and the woman Nise. When Florimant has left in a rage, Julie remarks to Céliane,

Qui t'a si bien instruite en l'art de courtiser?
Mille fois ma franchise à ta voix s'est rendue,
Et je brûle d'amour de t'avoir entendue.

(V, iv)

Not only does Céliane receive the compliment of having surpassed Florimant in the art of seduction, a superiority so effective in returning Filandre to Florante in *Célimène*, but she also continues to manifest her powers, this time visually, for the theatrical public. Her gestures with Julie, whom she begins to caress, are evoked in the text by the words of Nise ("les voyant s'embrasser" in the directions),

Mon amant à mes yeux en caresser une autre,
La baiser, l'embrasser! Infidèle, inconstant.

Céliane then demands satisfaction for "l'ardeur qui me presse" from both of the women present since it is the custom of "hommes de ce temps: / Quand ils n'en ont que deux, ils sont assez contens." The "agréables feintes" continue (V, viii) before two male lovers, Florimant and Pamphile, who are treated to even more sensuous performance than previously. Upon discovering the ruse, the principal male character whose infidelity caused the major imbalance in the pairing of lovers undergoes the same conversion to his first love that Filandre experienced. Like the latter he attributes his second change to the *feinte* of his mistress: "Dieux, que j'en suis touché! que sa

voix a de charmes! / . . . Heureuse invention!" Julie refers to his new
emotion as "l'heureux effet" (understand "de notre ruse") and
Céliane thanks the author of the disguise, Julie, whom she credits with
the resultant recapture of Florimant:
        Et toi qui m'as portée à cette invention,
        Que je suis obligée à ton affection!
                                                        (V, viii)
Julie explains at length to Pamphile and Florimant the source and
intention of the disguise, attributing to herself the most important
aspect of it—the pretended love of Nise and the male Céliane—but she
omits a number of steps in the psychological demonstration:
                . . . j'ai conçu cette feinte
        Pour bannir d'entre nous la tristesse et la plainte
        . . .
        Leurs crimes supposés, et leurs feintes caresses,
        Donnent à trois amans leurs premières maitresses.
                                                        (V, viii)
The elements of the explanation given here skip over precisely the
deep causal elements that are also omitted from Filandre's more
lengthy demonstration of the same effects in *Célimène*. The characters
who arrange the disguise seem to be aware of the pleasure and the
utility derived by the male characters who see themselves mirrored in
this imitation. But the creators of the disguise do not attempt to
translate the cause of this pleasure into words. In *Céliane* the various
roles or functions of the plot have been redistributed—Julie is the
internal *meneur-de-jeu*, Céliane is the principal actress and the disguised
woman but much less the active collaborator in the elaboration of the
internal plan, Florimant is the internal spectator although the dupe of
what he sees until near the end of the play. The two other male
characters are drawn into the role of spectators in different ways from
Alidor and Lysis, but the same mechanism functions. The male
declines to passive spectator position and the female rises to a position
dominating the erotic potential. The males of *Céliane* are, in this part of
the play (from the middle of the third act until the end of the last act),
moved even more into the periphery than in *Célimène*; unlike Filandre
they are not even aware of the emotional patterns which can exorcise
the unsatisfactory erotic bonds in which they are caught.
    More common than plays in which women consciously perform an
internal play (or "agréable feinte") for the male spectator, are those
plays in which the abandoned mistress directly replaces her former

lover with the given motivation of delaying or destroying his marriage
to the second woman. This occurs in Boisrobert's *Trois Orontes* when
Cassandre precedes her lover to Paris, assumes his name, and demands
the fiancée promised him. Caliste is already in love with Cléante and
has planned to avoid the marriage with Oronte, but finds this false
Oronte so attractive that she falls in love with "him." The situation
lasts for about one act and from the point of view of the subplot
"woman disguised as man" Caliste is simply the passive vehicle of
Cassandre's active love for Oronte. Again the male is conquered by
being replaced, eliminated from the center of the play, and cut off
from his sexual identity and his relationships with the other women in
the play. At the same time the true male lover of Caliste is reduced to a
secondary position of passivity during the time that his mistress is the
victim of Cassandre's disguise. Rotrou's Diane (in *Diane*) usurps her
faithless lover Lysimant's place in his engagement to Rosinde by
taking on the identity of her own lost brother Lysandre, her ready-
made familial male *alter ego*.

The direction taken by the theme of sexual disguise is clear from
these few examples of conscious, direct replacement of the male by a
female in the affections of the second woman whom he desires. No
connections, however, need be established either in emotion or in
family relationship between the women who fall into the trap of the
pretended male and the true male at whom the disguise is aimed or for
whom assumed. Many plays simply establish the attractiveness of the
disguised woman to other available female characters, in contrast to
the male's lack of noticeable or noticed beauty. The male's place is
preempted in reference to his potential conquests rather than to an
actual or intended one. This version of the episode of a woman's
mistaken love for another seems a step backwards from the more
explicit and self-conscious form the theme takes in plays in which the
heroine plans to provoke such a love

In Sallebray's *Amante ennemie*, for example, Flavine falls in love with
Claironde, disguised as Floridan, in what appears to be a purely
accidental subplot. Claironde's disguise is aimed at Tersandre, whom
she intends to kill in revenge for a brother's death. The double love of
Tersandre's sister Flavine and her confidante Clymène for the
disguised Claironde and Lucine, respectively, seems unnecessary to
the main action of the play. Yet this apparent subplot begin at the end
of the second act, occupies most of act IV, which contains amorous
dialogues and kissing (viewed by a male, Meliarque, whose place is

thus taken), and continues into the last act. Only in the last scene of the play do Flavine and Clymène discover the sex of their "lovers" although the male characters, beginning with Tersandre (V, ix), are aware of the disguise. Siginificantly, the hero decides to pretend to ignore Floridan's sex and to allow the internal play of disguise to take its course. He thus becomes an internal spectator and steps aside, so to speak, to see how Claironde will conduct her disguise and her retransformation into her original sex. This makes him an accomplice in the false love affair being lived by his sister and her confidante, a misunderstanding which lasts for three more scenes.

In a final resurgence of the theme of the contagion of a woman's love through a second woman to attain its ultimate destination in a man, Meliarque accepts Lucine's love after she wins Clymène. This means in effect that he prefers the love of the woman who disguised herself as a man and replaced him in the affections of Clymène to the love of the latter. While this last development of the play situates itself in the background, since it takes place among secondary characters, it demonstrates how the theme discerned in *Célimène* reduplicates itself in the interstices of other plays not based openly on the theme. *L'Amante ennemie* manifests in this way the implantation of a true system of feminine disguise which continues to operate even when it is depicted as an "accident" of the plot. Lucine wins Meliarque's love even though this was not her intention in assuming the identity "Dorimon."

Such accidents are a general occurrence in the theatre of sexual disguise. The heroine who assumes a man's identity for any number of reasons provokes the love of another woman without meaning to do so. This is often followed by a man's preferring the disguised woman to the other. The disguised character is often in no danger of losing the man's affection to begin with. The conquest of a second woman is simply a superfluous *tour de force*, all the more revealing of the integrity of the theme because of its gratuity in relation to the main action. Thus in Beys' *Hospital des foux* Méliane, who had eloped with Palamède at the beginning of the play, is loved by Eliante (act V) who believes Méliane to be a man named Clindor. Since Eliante has also fallen in love with Palamède (at the middle of act I), Clindor's accidental conquest is another case of a woman's replacing the loved man in the affections (albeit unwanted) of a second woman. Eliante's love is just another of those intercepting or mediating steps towards the reuniting of the separated lovers, a step which stands out here because of its relative uselessness in the very loose plot.[12]

To reinforce the displacement of the male from his role of love—certainly more than a simple sign of the male's identity—women often take a warrior's role in the same plays. Claironde/Floridan in *L'Amante ennemie* prepared to fight first to revenge her dead brother and then to protect her new love and the Doristée of Rotrou's play who frightens off robbers to defend a stranger are only two of the many valiant women as men who appear frequently in the plays of the period. By taking the traditionally male profession of arms the woman may simply usurp a male prerogative, that is, she may push the male out of the active center of the play as she does when she replaces him in another's love,[13] or she may invert the traditional roles by defending a man from attackers as in *Cléagénor et Doristée* when the heroine frees herself and the unknown Théandre from robbers (II, ii) and in *L'Amante ennemie* when Claironde defends her lover Tersandre in an armored combat with his rival.[14]

Tasso's Clorinda and Ariosto's Bradamante and Marphisa in the *Gerusalemme Liberata* and the *Orlando Furioso* were, of course, as courageous and skilled in warfare as the heroines of these plays. But unlike the heroines of these popular Renaissance epics, the Claironde of Sallebray's play and Rotrou's Doristée, along with most of their fictional contemporaries, do not dwell in a heroic world in which valor and femininity merge happily into one unified personality. Instead these French heroines participate in what are primarily masculine pursuits during a temporary and clandestine crossing of a barrier. Bradamante's combat with the evil Pinnabel (XXII, xcvii) in the *Orlando Furioso* has by no means the same significance as the heroine's defense of the hero in *L'Amante ennemie*. Claironde's armor is a disguise, unlike the costume of Bradamante. Claironde can only conduct herself in the way common to epic martial heroines through the creation of an illusory masculine identity, only by encroaching on the domain of the hero. Bradamante shared Rogero's power, while Claironde usurps that of her lover.[15]

This feminine usurpation of the masculine prerogatives does not lead to a final divorce between the main characters but instead to their reunion. The hero, like Filandre of *Célimène* and Meliarque of *L'Amante ennemie*, repossesses his male sexual prowess and chooses, not the woman he lost to the disguised woman, but the aggressive disguised woman. This choice can already be seen in the man's assumption of the position of spectator, accepting the woman's new, although temporary, identity. When Meliarque enters the scene unexpectedly at one point in *L'Amante ennemie* he sees "Dorimon" kissing Clymène (IV, vi). This insistence on watching, on the visual, in these plays points to the function of the masculine characters as mediators between the inner play of disguise and the play as a whole and its external public. Although he is passive in reference to the major emotional activity of the plot, acted upon more than acting, the male internal spectator most definitely constitutes the focusing element of the work. Just as he is the destination of the efforts of the women who disguise themselves, so he represents the viewpoint through which the public of external spectators can receive the message of identity radiated by the disguised woman. This spectator deserves in his turn to be observed, especially when he becomes a commentator on the effect of the disguise or when he participates, like Filandre, in the elaboration of the spectacle.

L'Hospital des foux begins with such a commentary from the principal male character, who describes for another man the disguise of his mistress Méliane. Palamède stresses to his friend Célidan the effect of the disguise:

Ayant quitté Tolède assez heureusement,
Elle se résolut à son déguisement:
Célidan, ses beautez en mon esprit empreintes,
Finissent mon discours, et font naistre mes plaintes,
Comme je l'imagine, hélas si je te dis,
Qu'elle parût charmante en ces nouveaux habits,
Sans doute, Célidan, il faut que tu confesses,
Qu'elle trompa les Dieux et ravit les Déesses,
Imagine toy donc que dans ce changement,
Elle changea de port, de voix, de mouvement,
Qu'elle fit des jaloux, et vainquit des maistresses.

(I, i)

Palamède carefully enumerates the particular codes by which sexual identity is conveyed and notes that Méliane changed her use of each one to arrive at a complete outward transformation. Like the first act of *Célimène* this speech sensitizes the public to these codes before the appearance of the disguised woman on the stage. More important, however, is Palamède's subjective reaction. He discovers new charms in his mistress because of her disguise and insists upon the *image* she has left in his mind. In addition he points out with satisfaction that

Méliane replaces men in the affections of other women and reduces men to the level of "jaloux." Méliane is not simply another man, when disguised she is the superlative of masculine charm, obviously surpassing Palamède himself by winning the love of the goddesses. Not only does the hero admire this broadened identity of the heroine, but he also draws his friend Célidan into the circle of spectators, perhaps even of *jaloux*.

If, however, the hero is not aware of the difference between appearance and reality in the sexual identity of the disguised woman his reaction is different. He may of course simply not notice the woman or be in any way affected by her, as happens in Boyer's *Fédéric*. If the woman while disguised, however, succeeds in attracting the male character's attention the hero finds himself thrust into an ambiguous relationship with what he believes is a male. This situation exploits the suggestions of a false male homosexuality. But the possibility of passionate love between two men, while being a visible part of the play (much more here than in plays about a man's disguise as a woman), is not explored in detail. Feminine homosexuality as touched upon in plays of the man's feminine disguise is given much more explicit treatment. The male who is attracted to a woman disguised as a man is cut off from physical sexuality entirely, rendered inactive rather than feminine. The situation of Tersandre in *L'Amante ennemie* illustrates this predicament.

When Tersandre first sees the disguised Claironde and Lucine, he and Meliarque (who serves as Tersandre's confidant-spokesman) are struck by the beauty of the two "boys." Meliarque echoes Tersandre's sentiments when he exclaims,

> Dans le ravissement d'une telle merveille,
> Certes, encore un coup je doute si je veille.
> Dieux! de combien d'appas tous deux sont-ils pourvûs.
>
> (I, ii)

By the middle of the second act the two males of the play, especially Tersandre, have become dependent on the friendship and the physical charms of the two disguised girls. Meliarque indicates the erotic potential of this bond by pointing out that the qualities he admires are those he hopes to find in a woman, a remark that leads Tersandre to declare,

> Que je serois content, si celle qu'Hymenée
> Doit ranger avec moy sous mesme Destinée,

Estoit toute semblable, ou bien par accident
Avoit à tout le moins quelque air de Floridant.

(II, v)

The two men are cut off from any active masculinity by a fascination
which makes them spend their time regretting the impossibility of
marriage with the two beautiful persons. During this time Meliarque
actually does find that his place in the affections of Clymène has been
taken by Dorimon (Lucine), the young person to whom he is attracted.
Tersandre and Meliarque are trapped by a vision of beauty which
they can never touch because of social taboo and which erodes their
eventual hope of sexual satisfaction elsewhere. Like Filandre, but in a
more desperate way, they are fascinated by the image of their own
alienated sexual power incarnated in the very beauty which they
would have wished to conquer. Unlike the hero of *Célimène* they have
no way of realizing that they will ultimately be able to recuperate the
sexual role they have lost.

Yet Tersandre, like Filandre and the other heros of these plays, will
recover that masculinity which the heroine, in her disguise, had taken.
Completing the cycle of the woman's disguise, the heroine surrenders
to the hero his own image. Then, his narcissism satisfied, the hero will
marry the woman who has succeeded in her disguise.

It is tempting to speculate about the popularity of the Célimène
pattern among the largely male audiences of the early seventeenth
century theatre. Why would they enjoy seeing a spectacle in which the
male assumes such a peculiarly passive role? Presumably Filandre's
obsession reflects and touches some deep and unconscious part of the
public's, as well as the playwright's, psyche. Could the hero's desire to
delegate a large part of his identity to the woman be linked with some
masculine change of role or "identity crisis" in the France of Louis
XIII and of the young Louis XIV? Although such a problem of
psycho-history requires the attention of a historian working outside of
literary texts, there may be grounds for linking this theme and the rise
of such phenomena as *préciosité*. The decline of the independent
aristocracy and the growing importance of the court with the
consequent imposition of a new set of manners and a new attention to
language among courtiers—changes in which women seem to have
played a large part—may be forces involved in a redefinition of sexual
roles as well. Perhaps the male, confronted with a world in which
courtly graces, somewhat feminine, and certainly more passive than
the talents required of an independent feudal nobility, could lead to

preferment as quickly as military accomplishment, subconsciously tried out a new role. He could, in fantasy, surrender or delegate his dominant, aggressive role to the woman, who would then possess both the old and the new powers. By possessing the woman after this transformation in a relationship like that between Filandre and Florante/Floridan the male could have, in fantasy, both the old power of the warrior and that of the woman and courtier.

Footnotes

1. Jean Rotrou, *La Célimène* (1633), ed. Viollet-le-Duc (Paris: Th. Desoer, 1820), II, 75-166. All future references to Rotrou's plays will be based on this edition.
2. Numerous studies have centered on Rotrou's use of illusion. Especially interesting are J. D. Hubert's "Le réel et l'illusoire dans le théâtre de Corneille et dans celui de Rotrou" (*Revue des Sciences Humaines*, XCV, July-September, 1958, pp. 333-350), Jacques Morel's *Jean Rotrou, dramaturge de l'ambiguité* (Paris: Armand Colin, 1968), Francesco Orlando's *Rotrou dalla Tragicommedia alla Tragedia* (Torino: Bottega d'Erasmo, 1963). Robert Nelson's *Immanence and Transcendence, The Theatre of Jean Rotrou* (Ohio State University Press, 1969) and Timothy Reiss's *Toward Dramatic Illusion: Theatrical Technique and Meaning from Hardy to Horace* (New Haven: Yale University Press, 1971) also illuminate Rotrou's use of illusion.
3. This effect is totally independent of the actual sex of the performer because it is conventional, like any code. Men having women's roles would be identified as such in women's costumes, as were the actors performing the parts of old grotesque women and the *nourrice*. In the French theatre generally at this period male actors having women's parts were limited to such roles (S. Wilma Holsboer, *Histoire de la mise en scène* [Paris: Droz, 1933], p. 216). On the other hand, the actress Marcelle in the troop of Genest in Rotrou's *Saint Genest* tells Plancien that she sometimes disguises herself to play a male on stage (IV, viii).
4. Venus appears for example as the divine force responsible for women's desire in the *Roman de la Rose*. Jean de Meun's Amour admits that Venus has charge of a domain which he does not command (10719-44). Later Venus swears that she will destroy chastity in women and asks Amour to do likewise for men (15800-07).
5. Otto Rank, *Une Etude sur le double*, trans. S. Lautman (Paris: Denoel et Steele, 1932).
6. Plays of the period which show the dangerous consequences of the existence of a double include Scudery's *Ligdamon et Lidias ou la*

ressemblance (1631) and Rotrou's *Sosies* (1637). In Rotrou's *Les Ménechmes* (1630-31) the theme of the double is somewhat less somber.

In addition to these plays in which there are meant to be two existing physical persons having identical features and often the same name, there are many plays in which the disguise of mistaken identity itself creates a spiritual double. In Brosse's *Les Innocens coupables* (1643), for instance, the heroine is mistaken for someone else and is, under her normal identity, given charge of the "other." This situation reappears in Thomas Corneille's *Le Geolier de soi-même* (1655). A woman competes against herself in Boisrobert's *La Jalouse d'elle-mesme* (1648).

7. R. J. Nelson in his *Immanence and Transcendence* situates Rotrou in his Christian context and finds in his thematic "virtually Christian motifs. . .accepted intuitively" (p. 14). In this perspective Nelson discusses transvestism and homosexual love, "a motif that is obsessional in Rotrou" (p. 55). While Nelson is assuredly correct in describing this motif as "an intense spiritualization" of love, he underemphasizes the person for whom this spiritualization exists, the male lover of Célimène and Florante. It is the image of the fictive being, Floridan, that enriches the physical charms of the disguised woman with a second, purely spiritual (or mental) identity.

8. The tragicomedies, comedies, tragedies, and pastorals in which this theme appears are: Anonymous, *Persélide*, TC (1645); Anonymous, *La Fille généreuse*, TC (1650); Baro, *Cariste*, PD (1648-49); Benserade, *Iphis et Iante*, C (1636); Benserade, *Gustaphe*, TC (1637); Beys, *L'Hospital des foux*, TC (1634); Boisrobert, *Les Trois Orontes*, C (1651); Boisrobert, *La Belle Invisible*, C (1656); Boyer, *Fédéric*, TC (1659); Brosse, *Le Turne de Virgile*, T (1645); Brosse, *Les Songes des Hommes éveillés*, TC (1644); Chabrol, *Orizelle*, TC (1632); Chevreau, *L'Advocat duppé*, C (1637); Corneille, *Théodore*, T (1645); Corneille, *Clitandre*, TC (1631); de Croisac, *Méliane*, P (1653-54); Desfontaines, *Orphise*, TC (1635-36); Desfontaines, *Eurimédon*, TC (1635-36); Desmarets, *Scipion*, TC (1638); Dorimond, *L'Ecole des cocus*, C (1659); Dorimond, *L'Inconstance punie*, C (1659); d'Ouville, *Aymer sans sçavoir qui*, C (1645); Durval, *Panthée*, T (1637); Du Ryer, *Lisandre et Caliste*, TC (1630); Du Vieuget, *Policandre et Basolie*, T (pub. 1632); Gougenot, *La Comédie des comédiens*, TC (1631-32); Grandchamp, *Avantures amoureuses d'Omphale*, TC (pub. 1630); Lambert, *La Magie sans magie*, C (1656); La Serre, *Climène*, TC (1642); *La Tour, Isolite*, TC (1630?); Le Vert, *Le Docteur amoureux*, C (1637); Magnon, *Tite*, TC (1659); Mairet, *Solyman*, T (1635-37); Mairet, *Les Galanteries du duc d'Ossonne*, C (1632);

Mareschal, *La Généreuse Allemande*, TC (1630); Mareschal, *La Soeur valeureuse*, TC (1634); Molière, *Le Dépit amoureux*, C (1656); Montgaudier, *Natalie* (1654); Pichou, *Les Folies de Cardénio*, TC (1634); Provais, *L'Innocent exilé*, TC (1632); Quinault, *Les Rivales*, C (1653); Quinault, *La Généreuse ingratitude*, TCP (1654); Quinault, *Le Feint Alcibiade*, TC (1658); Rampale, *Bélinde*, TC (pub. 1630); Rayssiguier, *La Célidée sous le nom de Calirie*, (TC (1634); Richemont Banchereau, *Les Passions égarées*, TC (1632); Rotrou, *Amélie*, TC (1633); Rotrou, *Céliane*, TC (1631-32); Rotrou, *Célimène*, C (1633); Rotrou, *Diane*, C (1632-33); Rotrou, *Cléagénor et Doristée*, TC (1634); Rotrou, *L'Heureux naufrage*, TC (1634); Rotrou, *La Belle Alphrède*, C (1635-36); Rotrou, *Les Deux Pucelles*, TC (1636); Rotrou, *L'Hypocondriaque*, TC (1628); Rotrou, *Laure persécutée*, TC (1637); Sallebray, *L'Amante ennemie*, TC (1640); Scudéry, *Le Prince déguisé*, TC (1634); Scudéry, *Le Fils supposé*, C (1634); Scudéry, *Le Vassal généreux* (1632); Tristan, *Amaryllis* (de Rotrou), P (1653).

9. Chapelain noted an example of a woman's disguise to pursue her lover as being contrary to dramatic probability in Desmarets de Saint'Sorlin's *Scipion*: "Dans la constitution Hyanisbé m'y a toujours fort déplu, et je ne puis souffrir qu'une Princesse quitte son Païs et devienne vagabonde pour exercer une vengeance qu'elle pouvoit faire par cent de ses chevaliers ou par une armée allant ruiner le païs de celuy qui l'avoit offensée." (Letter from Chapelain to Balzac, May 7, 1639, cited in Lancaster, *History of French Dramatic Literature*, II, 219).

10. Similar situations occur in Georges de Scudéry's *fils supposé* (1636), Rayssiguier's *Célidée sous le nom de Calirie* (1634), Dorimond's *Inconstance punie* (1661), and Rotrou's *Florimonde* (1654), *Céliane*, and *La Belle Alphède* (1639).

11. Boyer used this situation in his *Fédéric* (1660), as did Benserade in *Iphis et Iante* (1637) and D'Ouville in *Aymer sans sçavoir qui* (1647).

12. Lambert's *Magie sans magie*, Rampale's *Bélinde*, Rayssiguier's *Célidée*, Rotrou's *Cléagénor et Doristée*, Mareschal's *Soeur valeureuse*, Boyer's *Fédéric*, Chevreau's *Advocat duppé*, D'Ouville's *Aymer sans sçavoir qui*, and Magnon's *Tite* depict a woman's falling in love with, or being engaged to marry, a disguised woman.

13. The fighting woman may fulfill simultaneously a martial and sexual role by assuming a man's defense of his mistress. Astérie in Baro's *Cariste* fights in an ordeal by combat to save her rival Cariste, whom Astérie had earlier accused of being a sorceress.

14. The heroine also defends her lover in Quinault's *Feint Alcibiade*, Rotrou's *Belle Alphrède* and *Deux Pucelles*.

15. These differences make any study of the woman's disguise as a man which limits itself to noting traits common to the theatrical theme and earlier epic martial heroines not only incomplete but misleading. Carmen Bravo-Villasante's thorough account of the *disfraz varonil* in the Spanish classical theatre, *La Mujer vestida de hombre en el teatro español* (Madrid: Revista de Occidente, 1955), fails to penetrate to the special characteristics of this dramatic theme and its creation of an imaginary male being.

The Man as Woman: Théocrine

Poliarque, the hero of a play by Pierre Du Ryer, disguises himself as a woman, Théocrine. Although plots like this one from the first *journée* of *Argénis et Poliarque ou Théocrine*[1] are much less common than plays in which women are disguised as men, these works also form a pattern of relationships which undermines and then reconfirms the system of sexual identity imposed by the social order. The new definition of the relations between the sexes and between members of the same sex in these plays extends the patterns of *Célimène*. This time the hero actively undertakes a transformation of his own sexual identity. Yet the resultant relationships are not, in consequence, the simple inversion of what we have seen in *Célimène*. Surprisingly the same sort of taboo is transgressed in *Argénis* as in *Célimène*—a venture into an apparent feminine homosexuality. And the male's disguise does not address the heroine through a triangular relationship symmetrical to that of Filandre-Florante/Floridan-Célimène. Instead, what seems to be an adventure into an abnormal relationship exists to exorcise that abnormality; what seems to be a more violent renunciation of masculinity than in *Célimène* proves to be a preparation for the celebration of the male in his most masculine role. If there is then an opposition to be made between the two types of disguises it is in the greater emphasis on the hero's masculinity in those plays where disguise would seem to cancel that quality.

The first act, in three scenes, establishes the identities and motivations of the three male forces, whose conflict leads to the disguise. In the first scene Licogène, a Sicilian prince, declares his ambitious desire to marry Argénis, daughter of the king of Sicily, Méléandre. Poliarque (scene ii), who has seen Argénis's portrait, is also in love with her. He decides to leave for Sicily, even though, as king of France, he is prohibited by Sicilian law from marrying the princess. Méléandre (scene iii), refusing Argénis to Licogène, decides to shut her up in a castle to prevent Licogène's agents from reaching her. This series of actions establishes two visible opponents—Licogène and Méléandre—and a third male force as yet unknown to them. Poliarque must confront the physical obstacle raised by Méléandre against all males.

In terms of the preparation of Poliarque's disguise, an action not begun until act III, the first act is rich in significance. Already Poliarque's identity interferes with his love because of the prohibition of marriages between the French and Sicilian monarchies. The hero must divest himself of his identity as "king of France" in order to pursue Argénis. Since the walls of the princess's castle are closed to all males, Poliarque, in a second phase of his strategy, must also divest himself of his masculine identity. These indications of the necessary identity transformations point the way to a precise alternative among the many which we could designate under the heading "not king of France." Instead of canceling the geographical index "France," Poliarque's disguise must cancel primarily the index of masculinity contained in "king." There exist several ways of canceling or hiding this indication of identity—transformation into a neutral (non-human) object (as did Jupiter in becoming a bull to take Europa or into a golden rain for Danae),[2] apparent castration in order to pass as a eunuch (as in La Fontaine's comedy of that title), or disguise as a woman. It is the last alternative that Poliarque chooses, as do most of the male characters of the period when faced with this dilemma.

Poliarque decides on his disguise in act II, when he and his companion Gelanor learn that Argénis is sequestered. The first scene of the act emphasizes the essentially chaste and closed world in which the princess lives. No male is allowed, no passion can possibly arise in this place dedicated to feminine games and songs. Argénis is not even aware of the world of desire from which she is separated:

> C'est icy qu'Argénis esprouve des délices
> Que la mesme Innocence exempte de malices,
> Tout le temps qu'elle employe est si bien limité
> Qu'elle ne cognoist rien de sa captivité . . .
>
> (II, i)

Learning of this sexual prohibition which keeps males out of Argénis's castle, Poliarque expresses together the notions of metamorphosis and of the necessity of temporary impotence. The word "or" (used to bribe the guards) is placed in a pivotal position between "impuissance" and the mythological sexuality of the "pluye [d'or]":

> Quel effort ouvriroit le chasteau qui recelle
> Ce tresor de beautez à ma flame eternelle?

Si l'edit, qu'aujourd'huy l'on publioit encor
Donne de l'impuissance à la force de l'or?
Helas! s'il n'en falloit, qu'une agréable pluye
J'arriverois bien tost ou mon bon-heur s'appuye.
(II, ii)

Like Jupiter in his golden rain, Poliarque must find an attractive, even fascinating guise which is at the same time sexually neutral in appearance. Jupiter, as will Poliarque, feigns non-sexuality or sexual innocence by assuming, paradoxically, a form which adds still another level of sexuality to that already possessed by the hero.

In the first scene of the following act, Poliarque appears in his disguise before his confidant. His speech is designed to call attention to the visual aspect of the disguise, to his clothing and its sexual meaning. Of love he says, "C'est luy [l'amour] qui me fournit un habit de la sorte," and in the same monologue Poliarque uses the words *habit* (four times), *nuds* (twice), *habillier* (twice), and *robbe*. Poliarque's wearing a woman's costume is emphasized or excused flamboyantly on the verbal level, with reference to an inherent erotic quality. This differs considerably from Florante's procedure in *Célimène*. The male disguise in *Argénis* does not pass as a thing taken for granted as does the feminine disguise as a man. Indeed, while the elements of clothing and gesture in a woman's disguise are clearly designated, they are rarely justified by any theoretical considerations. Often they remain totally unexplained within the plot of a given play. Poliarque, on the contrary, during the first scene in which he appears thus transformed, gives a long justification for his costume, citing precedents for identity changes in the service of love and referring to his dress as if to palliate its embarrassment for the audience. The constant reference to his clothing draws the maximum effect from it, emphasizing the separation between his true masculinity and his disguise, probably provoking the spectator's laughter.[3] Another reason for calling such exaggerated attention to "Théocrine's" costume is that Du Ryer does not develop other feminine attributes in Poliarque's disguise. The hero's disguise is functional: it conveys a convincing sexual identity without lacunae to the characters of the play and involves dress, name, and gesture (he is able to sing like a woman). However, there is no attempt to show Théocrine superior to another woman in her specifically feminine qualities (as Floridan is in masculine ones) or even to attach a specific womanly character to this beauty or talent.

Although there are references to "her" grace and "her" beautiful voice, the femininity of these traits is not accentuated. By contrast, Floridan's masculine accomplishments are carefully underlined. The heavy-handed indication of Poliarque's new costume points to the limited nature of the man's transformation.

Poliarque's consciousness of the importance of the change of dress leads to the most concise and exact description of the principle of sexual disguise in the theatre of the period. Every incident of vestimentary change is potentially a synecdoche for the total message of identity. Poliarque, precisely because of his overdependence on a single identity code, makes this synecdoche most obvious. The change of identity which appears outwardly in his disguise corresponds to an internal redefinition of the self as a result of his love:

> Les amours sont tout nuz non seulement pour dire
> Qu'ils veulent que les coeurs soient nuds en leur empire,
> Mais afin de monstrer aux esprits curieux
> Qu'ils attendent l'habit qui les parera mieux.
> Si j'ay voulu loger dans mon coeur une fille
> N'est-ce pas la raison que ma peine l'habille?

> (III, i)

Sexual disguise is undertaken in order to conquer the person whose dress and sex one adopts, the destination of the disguise is also its form.[4] To conquer a woman's heart, the hero identifies himself with that object. In a sense the self is neutralized in favor of the greatest possible flexibility of visible identity, waiting, as Poliarque says, for the form which will best fit it in view of its pursuit. Like Florante, Poliarque is a kind of deforming mirror for his beloved. But unlike the woman who appears as a man, Poliarque is quick to minimize the change and to emphasize the aspect of deformation rather than accurate reflection present in this mirroring. His words indicate his costume but at the same time undermine its significance. Again seeking his justification in mythology, Poliarque invokes Hercules's dressing as a woman to please Omphale:

> Non, non, ne pense pas que le Destin desrobe
> La force, et la vertu, lors qu'on prend ceste robbe,
> Hercule en cet habit fit voir à la rigueur,
> Qu'il n'avoit pas perdu sa première vigueur.

This elaborate and apologetic citation of examples of masculine strength being disguised emphasizes a tension between the apparent identity expressed in the dress and the inherent force of the masculine identity which underlies the costume. This disguise has a built-in weakness, i.e. virile strength, which prepares the involuntary revelation of identity (act IV).

In addition to his dress, Poliarque changes his name to a feminine one (Théocrine) but maintains his rank and nationality (French royalty). He simply claims to be his own "sister" and eliminates his male self by reporting the death of the French king at the hands of a usurper. This maintenance of rank is another element in the construction of an identity as close as possible to that of the Argénis the hero pursues. While disguised as Théocrine, Poliarque is without the only quality which keeps him from Argénis—his sex—and possesses the beauty and rank which can bring them together. It is this similarity, approaching identification between them, that makes it safe from the point of view of the king Méléandre to enclose them together. Argénis and Théocrine do not complement one another, they tend to equal one another.

Like Florante's, Poliarque's disguise does not aim at deceiving only the pursued woman. But while Florante wished to draw the attention of a third party to herself, Poliarque wishes to pass unnoticed by the others. The immediate reason for Poliarque's assumption of feminine identity is to remove himself from the masculine population of the play so that he may overcome the barriers raised around the feminine center of the play. This external motivation and destination of Poliarque's disguise is prepared in detail. It is the substance of the play from the first scene of act III until the second scene of act IV. Like Florante's, Poliarque's change of identity has a male source in that it occurs in response to Meleandre's vigilance.

But beyond the external purpose of Poliarque's disguise lies the more mysterious relationship to be established between Théocrine and Argénis. Poliarque must create between them a relationship in every way similar to that existing between a man and a woman without revealing his sexual identity. He must not only please Argénis by his character, his talents, and his devotion, but must also please her by his physical qualities and his masculine achievements. Argénis must feel for him a true need resembling erotic attachment enough to give him the emotional satisfaction which he would receive as a male suitor obtaining the same attention. This difficult passage from his first approach of Argénis's governess Selenice to Poliarque's winning of Argénis occurs in the silence of the text, in the events not seen by the public, between act II, scene three, and scene two of the following act.

At the end of this transition, Poliarque makes a soliloquy which differs
little from that of a fortunate and clearly male suitor:

> Elle me dit souvent sans malice et sans fard,
> Qu'elle craint plus la mort, que mon triste départ
> Que je suis de ses maux le souverain remede
> Que je suis tout son coeur, qu'en moi je le possede,
> Et puisque le sort me fait present du sien,
> Pour vivre heureusement il luy faudroit le mien.
>
> (IV, ii)

If there is any difference between this monologue and one which retells
a woman's declaration to a man, it lies in the frankness with which
Argénis declares herself to Théocrine, a candor which rarely appears
in a woman's declaration to a man. Poliarque has, in fact, done more
than penetrate the barrier erected by Méléandre around his daughter
and the other aristocratic women of his kingdom. Through Théocrine
he also eliminates an internal barrier. The same restrictions which the
Sicilian king imposes by material means are installed in the
consciousness of Argénis herself by social and literary convention. By
awakening a deliberately unconventional passion, one beyond the
usual prohibitions which generate the suspense of love comedy,
Poliarque overcomes the ordinary mechanism of resistance.

Méléandre, the male possessor of Argénis, bars only the intruders
bearing *male* passion, and the society which he dominates and
represents prohibits illicit, unsanctioned, heterosexual love.
Poliarque's, or rather Théocrine's success opens an entirely new path
under the surface of the normal social patterns reflected by the
theatre.[5]

As if to recoil from the perspective opened by this love, with a
reticence not found in all the playwrights of the age, Du Ryer here
springs the tension of the separation between Poliarque and Théocrine
to bring out the masculine identity of the hero. The distance between
real identity and appearance is shown *en abîme* by the introduction of
the story of Poliarque into a tale told by Théocrine to Argenis and her
company. "She" recounts the expedient of a lover who pretends to
have left his country,

> Mais au lieu du pays, il changea seulement
> Sa parolle, son nom, et son habillement"
>
> (IV, ii)

in order to be near his lady. This semi-revelation, understood by the
public but not by Argénis, is followed by the other clue in the piece-by-

piece recreation of Poliarque's masculine identity, his proof of force against Licogène's emissaries. His valiant defense of Argénis and her father against his rival's attack confirms her affection for him but menaces, in Poliarque's eyes, the security of his disguise. The circumstances leading to the sudden ending of Théocrine's brief existence are, very significantly, accidental. The hero represents his confession as an involuntary one, coming only when the disguise has fallen into pieces, when the various elements composing it—dress and gesture especially—no longer form a whole. Poliarque emphasizes this disparity when he tells Argénis:

Princesse il n'est plus temps de contraindre l'Amour,
Dessous ce vestment qui le cachoit au jour,
Enfin il ne faut plus se feindre de la sorte,
Ou le sexe dément cet habit que je porte,
Non, je ne suis pas fille, et des faits si puissants
Ont peut estre desja desabusé vos sens . . .
                                        (IV, iv)

Poliarque says more here than he seems to wish, he makes a kind of literary pseudolapsus which does more than reveal *Amour*. Théocrine's love for Argénis had not been in question. Therefore Poliarque's declaration that his love can no longer be hidden plays on the sense of the words. *Amour* here, in the context of repeated references to the function of physical hiding performed by clothing—"Dessous ce vestement qui le cachoit au jour"—takes on a strongly physical and even phallic sense. This enrichment of the word *amour* finds a reenforcement in the affirmation "Théocrine n'est plus ou paroist Poliarque." When the physical qualities of the male appear in his strength ("des faits si puissants") and in the love hidden under his clothing, the feminine personality must disappear. In fact even the name "Poliarque" here seems to bear the burden of signifying maleness much the same way that the word *amour* does earlier. "Poliarque" is in this context primarily that which cancels the name Théocrine, which strips the bearer of that name of his previous femininity (a form of lack). In other words, Poliarque can only be the physical qualities no longer containable in the costume and comportment of the woman Théocrine.[6]

In *Argénis*, when Théocrine disappears, "she" leaves behind the memory of that identity which results in this play, as in *Célimène*, from the overlapping of two apparent personalities. For Florante/Floridan this shared basis of character appears even in the shared syllable of the

names. Although Poliarque does not dispose of a similar verbal device
for joining his two guises, he refers to the same central core of identity
when he asks Argénis,

> Conservez à mes feux descouverts à leur tour
> Le bien que Théocrine avoit dans vostre Amour.
>
> (IV, iv)

The abstraction made of the identity Théocrine in this plea is the
prelude to an episode which gives the play much of its interest as an
embodiment of the theme of identity. Théocrine continues to function
as a mediation between the two principal characters even after
Poliarque has concerted with Argénis a new disguise as a young male
foreigner (IV, iv).

Poliarque becomes, in the minds of some of the characters, the
goddess Pallas. Méléandre, entering after Poliarque's departure,
describes Théocrine as the goddess:

> Une divinité soubs ces habits couverte
> Delivre la Sicile, et detourne sa perte,
> Et Pallas elle mesme employa sa valeur
> A briser devant nous les traitz de ce mal'heur.

Méléandre really believes in this mythological explanation which
adds another level to Poliarque's disguise. The scene produces a
division of the identity Théocrine into two distinct and continuing
entities. On one hand the masculinity of Poliarque may reappear in
the form of a wandering knight, now that Licogène has overtly
violated Argénis's sanctuary and made the particular feminine form of
disguise no longer useful. Henceforth Méléandre's defenses are all
turned against a specific foe and not against men in general. The
prohibition which weighs on the French monarchy, previously not a
functioning obstacle (since the "woman" Théocrine was not touched
by it), now comes to the fore. Poliarque may become male but must
cease being king of France. At the same time the feminine identity thus
liberated or cast off is preserved by being transformed into a
superhuman abstraction, under which form it reappears in the
following act.

As well as producing the explosion of the hero-heroine's identity
into four different fragments (Poliarque, Théocrine, knight, and
Pallas), the fourth scene of this act raises the interesting identity
problem of the proof of Poliarque's claim to the French throne. The
question thus posed is nothing but a *fausse piste* in the mouth of
Selenice, when she asks Argénis, before Méléandre's arrival, how she

can be sure that Poliarque has told the truth about his origin. When Argénis ignores the important point thus raised, she demonstrates the tendency, in plays of sexual disguise, to limit the questioning of identity to one aspect. In *Argénis et Poliarque*, as in other plays of sexual disguise, the disguised male's position within a social class is not questioned. After the termination of the disguise "Théocrine" the heroine never doubts the truth of the identity "Poliarque." The action of the play depends on the exteriority of the change of identity and on Argénis's future complicity.

Argénis, having become priestess of Pallas at her father's order, uses the divine feminine identity of Poliarque as a device for her expression of love for him. In the third scene of act V Argénis publicly prays to Pallas while assigning the full identity of the goddess to Poliarque. In doing so Argénis is following a kind of secret code agreed upon in advance by the two lovers (according to Poliarque, V, i). Argénis prays, for instance,

> Je ne puis vivre sans te voir,
> (Déesse a qui je rends hommage)
> Aussi les loix de mon devoir,
> Me monstrent tousjours ton image,
> Ton agréable souvenir . . .
>
>   (V, iii)

Following Argénis's glance back towards the "agréable souvenir," we encounter the whole question of the relationship established by the disguised hero with the heroine. What is agreeable, to Argénis, about the memory of Théocrine?

The content of the relationship of Poliarque/Théocrine and Argénis is, in terms of function with the plot, identical to that of the love between "Daraïde" (the disguised king Agésilan) and the princess Diane in Rotrou's *Agésilan de Colchos* (1637). The affection which is simply alluded to in Poliarque's soliloquy (IV, ii) takes full dramatic form in Rotrou's play, in keeping with his propensity for elaborate plots of disguise and for making themes of illicit sexuality most visible. The third act of Rotrou's work is constituted by the gradual filling of the normal place of the male in Diane's life by "Daraïde" the woman. Clearly, the reaction of the two young women, Diane and her confidante Ardénice, is more important in establishing Daraïde's sexual identity than the actual feminine comportment of the disguised Agésilan. Although they always refer to Daraïde as a woman, the two women conduct themselves with "her" as if "she" —in her amorous

activities—were a man. Ardénie describes to Diane the sight of
Daraïde lying on her bed weeping and moaning, "O bel astre
d'amour." Ardénie quickly guesses that Daraïde is in love with Diane,
who asks, "Mais quel seroit le fruit de cette passion?" Ardénie then
makes the apology of sexual love between women:
> Le bien d'avoir suivi son inclination
> Et le plaisir d'aimer la beauté dans l'extrême
> Qu'elle ne peut trouver que dans son sexe même.
> En effet, la nature a d'un pinceau si doux
> Tiré les moindres traits que l'on remarque en vous . . .
>   (III, i)
Ardénie in turn discloses, after hearing Diane's praises of Daraïde,
expressed in terms of her physical qualities as well as her talents, that
> Je voudrois que l'amant que le ciel me destine,
> Si je mérite assez pour en espérer un,
> Eût tout, hormis le sexe, avec elle commun:
> Elle n'a rien en soi qui ne me satisfasse,
> Et ne fait action ni pas qui n'ait sa grâce.
The two women declare thus their rivalry—"je te vois déjà d'un oeil
un peu jaloux. / Il me fâche déjà d'avoir une rivale"—and conclude
that their quarrel over Daraïde can be solved by "un duel de baisers."
The love here expressed for Daraïde in terms appropriate for the love
of a man, including the decisive element of jealous rivalry (however
edulcorated), which gives the relationship of Ardénie and Diane the
structure of competition so overwhelmingly familiar in plays based
overtly on heterosexual love, is continued in the third scene of the act
by a physical confrontation between the three interested characters.
Ardénie returns to the scene to find Daraïde kissing the lips of the
sleeping Diane. When Diane's confidant jealously demands her share
in the attentions of their common object, Daraïde, the latter replies:
> On ne le peut nier, belle et sage Ardénie,
> Vos attraits sont puissans, votre grâce infinie;
> Je ne vous saurois voir sans beaucoup de plaisir,
> Et, mon sexe changé, j'irois jusqu'au désir . . .
"She" insists however that only Diane is worthy in her eyes of
adoration. When Diane wakes and becomes the judge of the quarrel,
she hears expressions which come directly from the amatory language
of the period as it is usually applied to members of different sexes:
"l'encens que je brûle pour vous," "un coeur qui vous est destiné,"
"enflammée." Diane's decision is that Daraïde love both women,

J'ordonne qu'à toutes deux
Daraïde offre des voeux,
Et qu'elle aime beaucoup, étant beaucoup aimée.

It is understood, however, that Daraïde's personal penchant for Diane
is given priority and meant to continue under the externals of her
attention to Ardénie. The scene ends with Daraïde's bestowing three
kisses on Ardénie.

This section of the play abandons the point of view of the disguised
male—the preparation for his disguise, his justication to himself and
his confidante—for that of the women in order to explore the effect on
them of the fictive identity. In this way the women characters disclose
some of their affective and libidinal traits. The exposition of a
homosexual capacity in the heroine, rather than seeming a difficulty
to be swiftly passed over (it is of course essentially present but
understated in *Argénis*) is on the contrary explored at length in two
scenes, one of 89 verses and the other of 102 verses, in *Agésilan*. Like the
dramaturgy of the disguised woman (*Célimène*) that of the male
transvestite tends to bring about on the stage the spectacle of women
falling in love with other women and demonstrating this affection in
physical terms. In the theme of Théocrine and of Daraïde this current
abnormality is, in a sense, more explicit and closer to the full violation
of the taboo. Diane loves a woman in all consciousness of the
impossibility of social fulfillment of her love; as Ardénie says, Daraïde
would be the perfect mate "hormis le sexe" (cf. Meliarque in *L'Amante
ennemie*). In both types of sexual transformation the heroines are kept
from expressing consciousness of the abnormality of their acts. In
Célimène this is accomplished by keeping the heroine within the
bounds of conventional sexual normality and projecting the sense of
abnormality into the minds of the spectators (including the internal
spectator) through a knowledge of the disguise. In the Théocrine plays
the sexual abnormality is considerably greater and leads toward an
infraction of the social code by the "innocent" heroine; no explanation
is given or assumed for Diane's and Ardénie's frank acceptance of this
unusual love. This form of moral blind spot in the characters
themselves is compensated for by the consciousness of the audience
that there is no crime in fact, however things may appear within the
play. The two types of play involve, then, an illicit love which appears
licit to the heroine (Célimène) on one hand and on the other a licit love
which appears illicit to the heroines who experience it.

In this second use of identity disguise as a vehicle for the
"forbidden" theme of feminine homosexuality by placing the full
responsibility for her affection in the mind of the heroine, the author is
playing with an "innocent perversion," one which gives pleasure,
leads to no painful catastrophe, and leaves no remorse—all thanks to
the magic of identity transformation. Such a disguise, or rather the
termination of the disguise, has in the denouement of the play a
function analogous to that of the literal *deus ex machina* at the
conclusion of Benserade's *Iphis et Iante*. In both cases the device, either
the revelation or the true and permanent metamorphosis, justifies or
consecrates a situation of sexual relationships which is socially
prohibited.

There are plays in which the heroine comes still closer to being
involved in a love portrayed as a crime and an abomination, works in
which the ultimate disculpation provided by the disguise seems to be
the only way to redeem the theme, or the heroine, for a comedy. This is
the case in Gougenot's *La Fidelle tromperie* (1633), based on the same
plot (taken from the same source, the *Amadis de Gaule*) as Rotrou's
Agésilan. Gougenot moves farther towards explicit infraction of the
sexual taboos than does Rotrou, whose text remains free of the guilty
conscience which could ruin the innocence of Diane's comic world.
Gougenot inserts the social condemnation into his text, thereby
contaminating the work with a theme of crime which not only leaves
the *bienséances* in shambles but makes the heroine Alderine (the exact
counterpart of Diane) worthy, in her confidante's eyes, to be classed
among the tragic heroines, of whom she names several, including
Phaedra. Florinde, hearing of Alderine's passion for Lucide
(Armidore in disguise), says,

> Ces amours sans espoir se tournent en fureurs,
> Et ne laissent en fin que des cris et des pleurs.
> Un amour légitime après la patience,
> Attend de ses labeurs l'heureuse récompense,
> Mais nature manquant à ceste passion,
> Elle ne peut donner que de l'affliction.
> Ou void-on une Dame aymer une autre Dame?
> Ce penser seulement ne peut toucher mon ame,
> Toutes choses s'opposent à de telles amours.
> La biche ayme son cerf, et l'ourse aime son ours
>
> (II, ii)

Alderine simply replies, "Mais pourquoy blasmez vous ces aymables desirs?" After the mutual flatteries of Lucide and Alderine, Florinde comments,

Mais ou pourroit-on voir des flames plus ardentes,
Peut-on mieux exprimer des amours violentes?
Quel Amant pour sa Dame a jamais tant souffert?

These quotations from Gougenot are not displayed simply to demonstrate the existence of the theme of feminine homosexuality in the French theatre. In itself, the existence of such a traditionally asocial act would be no more surprising than the well-known incest theme in tragedy. What is, however, more striking is the presence of a fully developed tragic theme, complete with comparisons of the heroine to other tragic figures, in a comedy. This insertion of homosexuality into the comedy is possible only through the magic of identity transformation, which makes the guilty innocent and makes the crime itself an illusion.

It is essential to note the great explicitness characteristic of the treatment of feminine homosexuality compared to the restraint of the much rarer suggestions of a masculine perversion of the same nature. The closest analogy with the situation of Argénis in the plays of feminine transvestism is that of Tersandre and Meliarque in *L'Amante ennemie.* The latter play confines itself, as noted earlier, to comments of the sort,

Que je serois content, si celle qu'Hyménée
Doit ranger avec moy sous mesme Destinée,
Estoit toute semblable, ou bien par accident
Avoit à tout le moins quelque air de Floridant.

(II, v)

There is no weeping, wasting malady, or—the most significant detail—rivalry between two men for the love of another. In addition men are restricted in the physical gestures of affection between them and are never placed in a position of taking physical pleasure together. Women, however, at least in the stage tradition and possibly also in society, are granted much more freedom in physical expression of affection.

The classic example which haunts the tradition of the pastoral novel and play is the kissing contest of the Megarensian maidens in Guarini's *Pastor Fido* (II, i). Mirtillo, who had disguised himself as a girl in order to be near his beloved Amarilli, tells his friend Ergasto of the occasion on which he was able to kiss her. One of the troup of Megarensian girls suggested,

> proviam oggi tra noi così da scherzo
> noi le nostr'armi, come
> contra gli uomini, allor che ne fie tempo,
> l'userem da dovero.
> Bacianne, e si contenda
> tra noi di baci; e quella, che d'ogni altra
> baciatrice più scaltra,
> li saprà dar più saporiti e cari,
> n'avra per sua vittoria
> questa bella ghirlanda.[7]

Amarilli is chosen, as the girl with the most beautiful mouth, to be the receiver and the judge of these kisses. Mirtillo, as a girl, kissed his beloved and describes from his experience that of all the girls who were fortunate enough to participate and kiss

> quella bocca beata,
> quella bocca gentil che può ben dirsi
> conca d'Indo odorata
> di perle orientali e pellegrine;
> e la parte che chiude
> ed apre il bel tesoro,
> con dolcissimo mèl purpura mista.
> Così potess'io dirti, Ergasto mio,
> l'ineffabil dolcezza
> ch'i sentii nel baciarla!
> Ma tu da questo prendine argomento,
> che non la può ridir la bocca stessa
> che l'ha provata. Accogli pur insieme
> quant'hanno in sé di dolce
> o le canne di Cipro o i favi d'Ibla. . .

(171-85)

Mirtillo received the prize from Amarilli, who found his kisses "più di quelli d'ogn'altra saporiti," in other words, the masculine passion of Mirtillo's kisses is the key to the best kind of kisses, even those exchanged by women. It is this freedom in physical contact between women, in all innocence and social acceptability (within a closed society) that makes possible the affective developments in *Argénis et Poliarque* and *Agésilan de Colchos*. The kisses between the Megarensian girls are described not only with all appearance of innocence but in a context of pure sensuality in terms of "savor" and "sweetness," "honey," and "perfume." Amarilli merely judges Mirtillo the most skilled of her companions in the physical delivery of her kisses, the skill as well as the inherent buccal "equipment." In the French plays this naïve sensuality has been developed into a passionate desire, a love of the whole person of the other, in terms of the physical as well as the spiritual qualities of the second "woman." Even more, in fact, occurs in the French plays, since the man disguised as a woman is the object of rivalry between the heroine and another woman. With *Argénis* and even more with *La Fidelle Tromperie* the torment of the impermissible and the unnatural penetrates into the garden of the pastoral comedy. These plays and, in particular, the scene from Guarini's *Pastor*, cannot but bring to mind several of the scenes in *L'Astrée*. Although the domain of disguise and illusory identities in the novel is too vast to explore here, d'Urfé's work imposes itself in the minds of most readers as the prototype of masculine sexual transformation. *Astrée* furthermore was considered as a kind of tragicomedy in five acts.[8] The love story which forms the center of the work, the separation and reconciliation of Célidon and his beloved Astrée, is essentially a long series of disguises and apparent metamorphoses which tend towards a complete confusion and reversal of the social and sexual identities of the lovers. Céladon transforms himself in appearance, taking that of a woman, three times; once, at the chronological beginning of the adventure, into a shepherdess named Orithie, then, briefly into Lucinde, and finally, in the longest adventure, into the druidess Alexis. Astrée's lover took upon himself the identity of Orithie in order to penetrate a private and religious contest of beauty between three chosen shepherdesses who are compared, unclothed, by a fourth girl. Céladon-Orithie is elected to be that judge and profits from the situation to contemplate Astrée and to extract from her a promise to love "her," Orithie, more than anyone. Another time Céladon disguises himself as Lucinde in order to escape the captivity of the amorous nymph Galathée. And finally, during the longest episode of his loves, Célidon presents himself under the name of the druidess Alexis. In this form he lives intimately with Astrée, winning her love because of a resemblance to the deceased Céladon.

The transformations in the outward sexual identity of the two characters continue through their exchange of clothing as they attempt to arrive at the most complete identification of the subject with the loved object. Céladon/Alexis becomes Astrée, Astrée the druidess Alexis. Then the new "Alexis" becomes the *serviteur* of the new "Astrée," called "maîtresse." As Alexis/Céladon says to Astrée, "J'ordonne donc qu'Astrée sera Alexis, et qu'Alexis sera Astrée, et que nous bannirons de nous, non seulement toutes les paroles, mais toutes les moindres actions qui peuvent mettre quelque différence entre nous."[9]

At the moment when the disguises reach their peak of complexity, Céladon is disguised as the druidess Alexis, disguised as the shepherdess Astrée, while Astrée is disguised as the druidess Alexis, disguised as a male suitor of the same name. These complex transformations and exchanges of identity can be shown in diagram A.[10]

Céladon (m)	Astrée (f)
"Alexis" (f)	Astrée (f)
"'Astrée'" (f)	"Alexis" (f)
"'Astrée (f)	"'Alexis'" (m)
Céladon (m)	Astrée (f)

Diagram A

Although the *Astrée*, primarily because of its length, can display in more detail the phases of sexual disguise and discovery, it is grounded in the same thematic, or the same obsession, as *Argénis*. Like Poliarque, the hero Céladon/Alexis finds partial satisfaction in achieving complete identification with the object of his desire. Even more than Poliarque, Céladon merges completely with the woman and becomes Astrée. D'Urfé abandons the use of the name and masculine gender of the hero during most of the feminine disguise. In fact, the narrator still refers to the actions of Alexis even after Astrée knows the true identity of her lover. Astrée, however, in comparison to the feminine principals of the plays like *Argénis*, bases her actions and her attitude towards Alexis in a constant reference to normality: her love for the druidess springs from the latter's resemblance to Céladon. Thus while plunging deeper into levels of disguise, Astrée is simply appealing to the original order which she regrets having lost. Yet the reign of this normality, of the zero degree of disguise, is shorter-lived in the *Astrée* than in Rotrou, Du Ryer, and Gougenot. Even the recourse of the theatrical hero, the unavoidable bursting through the physical bounds of his disguise, is closed to Céladon the recidivist. His feminine disguise is prolonged until in the end only the intervention of the druid Adamas can win for him the right to reappear as Céladon.

Throughout the *Astrée* the design of the novelist is clearly to maintain the characters in a state of sexual suspension by inserting the transexual disguises as a kind of prolonged parenthesis which separates the opening and closing of the basic givens of the plot (the love of Astrée and Céladon in spite of the hostility of their families and the jealousy of rivals). While Astrée and Céladon act out their love under different identities they exploit the freedom of love from social restraint.

The exploration of the temptations of the forbidden sexual combinations typified by Argénis is possible because of the existence within the pastoral tradition of this return to a state of sexual or presexual innocence in the enjoyment of the sensual world, a pleasure taken within the closed garden of women. Armarilli and her companions live in expectation of the reality which will follow their games and give them meaning. Mirtillo already, by his disguised presence, violates this state of innocence by attaching a passionate significance to Amarilli's kisses, a significance which she does not place in them and which is generated only by the self-appointed "receptor" of her love.

In Argénis and still more in the other French plays mentioned, this passionate and therefore forbidden meaning is attached to the kisses and caresses by the heroines themselves. It is as if Amarilli had begged a kiss from Mirtillo, disguised as a shepherdess. In Gougenot's play the interdiction which weighs on such kisses and by implication the meaning of the gesture itself (i.e. passionate love appropriate only between man and woman) is stated and restated by the author, through a character functioning primarily as a commentator.

Through the dramatic function of the man disguised as a woman the French tragicomedy can introduce the most explicit and systematic violations of traditions of licit sexual desire into the pastoral garden and the castle of romance while redeeming the works for presentation to the very society whose traditions and prohibitions the genre so insistently violates and mocks. Théocrine is to Argénis both the occasion of her sin and the redeemer of her status in the realm of heterosexual feminine identity.

The fictive sexual beings "Théocrine" and "Daraïde" provoke the heroines' potentially heterosexual love and direct this love towards a character incapable of satisfying them in a public union. The heroines of Du Ryer's and Rotrou's plays point out the specific inaptness of the object of their love, indicating that their love could prosper, "hormis le sexe." At the same time the transvestism of the male makes the possession of the masculine gender most apparent, his virility bursts through the confines of his role and his costume. In a sense the force with which the male's identity comes into the consciousness of the characters is proportionate to the perversion it corrects, or rather, justifies; a superabundance of masculine normality effaces the feminine perversion which precedes it. Finally both normality and abnormality are found to spring from the same source, the male's desire.

The theme of the man's disguise as woman is a theme for two characters, Argénis and Poliarque, as opposed to the woman's disguise as a man which involves three, Célimène, Florante, and Filandre. A second woman character added to the plays of masculine transvestism may also desire the love of the disguised man, as does the Ardénie of Rotrou's *Agésilan de Colchos*. But such characters not only remain decidedly secondary, almost as faceless as the Megarensian maidens of Guarini, but serve at most as a shadow of the love between the two principals. More important is the fact that such additional secondary characters are women.

There are few works based on a man's mistaken love for another man disguised as a woman. When, moreover, such a situation does arise it is designated in the situational language of the classical tradition as farcical. One clearly reads here the situation of the Pautean *senex* who commits the error of falling in love with the disguised hero; there is never an amorous conjunction of two young men capable of feeling and creating sexual desire. Instead the senile king, a being emptied of physical sexuality, compounds the Roman Old Man's stupidity of falling in love with a young person by mistaking the gender of his object. In Desfontaines' *Eurimédon* (1637), Archelas, king of Troade and father of Pasithée, becomes enamored of the "Amazone" who saves his kingdom. This amazon is, of course, Eurmédon himself, exiled by Archélas because of his temerity in loving Pasithée. He returns in disguise seeking to persuade Archélas to permit the marriage of the two lovers and to penetrate the material barriers raised by the king around his daughter. In Maréchael's *Cour bergère* the king's senility or stupidity is established from the first scene by the recital of the ridiculous precautions he takes against the fulfillment of an oracle and then (I, ii) by his choice of the dullest inhabitant of the countryside to be his daughter's tutor. With this introduction to the king's character, the spectator is not led to take seriously his love for the "amazon" (III, iii). King Bazyle's masculinity, as his intelligence, is made suspect by his queen's love for Prince Pyrocle, whose sex she recognizes despite his feminine disguise. These examples of the duped old man underline the fact that the hero's love is addressed directly to the heroine, not to a second male as an intermediary. Célimène is essential to the relation between Florante and Filandre, but neither the amorous old king nor the jealous confidante is necessary to the relationship of Argénis and Poliarque.

This comparative simplicity in the emotional relationships is possible because of the disguised male's singular sexual valence. His masculinity is meant to be progressively proven, not diluted by a feminine role imposed by the love of a credible (i.e. young) second male. The man's love steadily invades the innocent and totally monosexual world of the beginning of the play (the castles of Argénis and Diane, from which sexual love is supposed to be excluded) by the expectation of a male presence. The disguised hero first creates a lack and a need in this world before revealing this true sex in reply to the growing sexual tension.

Despite the differences in the themes of masculine and feminine disguise between the actions of Florante and those of Poliarque one detects a similar male role in both types of plays. Filandre is the author of Florante's disguise, as Méléandre makes Poliarque's sexual disguise necessary. No direct connection can be drawn between the functions of Filandre and Méléandre as individuals, but by considering together the activities of Méléandre and his opponent Poliarque, by fusing the two men together under the dramatic function attributed here to maleness, one perceives more clearly the essential male position in the whole theme of sexual disguise. Indeed the male of *Argénis* is both the possessor, controlling the established order with its implicit sexual dominance, and the character who desires to undermine that order and its privileges. Are not these two functions of domination and of subversion the role of Filandre? The latter possesses the love of Florante and could conceivably win Célimène (despite the experience of rejection). He wishes to subvert the social order which gives both women to him as a male by initiating the transformation of the woman's role into that of a man. Filandre voluntarily destroys the conventional relationships which make him the object of the women's affection by creating—temporarily, to be sure—a new order in which the women seem to become a self-sufficient group. Poliarque, as Théocrine, in order to obtain Argénis also subverts the social-sexual order in which the heroine's destiny belongs to the male. He circumvents the physical barriers erected by the father and then incites Argénis to transgress the internal (or natural) limitations of her mating role, a role in which he has an interest as a potential husband or lover.

Thus the male characters in both groups of plays, in both major myths of transformed sexual identity, have the paradoxical role of undermining their own possession of the woman whom they desire. This temporary surrender of the object of desire or, in the plays like *Célimène*, what amounts to a conscious alienation of the hero's very maleness in the affective system, is only a step in the dramatic game of alienation and repossession, rupture of stability and restabilization, which is such an evident foundation of comedy.

The theme of the disguise of the woman as man is much more complex than its converse and much less motivated (as far as furnishing literary verisimilitude to excuse this variance from normality). The division of the dominant male roles into two, the old king and the young prince in *Argénis*, gives the young male's renunciation of his virility a tactical justification and a pretext for the acting out of a more internal conflict. When this happens the struggle is removed from the hidden consciousness of Filandre onto the stage. There it becomes an external opposition between two phases of the male character expressed as separate individuals.

Within the many texts which belong to the thematics of disguise of sexual identity, broad patterns thus emerge, drawing out two myths of transformation which are profoundly related. Both of them hinge on the male function, a curiously active but invisible maleness which, by its absence, by apparent abdication, prepares in two different ways its final triumph.

Footnotes

1. Pierre Du Ryer, *Argénis et Poliarque ou Théocrine, première journée,* (Paris: Nicolas Bessin, 1630). The play is based on a popular contemporary novel, *Argénis* by John Barclay (Joannis Barclaii *Argénis.* [Paris: N. Buon, 1621]). The catalogue of the Bibliothèque Nationale lists ten editions of this novel in the seventeenth century and four editions of the translation of Pierre Marcassus: 1624, 1625, 1632, and 1638. The theme of man's disguise as a woman occurs in only fourteen of the two hundred forty-four plays about mistaken or disguised identity discussed in this study. Such plays include Thomas Corneille, *Le Berger extravagant* (Paris: A. de Sommaville, 1656), Desfontaines, *Eurimédon* (Paris: A. de Sommaville, 1637), Desfontaines, *Orphise* (Paris: A. de Sommaville, 1638), Desfontaines, *Bélisaire* (Paris: A. Courbé, 1641), Gillet de la Tessonerie, *Francion* (Paris: T. Quinet, 1642), Gougenot, *La Fidelle Tromperie* (Paris: A. de Sommaville, 1633), La Morelle, *Philine* (Paris: M. Collet, 1630), La Serre, *Climène* (Paris: A. de Sommaville and A. Courbé, 1643), Maréschal, *Lizidor ou la Cour bergère* (Paris: P. Rocolet, 1631), Rampale, *Bélinde* (Lyons: P. Drobet, 1630), de Rayssiguier, *Les Amours d'Astrée (Paris: N. Bessin, 1630),* Rotrou, *Agésilan de Colchos* (1637), Scarron, *L'Escolier de Salamanque* (Amsterdam: R. Smith, 1656).
2. Of course Zeus was capable of a true transformation while the human heroes of these plays only superficially alter their appearance.
3. There exists an example of the man's reaction to seeing another man disguised as a woman in the theatre of the period. In Scarron's *L'Escolier de Salamanque* (Amsterdam: R. Smith, 1656), Crispin and Pèdre (V, i) have just helped the count escape from prison disguised as a woman. Crispin remarks,

Ce grand Comte en femme travesty,
Avoit plus peur que vous alors qu'il est sorty,
Déguisé d'une robe, et couvert d'une mante,
Il sentoit son fantosme, et non pas sa servante.
Au reste il cheminoit si masculinement,
Que je me divertis d'y songer seulement.

4. Jacques Ehrmann (*Un Paradis désespéré*: Paris: l'Institut d'Etudes françaises de Yale, 1963), p. 82) when he notes that in the *Astrée* the two principal characters exchange their clothing in order to attain the maximum identification with the loved one.

5. *Argénis* comes close to the subversive thematic of Benserade's *Iphis et Iante*, in which a woman consciously loves another and actually does marry her in a plot drawn from Ovid.

6. Poliarque's disclosure of the physical traits which mark his identity is similar to that of Prince Pyrocle disguised as the amazon Zelmane in Maréchal's *Cour bergère*. Here too the male's sexuality is precisely designated as a physical characteristic which cannot be hidden. Queen Gynécie, in Maréchal's play, demands Zelmane's erotic attentions:

Gynécie: Je cherche la pitié, non pas d'une Amazone.

Zelmane: Dieux! je suis découvert, sa parole m'étonne.

Gynécie: Mais plustôt le secours, (diray-je mon péché?)

Que dessous cet habit la Nature a caché.

Maréchal, *Lizidor ou la Cour bergère* (Paris: T. Quinet, 1640), (III, iii).

7. B. Guarini, *Il Pastor Fido*, ed. G. Brognoligo (Bari: G. Laterza, 1914), v. 129-138. Other citations from the Pastor Fido are taken from this edition.

8. As Baro, d'Urfé's friend who completed the *Astrée* after the original author's death, writes in the "Avertissement" of the fourth part, "il m'a fait autrefois l'honneur de me communiquer qu'il vouloit faire de toute son oeuvre une tragecomedie pastorale, et que, comme nos François ont accoutumé de les disposer en cinq actes, chasque acte composé de diverses scènes, il vouloit de mesme faire cinq volumes composez de douze livres. . ." (ed. Vaganay, IV, v).

9. Honoré d'Urfé, *l'Astrée*, ed. Hugues Vaganay (Lyons: Pierre Masson, 1927), IV, 44.

10. In this diagram (m) and (f) indicate apparent masculine and feminine guise according to outward appearance. Continuous vertical lines indicate the exchange of identity (the outward guise or appelation) between Astrée and "Alexis."

The Unknown Woman les Fausses Véritéz

The theatre of these years is haunted by the theme of the masked or unknown woman. Plots in which the theme appears follow a familiar pattern. A young nobleman comes to Paris from the provinces. A relative stranger to the metropolis, he has a few friends there. He has come, perhaps, to marry a girl chosen for him. He soon encounters a fascinating and mysterious woman while he is walking in a public place—theatre, church, or garden. She refuses to say her name; her face may be covered. The hero may see only her hand when it is uncovered in prayer or to take water from the holy-water font. Her voice is unforgettably sweet. Her dress shows that she is of good birth. Throwing himself wholeheartedly into the search for her identity, the hero resolves to marry no one but her. Surprisingly, though he is a stranger to the city, his name is known to her, yet she remains mysterious to him. When his valet inquires of her coachman who his mistress is, the reply is ambiguous. Perhaps no one in the city has ever heard of that marquise or that countess. Is the unknown woman really noble after all? Why is the young lover unable to find her house? The hero wonders if he is committing some crime by loving her. This may be the reason why she is unwilling to show her face. She may already be married or she may be the mistress of his friend of relative.

This pattern creates a comic paralysis, a situation in which a character's ignorance of another identity makes him collide with certain important social obstacles to marriage. Although this type of play seems at first glance quite different from the comedy of disguise of sex, the plays of the masked or unknown woman also exploit a kind of dreamlike succession of activities which are normally forbidden by society.

D'Ouville's *Les Fausses Véritéz* (1643) opens with a typical situation. Florimonde, a Parisian *demoiselle*, confides in her servant Nerine her love for Lidamant, a noble from Languedoc, whom she sees often but secretly in the Tuileries. She thus escapes from the strict confinement imposed by her brother Léandre in order to preserve the family honor

from her potential indiscretion. Léandre even refuses to allow her to
meet his friend and guest Lidamant. The young provincial lives in a
separate part of the house which can be entered only by a door on the
street. Florimonde fears, as she tells Nerine in the first scene, that
Lidamant's sense of honor might cause him to leave her if he found
that she is his friend's sister. The young woman, moreover, in addition
to having the advantage of knowing all of the characters' names and
relationships, remembers the secret of the concealed internal doorway
leading from her part of the house to Lidamant's.

From the beginning the question of identity occupies the center of
the intrigue and grows into a framework which will control the action
of the forty-three scenes of the five acts. This first expository scene
between Florimond and her confidante Nerine establishes the system
of knowledge of identity determining the relationships among the
characters, on one hand, and between the spectators and the text as a
whole on the other. The two characters of this first scene are presented
as the party of strength, that group which possesses fully certain
knowledge which the other characters do not have. The public
becomes the accomplice of this first group by sharing this knowledge
and assuming a stance of irony in relation to all characters except
Florimonde and Nerine.

The public's participation in situations of irony through superior
knowledge is common in comedy. In Florimonde's case strength
comes specifically from knowing an important identity—her
own—which is concealed from the other characters. The concealed
knowledge is minimal. Yet simply by withholding the power of
classifying herself from others who are themselves fully categorized,
Florimonde holds the key to all the action.

Her identity is suppressed in her relation to Lidamant, in the
encounters described in this first scene, simply by concealment of
name. Her sex, her physical appearance, and her apparent class
identity are all apparent to her suitor. He lacks only her name, that
clue which would allow him to place her within the bounds of a family.
Florimonde, however, knows not only that Lidamant is a man and a
noble but that he is her brother's friend. Progressively the element of
family name and kinship becomes the crux of the curious system of
power resulting from the heroine's secret.

In order to understand Florimonde's motive in keeping Lidamant
from knowing her name, the viewer must seize the importance with
which the family is invested as an obstacle to marriage and the

concomitant significance of the outside room of Léandre's house. By inviting Lidamant to live with him, Léandre in effect confers upon his friend not only a privilege but also the duties of a kind of kinship. Scenically the metaphor of the house, the roof under which Lidamant and Florimonde live together, conveys this sense of an enlarged family group. The heroine becomes (or risks becoming) in this way a kind of sister to her lover. Only the wall which separates his section of the house from hers prevents Lidamant's discovery of this adoptive kinship and a resultant kind of dramatic "short circuit." Later in the play (III, i) the strength of the feeling of kinship between Lidamant and Léandre is accentuated by Lidamant's decision that his Unknown is Léandre's mistress and therefore forbidden him by his bond to Léandre. The spatial metaphor for this relationship, the house in which he lives with Florimonde, separated by a wall, marks the situation from the beginning of the play with the sign of the incest taboo. On the same psycho-symbolic level, Florimonde's knowledge of the internal doorway signifies her control of the system of relations between the characters.

The heroine's knowledge of the identity of her brother's friend and houseguest enables her to withhold a name which is henceforth dangerous to her if it falls into the possession of two persons, Lidamant and Léandre (the latter because of his potential anger at the betrayal of his honor). By concealing her identity appropriately from Lidamant, Florimonde entices him into a transgression of the prohibition that weighs on them both.

In this anonymity, Florimonde leaves room for assumptions by other characters about her. From early in the play as spectators we become the only witness of the various false identities which are ascribed to Florimonde (and, at certain moments, to the masculine characters). Thus while we never cease to be aware of the true identities involved we participate in the characters' conceptions and misconceptions. Each new identity assigned by any character becomes a kind of imaginary character in the play towards whom the other characters are acting and reacting. In this way each of the different identities assigned to the Unknown becomes a functional entity in the *Fausses Véritéz*. Such identifications are the basis for new twists in the multilevel language and action of the work. Florimonde's acts constantly generate new identities in the other characters' "minds", that is to say, their comportment and language on the stage and their relations to the other characters.

After the first act of the play Florimonde attempts to maintain her
initial fortuitous liberation from the identity imposed on her by her
relation to Léandre and by her family or *maison*. She receives
permission to use the house of Orazie, Léandre's mistress, for a rendez-
vous with Lidamant. This meeting in a place free from the constraints
of the implicit incest taboo of her own house, takes place in act II. As an
unexpected consequence, however, Lidamant confuses Florimonde
with Léandre's mistress. Léandre, too, begins to doubt Orazie's
fidelity after glimpsing an unknown man (Lidamant) in her house.

Thus at the very beginning of act III, Lidamant, who has never
learned the name of Orazie, informs his valet that they must leave
Paris in order to avoid a dishonorable rivalry with Léandre.
Florimonde has, at this point, succeeded in projecting her identity
from one extreme of the erotic identity pattern to the other. Although
she is Léandre's sister, as the public and Florimonde know, and
ineligible for this reason to be loved by Lidamant, she has so separated
herself in his eyes from Léandre's kinship that her lover assumes that
she is Léandre's mistress. Florimonde, however, believes that
Lidamant's planned departure is based on an accurate knowledge of
her true identity and therefore on the functioning of the original taboo
of "adoptive kinship" or "blood brotherhood" outlined in the first act
(III, ii). The succeeding scenes of act III develop the fluctuations in
Lidamant's suppositions about the Unknown's identity. Florimonde
finds that he does not know her identity but convinces him
accidentally once more than she is Léandre's mistress (scene iii). Then
Léandre seems to confirm this belief (iv) before Orazie's arrival shows
Lidamant that his mistress is not Léandre's (v). Finally the masked
figure of Florimonde becomes in Orazie's mind a feminine rival for the
affections of Léandre, a certain Iris (vi).

Once more, this time in Orazie's perception, Florimonde is
projected into an imaginary identity in which she is no kin to Léandre
and can marry him. Thus identified as "Iris," Florimonde again seems
about to have an amorous connection with Léandre. We see her
placed, though only in the assumptions of one of the characters, in a
position of formal violation of the marriage customs of her society. Yet
Orazie's identification of the Unknown is not a purely subjective or
psychological event in the play. All identifications in *Les Fausses Véritéz*
are immediately translated first into sexual pairings or possibilities of
sexual unions which are permissible according to the various social
groupings and categorizations, and secondly into reactions on the part

of a character whose own intended place in the sexual economy of the text is occupied by the newly identified character. No identification remains subjective or gratuitous, purely internal or lyrical cognition. Orazie at the end of act III spurns Léandre and leaves him in a rage, an action which leads to a number of other actions important to the plot in the following act. Lidamant had behaved in a similar fashion in the beginning of the third act, after his decision that the Unknown must be Léandre's mistress. In both cases the act of identification leads to immediate consequences for all the characters.

This constant search creates a system of simple binary oppositions which is repeatedly employed to classify the Unknown. Through her single identity the work displays a definition of the concept of identity within its miniature social world. Florimonde is classified, according to the different names and family identities projected upon her by Lidamant, Orazie, and Léandre, in reference to her relationship to Léandre. Both Lidamant and Orazie fear that she is Léandre's lover, a situation which would keep them from the positions they covet. Florimonde, on the other hand, fears the evidence which would prove that she could not possibly be Léandre's lover within the marriage system of her society. The pair of Léandre and Florimonde (the Unknown) are frequently linked during the play. The public and Florimonde know that this pairing occurs through the nonsexual union of brother and sister while the other characters, including Léandre himself at moments, believe that the two are linked in the potential bond of lover and mistress. Since Léandre's identity is viewed by all as stable (unchanging in kinship, name, social position, and sex) it is around him that the Unknown's identity orbits. The others seek to deduce her name and all her identity attributes from her relation to him (a kind of identity puzzle which appears also between Pulchérie and the two young princes of Corneille's *Héraclius*). This enigma is the reverse of the more familiar social practice in which people's names are known and their possible marriage partners determined by inserting this family name into the place reserved for it in the preestablished schema of mating custom. D'Ouville's plot simply reverses this usual procedure in order to rise from the prohibition, implicit in the Unknown's behavior, towards the identity which falls under this prohibition.

Léandre's own perplexity about the identity of the Unknown appears in his potential violation of the prohibition surrounding his sister. At the end of act III when the masked woman flees the room where she had been hiding from Léandre after talking to Lidamant, Léandre tries to follow her but Orazie stops him. One presumes that his motivation is curiosity, but no explanation is advanced and there is no way of distinguishing here the pursuit (in its simple literal sense) from the usual amorous metaphor of pursuit of an attractive and mysterious woman. In this instance Léandre wants to pursue the Unknown, even when he knows that she is not Orazie and even at the expense of sacrificing a conversation with his beloved. Yet he offers her no explanation of his attempted pursuit and makes no apology. Why does Léandre not explain to Orazie that the masked woman might be of nonmarital interest to him, in other words, one of his kin?

By the end of the third act the system of identity within the play is functioning primarily with reference to Léandre's potential relationship to the Unknown and the consequent frustration of the desires of the three other characters: Florimonde, Orazie, and Lidamant. Neither Orazie nor Lidamant is aware that Léandre simply cannot licitly feel an amorous interest in the Unknown. In fact, as we have seen, Léandre himself does not know of this barrier which is at the same time the link which ties Florimonde to her identity. Only Florimonde, Nerine, and the audience are fully aware of the Unknown's identity. Orazie knows that her friend Florimonde is the unknown woman Lidamant loves, but she does not know that the masked woman supposed "Iris" (III, vi) is the same as Lidamant's Unknown.

The last two acts of the *Fausses Véritéz* exploit the confusion of the Unknown's potential (apparent) relationship to Léandre by making both men believe that they are courting the same coquettish woman. D'Ouville here explores further the comic value of the confusion between Léandre's perfectly acceptable love for Orazie and an apparent rivalry with Lidamant for the hand of his own sister, an impossible love in terms of comic dénouements. The fourth act is largely a preparation for the confusion and rapid chasing around the stage which fills the last act. Florimonde, at her brother's request, asks to be allowed to spend several days at Orazie's house in order to spy on her. Orazie simultaneously asks Florimonde to let her stay several days in Léandre's house in order to spy on Léandre and his Iris. They finish by deciding to exchange houses and *suivantes* for a few days (scenes ii, iii). Lidamant meanwhile decides to stay in Paris now that he knows that the Unknown is not Orazie (because of the confrontation in act III) as he tells his valet (iv). He receives a rendez-vous from the Unknown, set at her house (Orazie's house, v). Léandre and Lidamant set out together for this house. In these two acts the house continues to serve as an outward sign of identity, a meaning which it retains from the first act. In act II another house with two doors is the ambiguous sign or Orazie's identity usurped by Florimonde. In the final act this confusion is repeated and intensified; to the house the *suivante* is added as another exchangeable sign of identity. Léandre and Orazie persist in their errors of identification of the Unknown until the seventh scene. During this period the confusion between Orazie and Florimonde becomes complete for Léandre; the two houses, the darkness and the secret exit from Lidamant's room lead to physical confusions between the two. Léandre at one point seizes Florimonde (V, vi), thinking that he has caught Orazie in open violation of her faith in Lidamant's room. Then Orazie enters the room through the secret door expecting to find Léandre with "Iris" but is herself grabbed by her lover when, in the dark, Florimonde manages to escape. In this way the action continues to take the woman Léandre holds back and forth across the frontier separating the permissible love from the impermissible love, i.e. the incestuous. The public is conscious of these errors, but the characters are oblivious to the significance of their actions. Each of them possesses only a fragment of the identity puzzle of Florimonde. Lidamant knows throughout the act that the Unknown is not Léandre's mistress. Léandre remains more ignorant than Orazie or Lidamant. The brother's ignorance is more important and interesting than that of the others becasue Florimonde's identity is defined precisely by her relation to him. For Léandre any discovery concerning this identity is intolerable. If the Unknown is Orazie or another woman he could marry, she is already unfaithful to him. If she is a woman whom he cannot marry (a member of his family), she has dishonored him. Léandre does not raise this question openly until the last scene, but Florimonde worries about it all along.

The play concludes, of course, with the disclosure of Florimonde's identity as the Unknown, Léandre's rage at his dishonor (he is on the verge of killing his sister with his sword) and the subsequent peaceful granting of Florimonde to Lidamant when he asks for her hand. Léandre is doubly impoverished by this dénouement. Losing the total possession of his sister he loses a valuable item through which he can achieve alliances with other families. As an unchaste or uncontrollable woman his sister destroys one of his points for barter and reduces him

socially. Moreover, specifically because of the apparent transformation of identity brought about by the revelation of Florimonde
as the Unknown, Léandre is robbed of a potential sexual object. Once
the Unknown's identity is clear the various social inhibitions which
normally weigh upon the characters are reimposed. Because of this
new inhibited state the characters are at once fixed, frozen into a single
and apparently permanent set of relationships. The irony of the
spectator's vision ends.

Curiously d'Ouville had used an almost identical theme of disguise
for the plot of his *Esprit folet* (1638). The title of the earlier play refers to
the additional use of the secret door for the purpose of playing ghost
and frightening the guest's valet. Otherwise the plots are much the
same. Angélique, the sister of the Parisian gentlemen Liandre and
Licidas, is in love with Florestan, a young noble from Languedoc. The
use of the house, the guest's room, the strong bond of friendship
between her lover and brothers' severe regulation of the heroine's
activities (despite her status as a young widow) remain the same as in
Les Fausses Véritéz.

The earlier and more farcical *Esprit folet*, however, gives more
importance to several significant incidents. At the very beginning of
the work Angélique is in love with a young stranger (during the act she
learns that he is Florestan and that he will live in her house). They met
when he helped her escape from her brother who had followed her out
of the comedy where she had gone secretly and without permission.
This pursuit is ambiguously motivated. Apparently the brother did
not recognize Angélique but wanted to see the face of the beautiful
woman everyone was staring at. The play thus begins with a comic
impropriety on the part of the brother whose galant pursuit is
inconsistent (as the public knows) with the identity of the girl he
chases. The arrival of the young stranger who throws himself between
the heroine and her brother is perhaps even more significant. This
opening conflict sums up the underlying relationships which lead to
Angélique's subsequent attempts to escape from her family identity
and join herself to Florestan. In the last moments of the play, before
Angélique and Florestan receive her brother's permission to marry,
the same interposition—of lover protecting a woman from her
brother—occurs again.[1]

This confusion of the roles of brother-possessor-protector and that of
a man in pursuit of a mistress is a striking formal reversal. Angélique
arrives on the stage in the first scene still showing the signs of the

exertion of fleeing. The future lover has just prevented both the outcome Angélique fears (her brother's rage) and that which Licidas anticipates (discovering a beautiful and mysterious woman). At the end of the play two similar reversals of roles occur and the question of identity of a sister again comes to the fore. Angélique is once more threatened by her brother who, however, swallows his rage when Florestan asks for her hand. Then Angélique objects that Florestan seems to be engaged already to another woman whose portrait she found among his belongings. Florestan identifies this woman as his sister. Her relationship to Florestan is therefore no more an obstacle to his marriage with Angélique than was Licidas's pursuit of his sister before the first scene. Both the beginning and end of the play contain identity confusions which must be resolved before the characters can proceed with their love and marriage. These two situations are the result of a failure to recognize a kinship which makes two unions impossible (diagram B).

Licidas		Angélique
marriage	marriage	marriage
possible	prohibited	possible
Soeur de		Florestan
Florestan		

Diagram B

The dilemma of d'Ouville's protagonists illustrates clearly the dramatic effect of the pursuit of the "masked woman." The spectator witnesses the struggles of a protagonist trapped and rendered indecisive by his ignorance of an identity which is known to the public. The confusion and powerlessness which the spectator finds comic (in addition to the comic produced by an incongruity of relationships which only the public sees) results from the character's fear that he may, because of an ignorance of identity, transgress some social prohibition. He is frustrated by an imagined obstacle which he projects into the "empty space" left in his perception by this question of identity. In d'Ouville's two plays the social impropriety feared by the primary hero, the young provincial who falls in love with his host's sister, is the violation of a social rule forbidding a close friend or an adopted brother from being a rival for the hand of a woman loved by the friend or brother.[2]

The two masculine characters—the suitor and the brother—are not equally conscious of the risk they run of violating some important social rule. The spectator's perception of this risk or of the incongruous relationships the characters form is the source of the comic which occurs even when the latent violation of the taboo is purely formal. Thus Léandre's pursuit of his sister, a movement of curiosity which is inseparable from the suggestion of amorous pursuit (III, vi) is by no means an intentional incestuous act. Nothing would be farther from his mind than erotic interest if in fact he caught his sister. Yet the violation of the prohibition which occurs here—in the events which precede the opening of the *Esprit folet*, and in the heroine's suspicions about the portrait in her lover's baggage in this play—points to a potential or formal violation of the social pattern which only the spectator perceives.

In a different way, other plays of the period exploit the comic possibilities of the latent or unconsummated incest through an ignorance of the woman's identity. Rotrou's comedy *La Soeur* (1645) contains a more explicit reference to the incest taboo. The hero Lélie, who lost his mother and sister in infancy, is sent by his elderly father to Constantinople where the two women have reportedly been found. While on his way to Turkey, however, Lélie falls in love with a Venetian girl named Sophie, marries her, and then returns with her to his father's house. There he pretends that Sophie is his sister Aurélie whom he found, without their mother, in Turkey. These details, exposed in a dialogue between the hero and his friend Eraste (I, iii), clarify the situation of the characters in the first scene. Lélie is alarmed at the marriages ordered by his father and Eraste's father. Lélie is supposed to marry Eroxène, whom Eraste loves, and Eraste is expected to marry Lélie's "sister" Aurélie. The only propsoed solution is that offered by his valet Ergaste (I, iii) who suggests a pretended marriage followed by a clandestine and habitual nocturnal exchange.

The hero is guilty only of having married without his father's consent and allowing this marriage to distract him from his family duties—certainly a dilemma for a comic character but not an infraction of a deep social rule which would result for comic heroes in anything like tragic guilt. All this worry and confusion in the first act simply bring to the public's attention the difference between the reality of Lélie's relationship to Aurélie and his apparent kinship with "Sophie." The two kinds of kinship, that of brother and sister and that of husband and wife, are mentioned, contrasted, and shown to exclude one another. The comic effect derived from the hero's attempt to maintain the two contradictory identities of the girl he loves is fairly evident. From scene to scene the spectator complacently watches the contrast between the "correct" view of this relationship (II, i—Lélie and Aurélie) and the outsider's misinterpretation of it. For example Lélie's father Anselme sees the tenderness between the siblings as a danger and an evil (II, ii). The fear of incest exists in these "ignorant" outsiders, but we know, along with Lélie that this fear is unjustified. As Anselme says to Ergaste:

> Il en usent pour Nole avec trop de license;
> Et, quoique leur amour ait beaucoup d'innocence,
> Je ne puis approuver ces baisers assidus,
> D'une ardeur mutuelle et donnés et rendus,
> Ces discours à l'oreille et ces tendres caresses,
> Plus dignes passe-temps d'amans et de maîtresses,
> Qu'ils ne sont en effet d'un frère et d'une soeur.
> (II, ii)

Yet in the fourth act, the public and Lélie are surprised and shocked to discover, through the revelations of Lélie's mother Constance who finally does appear, that Lélie's Aurélie is really his sister. The false identity becomes the true one, retrospectively the father's fears are justified. Lélie and Sophie are trapped in the disguise which they had prepared for the others. The mother-daughter recognition (IV, iv) confronts the mother and her children with a knowledge of the incest and converts the audience's feeling of contented superiority and comical irony (over those who fear the sin) into a shocked apprehension of a tragic accident. Because *La Soeur* is a comedy Constance reminds her son that he has committed no serious sin. After all, he and Aurélie were ignorant of their kinship when they married and they will commit no sin if they simply cease marital relations:

> Ayant cru contracter un hymen légitime,
> Vous n'avez point péché; l'erreur n'est pas un crime,
> Et n'a point fait d'outrage à ses chastes appas,
> Pourvu qu'à l'avenir vous n'en abusiez pas.
> (IV, iv)

This appeal to contemporary casuistry seems stunningly inappropriate as an excuse for incest. Certainly this sin is not so easily pardoned in the tragic tradition in which incest is most familiar to the theatrical public.[3] Significantly, the spectator is not given time to dwell on the implications of this discovery for more than two scenes

(IV, v, vi) while, moreover, the action on stage displaces interest from the major characters to the minor figures of Eroxène's uncle Orgie and her servant Lydie. In the first scene of the last act Lydie reveals to Anselme, Lélie's father, that because of a substitution of children the girl believed to be Sophie, Lélie's sister, is in fact the true Eroxène and that the supposed Eroxène to whom Anselme wished to marry Lélie, is Lélie's real sister. Anselme is relieved at having avoided forcing Lélie into an incestuous marriage. Aurélie and Constance learn the truth (V, iv) before Lélie. He, like most of the protagonists of the plays of the masked woman, is the last to understand the true identity of the woman he loves (V, vi).

Between d'Ouville's two plays and Rotrou's *La Soeur* there is a great difference in the characters' consciousness of the moral status of their acts. What remained primarily formal in d'Ouville, a juxtaposition within the spectator's omniscient mind of illicit actions which the characters believe licit, is represented in Rotrou as the characters' own realization that they have broken a social rule. Lélie is, in fact, because of this consciousness, more a pseudo-tragic hero than a purely comic one. Until the fourth act he is a comic character. Then his lies become "true" and hence, because of the gravity of his mistake, tragic. In turn this truth once more becomes a fallacy. This theme, in which the hero is either simultaneously or alternately guilty and innocent of a serious moral fault, creates a complex relationship between the spectator and the character who acts out the crime. The spectator is, like Lélie, scarcely willing to accept the reality of his sin, an act which in the beginning and then in the end appears to be guiltless. Yet for a moment, because of an error of perception, this act seems a crime.

Rotrou's play is a comedy, but the characters risk committing a serious fault, one usually associated with tragedy. The astonishing ease with which the theme thus crosses conventional generic boundaries is illustrated by the Dircé-Thésée episode of Pierre Corneille's version of the Oedipus legend. This "tragedy" is based on the drama which is the Aristotelian prototype of the genre and uses the incest theme in a way similar to the way Rotrou uses it in comedy.

Corneille's play offers a striking example of the conversion of a terrifying and tragic subject into what has been described as "une féerie de l'équivoque."[4] By adding the couple Dircé-Thésée to the Oedipus legend, Corneille draws the attention of the spectator until the middle of the third act to a story of young love. Until then there is no suggestion of a possible incest or of the death of Oedipus. The rumor that the son of Laius is still alive (III, iv) brings about Thésée's confession that he is this son and guilty of incest. This avowal prepares the first scene of the fourth act, in which the spectator views what seems to be the continuation of the same love story (with which the public is intended to sympathize) become an incestuous love without losing its appeal. Although the spectator is enlightened, along with Dircé, as to the fallacy of this suspicion of incest (end of IV, i) the public does not learn of the true incest predicted by the oracle before the third scene of the fifth act. Corneille thus minimizes all references to Oedipus's incest by attaching the public's attention to the spectacle of the false incest which may be less repugnant than the sexual love between mother and son. The Theban king's sin occupies only nine verses while the imaginary incest of Dircé and Thésée forms the subject of at least seventy-three verses.

However short, this subplot of false incest stands out in *Oedipe*. In the beginning of act IV, Corneille uses the device of the unknown identity, in this case a voluntary disguise, to produce simultaneously a sexual equivocation, an effect of pure verbal pleasure derived from play on double meanings, and a kind of detective game in which the spectator could guess Thésée's revelation before Dircé. Thésée, having shown some vague doubts about the truth of his claim to be Dircé's brother by saying

Et de mon sort douteux l'obscur événement
Ne défend pas l'espoir d'un second changement
(1219-20)

plunges into a declaration of love which appears to Dircé and to the spectator to be incestuous:

Mon coeur n'écoute point ce que le sang veut dire;
C'est d'amour qu'il gémit, c'est d'amour qu'il soupire;
Et pour pouvoir sans crime en goûter la douceur,
Il se révolte exprès contre le nom de soeur.
(1237-40)

These verses provoke a naïvely incestuous reply from Dircé, who is not aware of any insincerity in Thésée's claim of fraternity:

J'aime en ce douteux sort tout ce qui m'embarrasse;
Je ne sais quoi m'y plait qui n'ose s'exprimer,
Et ce confus mélange a de quoi me charmer,
Je n'aime plus qu'en soeur, et malgré moi j'espère.
(1258-61)

When Thésée then at last reveals his stratagem in the following reply the *quid pro quo* has lasted for sixty-four verses. Corneille, proud of having spared the spectators the "dangereux spectacle" of Oedipus's bleeding eyesockets, as he notes in the *Examen*, is pleased with his invention of the supposed incest of Thésée. Corneille refers to this love as "l'heureux épisode des amours de Thésée et de Dircé." In this way the "happy incest," or the love which redeems itself from the guilt of incest, makes its way into the tragedy, forming a comic subplot which almost hides the original painful theme of Oedipus's punishment and guilt. Corneille saw that to the sensibility of his period there were two radically different ways of treating this forbidden love, and he contrived to insert the second and lower form of the theme within the classic example of its higher treatment.

In this way Corneille's tragedy crosses the border into the comic through a portrayal of the same action in which Rotrou places his comic hero in the shadow of the tragic. Lélie, in *La Soeur*, had in fact exclaimed, upon learning the crime into which his mistake in identity had led him, "Quel supplice assez grand expîra mon forfait?" He also demonstrates the persistence of his love in spite of the recognition:

Je doute quel des deux est moins m'assassiner,

Ou de la retenir, ou de l'abandonner.

(IV, iv)

The two stories are based on the continuation of the same love under different social circumstances of approval and disapproval. Lélie, Sophie, and Dircé are made aware (and Thésée seems to the public to be aware) of an incestuous relationship which they are loath to interrupt, having begun it in all innocence. Thus Dircé explains how her love "Se révolte exprès contre le nom de soeur." The impetus of her original passion makes it impossible for her to stop loving simply because of its new sinful status. She pleads with Thésée,

Ah! prince, s'il se peut, ne soyez point mon frère,

Et laissez-moi mourir avec les sentiments

Que la gloire permet aux illustres amants.

(1262-64)

In this type of rapid alternation between the permissible and impermissible, between two radically different types of love and sexual relation, it is not the psychology of the characters but the spectator's attitude toward this situation and these characters which deserves comment. If anything is foreign to the plays of the masked woman, it is concern with introspection in the characters and any attempt to guarantee some kind of truth or unity to the individual's emotions as they relate to his actions. Unlike the situations of purely formal violation of the moral code which exist, for example, in d'Ouville's plays, in *Oedipe* and in *La Soeur* the characters and the public share a consciousness of wrongdoing. In Rotrou's play they are equally surprised to discover that Lélie has married his true sister (or almost so, since the public knows that there is some mystery attached to Orgie and thus to Eroxène's kin). If the spectator had known from the beginning of the incestuous nature of the hero's love, the emotion would perhaps appear less deserving of sympathy than it does when the spectator is surprised in his complicity. The spectator looks upon this protagonist as a man who has involuntarily committed one of the gravest social faults. Yet his recognition of the fault is not followed by punishment. Instead, what was a crime, again becomes licit soon afterwards. Even when all are aware of the criminal love which continues in spite of the new knowledge, there are various attempts to circumvent the prohibition or to excuse its violation. Constance in Rotrou's play tries to persuade her children that they have committed no sin since there can be no evil without consciousness; Dircé also evinces a desire to continue the love she has for Thésée simply by wishing away the unwanted kinship. It is this refusal to accept the sin as a permanent condition and a definitive sentence which prepares the return to normality which follows in both cases. Licit love becomes sinful and then licit again, all the time maintaining the public's sympathy for the characters and their love.

In these plays unlike the *Fausses Véritéz* the spectator does not have the pleasure of an ironic superiority to the characters and cannot therefore find the pleasure of laughter from the sense of incongruity between the character's actions and the social taboo such actions violate. The comic in plays like *La Soeur*, in which the spectator's knowledge is usually as limited as that of the fictive beings he watches on stage, comes from the feeling that a taboo has been avoided. The characters, and with them the spectator, have succeeded in achieving what they desired without transgressing the social limit of permissible marriages. The prohibition is not finally conquered, not violated with impunity but, to our relief, the danger of its violation falls away. The spectator shares with the characters complicity in the desire to commit the sin (or, at least, forget the rule) and finds that he is spared the guilt of having sympathized with a true violation of his social code.

The result is that the desire has been accomplished, the obstacle of social convention rendered inapplicable. It is the taboo which seems to have retreated rather than the characters. Of course the moral code of society, both within the text and outside of the theatre remains the same, but for a brief moment what was forbidden (if only in name) becomes permissible (if only because of a name). The dramatic effect is thus to reaffirm the importance of the moral code as well as to permit in fantasy the transgression of the taboo by sympathetic characters who draw the public into a kind of complicity. By creating such an attitude towards the protagonists' possible sin and ultimate sinless happiness, the author contributes to the "comédie galante de l'inceste" (as Brasillach called it), analogous to Northrop Frye's "comic Oedipus situation."[5]

While the use of unknown of disguised identity to introduce the incest theme into comedy is the most striking aspect of the "masked woman" plays—because of the disparity between the seriousness of the potential error and the comic effect it produces—other situations arise because of the mystery surrounding the woman. The protagonist's failure to identify the woman leads to other comical confusions and temporary distortions of marriage customs.

The hero may fall in love with a woman whose family and social status is unknown to him. Here a conflict can arise because the hero prefers the love of an unknown and possibly poor woman to the wealthy match arranged by the father. Or the hero may wonder whether the woman whom he pursues is of the proper social rank for him to marry her, since a crossing of the boundary separating the bourgeoisie from the aristocracy, or the commonality, is implicitly excluded.[6]

Sometimes, as in d'Ouville's *La Dame suivante* (1645) or in Thomas Corneille's *L'Amour à la mode* (1653), the heroine changes the outward signs of her membership in a certain class in order to gain a better knowledge of the hero while remaining herself unknown and uncompromised. In d'Ouville's play the woman Isabelle appears to the hero first as a masked woman whose nobility is apparent (act I) and then takes on the guise of a servant in order to enter the service of Léonor, the original mistress of her newly chosen lover Climante. Subsequently Isabelle has her own servant Dorise dress herself as a *dame* to take her place masked in the third act. Isabelle appears to Climante in her role as servant to Léonor, under the name of Dorothée.

By utilizing this multiplication of guises Isabelle approaches her beloved from several different directions and profits from the apparently contradictory advantages of the poor woman (the familiarity with which she can speak to the hero and circulate unobserved) and of the rich lady (the obvious possibility of a marriage, the impression of great wealth, titles, etc.). Disguised as Dorothée, Isabelle runs after the masked woman (played at this moment by Dorise) to see who it is (III, iv). She returns to Climante to describe the woman's beauty (speaking of herself), her wealth, and her love for Climante but does not tell him her name (III, vi). Finally the hero is allowed to guess (IV, i) that Dorothée is the unknown woman, revealing her name but concealing her class. In the last act (viii) Isabelle appears to Climante both unmasked and dressed as a lady, but she continues to conceal her true name, calling herself Lizène (and occupying the house of a woman who is actually named Lizène). Isabelle maintains the secret of her double identity until the very last scene of the play when she surprises Léonor and reveals to all that the identity of Dorothée was the false front behind which her true nobility was hidden.

Isabelle thus passes through a number of partial disguises. She appears as the masked lady in act I, the unmasked servant in the next three acts, and finally as herself, the lady Isabelle (V, viii). She also temporarily assigns the identity of the masked lady to Dorise, who plays that role in act III (scenes i, iv). At no time before the final scene do face (personal identity), class identity, and house (family identity) merge for the protagonist into one person, a woman whom he can marry in all honor. Until that moment he does not have the knowledge necessary for him to act within the framework of his class.

In *La Dame suivante*, as the title suggests through the conjunction of the two guises of Isabelle as lady and servant, the comic effect derives largely from the assumption by the heroine of at least two contradictory social identities and the necessity for a resolution of this illusionistic duality before the hero can marry her. This amusing metamorphosis plays on the public's sense of the disparity between the flexibility of a character's social standing and that of the real world in which economic categories are much less supple.

In other plays the identity of the woman is not so deliberately and explicitly distributed over several different classes. In Corneille's *Le Menteur* the extremely successful use of the theme of the liar or braggart which gives the play its title is inserted into the framework of a play

about confusion of identity. While this play begins with the hero
Dorante's attempt to mystify two women he meets soon after his
arrival in Paris (I, ii) and to impress the one woman who particularly
attracts him, it is he who is soon mystified. His attempt to conceal his
own identity and profession quickly turns to the usual situation of
amorous identity intrigues—the woman learns the hero's identity and
keeps him in doubt or confusion until the end of the play.[7] Thus
Dorante fails to interpret correctly the coachman's statement, "La
plus belle des deux. . .est ma maîtresse, Elle loge à la Place, et son
nom est Lucrèce" (I, iv). From the beginning of the second act, in a
scene between Clarice (whom Dorante assumes to be Lucrèce) and
Dorante's father Géronte the girls' names are apparent to the
spectator. Thereafter he watches Dorante work out his misidentification to its extreme conclusion, in which he declines the hand of the
woman he esteems and demands the other's hand because of his
confusion of names. In all of this confusion of the feminine identity the
question of disguise or mistake of membership in a social class is not
raised. Yet Dorante's mistake is a profoundly social act. By loving
"Lucrèce" instead of "Clarice" he disobeys his father, risks his family
alliances, and turns his own love into the weakest and most ludicrous
failure of the marriage system. By contrast the figure of the benevolent
father, representative of the order which Dorante refuses and which is
the origin of the names and *maisons* confused by the hero, is exalted and
justified.

Comparing Molière and Corneille, Charles Mauron points out this
abasement of the young hero and the triumph of the father in the plays
of Corneille: "Le ridicule, dans le théâtre de Molière, atteint surtout
les personnages paternels . . . . Il est attaché, au contraire, dans les
comédies de Corneille, à un personnage de fils amoureux: Alidor (*La
Place Royale*), Matamore (*L'Illusion comique*), Dorante (*Le Menteur* et *La
Suite du Menteur*)."[8] Yet Dorante's mistake and his loss of control of his
own destiny is not an isolated or exclusively Cornelian comic situation.
Works involving a masked or unknown woman often call for the
degradation of the hero and a reversal from the position of strength for
the male (at the beginning of the play) to a dominance by the woman
(in the middle and end of the play) through changes in the knowledge
of identity possessed by each.

One could describe these plays in terms of a generalized
disintegration of the hero's perception of the world—that is, the social
world in which he acts—with the woman and her identity and

attributes at the center of this disintegration. The dramatic world of the *Fausses Véritéz* and similar plays is characterized by a profound fragmentation of the woman's identity in the hero's perception. The elements which compose her individual character are separated and maintained in suspension for the duration of the play.

In d'Ouville's play, the woman's name, face, and family (including the physical sign of the family, the house) are separated in the hero's vision. Other authors fragment the person of the heroine in even more intimate ways. Thomas Corneille's *Charme de la voix* (1658) separates the heroine Fenise from her voice, which the Duke of Milan has heard and loved without knowing whose singing it was. Seeing Fenise at a ball without knowing her, the duke shows no interest in her. Léandre, hero of Boisrobert's *La Jalouse d'elle-mesme* (1650) falls in love with a woman whose beautiful hand he has seen (I, iii) but cannot identify the woman by name or face, since she is masked. Angélique, the heroine, even describes herself in terms of this fragmentation:

Je me voy, quoy qu'unique en trois parts divisée,
Il n'en doit aimer qu'une, et je sens toutefois
Que je suis sans raison jalouse de ces trois.

(V, ii)

Only at the very end of the play does he realize that the hand and voice of this woman belong to Angélique, his intended fiancée. In the same author's *L'Inconnue* (1655)[9] Dom Felix knows neither the name nor the house of Climène and cannot persuade her to show her face (I, i). From her clothing he determines her probably social class. In Boisrobert's *La Belle Invisible* (1656) the unknown masked woman's identity is so entirely fragmented that her social existence is unknown to all but one other character (in act I). No woman is known to have been born to her family, for her parents disguised her as a male in her infancy. Olympe is therefore separated from her sex and name. Don Carlos, the hero, knows only her voice and shape and cannot associate these characteristics with any person existing in his society. His knowledge of the heroine is so divided that he cannot recognize her by joining the voice and the face for example, even when Olympe appears unmasked (act IV) to warn him of the danger presented by the love of the *belle invisible* (who is, the public knows, herself).

The protagonist of such plays begins with a partial glimpse of the heroine's identity, but the plays proceed in such a way that further revelations of portions of the woman's identity do not fit together in his mind but instead create greater confusion. Because a certain key is lacking, the hero's perception seems gradually more and more warped. Eventually, even when he has all the necessary pieces of the identity puzzle, he cannot reach the conclusion to which he is invited. The final collapse of the hero's perception often culminates in a confrontation between the hero, now rendered blind to and by all the evidence, and the unmasked woman, the object of his quest. The hero refuses to see this woman as the one he loves. When Boisrobert's Don Carlos talks to Olympe in *La Belle Invisible* (IV, iii) her face is uncovered and her dress suits her rank and sex. Only the protagonist's perception is clouded. In fact the proof of this blindness is sometimes imposed by the heroine herself before she accepts the hero's love. In *La Jalouse d'elle-mesme* Angélique, in the dark, demands the Léandre not only renounce but insult Angélique. Only after he does this, believing that he is speaking to the "marquise" he loves, will the single heroine Angélique accept his love (V, iii).

This fragmentation of the heroine's physical and moral being translates identity into spatial signs. This characteristic is already clear in the *Fausses Véritéz* where the place of the unknown woman's appearance and the relation of each character to a house or a room is an outward sign of identity. The use of the *maison* moreover is simply the most obvious example of the practice of dividing the identity of the physical object into pieces which are not shown together in the same space at the same time. The woman then becomes in the hero's mind a series of incomplete objects, associated with different places, never cohering in the same space. The heroine's hand exists in a different space and time from her face, her voice from her body, her house from her sex, her face from her name. The woman is a kind of disincarnate presence which haunts the hero's world. The segments of her person are isolated and scattered throughout the scenes and places of the theatre. As Pedro in Scarron's *Les Trois Dorothées* exclaims:

Quoy, bons Dieux! Dorothée à Dom Diegue aussi!
Dorothée à Madrid, et Dorothée icy!
Et Dorothée en chambre, et Dorothée en chaise!
(IV, iii)

This dislocation of the object of the hero's desire into physical fragments is not merely coincidental to the themes of false incest and disguise of social class. In both spheres, the physical (that of the corporeal presence apprehended in its totality) and the moral (that of the conventions regulating actions and especially actions relating to other persons), the hero's vision becomes confused. His divided view of the identity of others and his consequent difficulties in respecting the proper marriage patterns seem almost dreamlike. And as in a dream certain actions and visions seem possible which, upon awaking, are shown to be forbidden. The plays of the masked woman are similar to dreams in the way they seem to dissolve the social structure and identity patterns before reestablishing them in the final scene.

Footnotes

1. The only functional explanation for the existence of two brothers concerns this moment in the play. The conflicting elements of the brother's relationship to the young provincial are made more explicit in the *Esprit folet* than in *Les Fausses Véritéz*. In the later play they are condensed into a single person. By separating the two tendencies in the earlier play, d'Ouville underlined the very real rivalry between the lover and the brother.

2. This is at least a kind of social convention which the play itself projects and utilizes. There are, of course, plays of the period which take the rivalry of brothers as their subject, e.g. Beys, *Céline ou les frères rivaux* (Paris: T. Quinet, 1637), Boyer, *Tyridate* (Paris: T. Quinet, 1649), Corneille, *Rodogune* (1644).

3. There are a number of plays of the period in which incest leads to an unhappy tragic end. Boyer's *Tyridate* (1647), Dalibray's *Torrismon* (1635) and its Italian source in Tasso (1587), Corneille's *Oedipe* (1659), Desfontaines' *Véritable Sémiramis* (1646). It is probably a greater problem for the modern reader to see these plays which end unhappily as exceptions to the prevalent comic or tragicomic use of incest before Racine.

4. Robert Brasillach, *Corneille* (Paris: Arthème Fayard, 1938) p. 361.

5. Northop Frye, *The Anatomy of Criticism (1957; rpt. New York:* Atheneum, 1967), pp. 180-181.

6. Plays in which the hero is puzzled by the woman's social origin include Baro's *Cariste* (1648), Boisrobert's *La Belle Invisible* (1656).

7. Other plays in which the woman keeps the man mystified until late in the play are Boisrobert's *L'Inconnue* (1654), his *Jalous d'elle-mesme* (1648), Thomas Corneille's *L'Amour à la mode* (1651), *Les Engagements du hasard* (1649), *Le Charme de la voix* (1656), Lambert's *Les Soeurs jalouses* (1658), Scarron's *Les Trois Dorothées ou Jodelet souffleté* (1645), the Five Authors' *Comédie des Tuileries* (1635).

8. Charles Mauron, *Psychocritique du genre comique* (Paris: Corti, 1964), p. 150.

9. Based on Calderòn's *Casa con dos puertas mala es de guardar*, the source of his brother d'Ouville's *Fausses Véritéz*.

The Unknown King: Héraclius

The confused gallantries of the plays of the masked woman revolve around identities defined in terms of certain social and economic structures. The latent political significance of the individualistic, often middle-class concerns of the *Fausses Véritéz* and the *Belle invisible* becomes manifest when the same structures are depicted on a higher social plane. With surprisingly little change in the actual form of the identity confusions involved, what elsewhere seems simply amorous play becomes decisive in determining the reunion of nations and the legitimacy of rulers. These grave events are not only united to a theme of love, as they are in the broadest sense in most Cornelian and Racinian tragedy, but in a certain number of works these heroic and tragic consequences hang on the outcome of the same problems of unknown identity, involuntary incest, and class confusion as in the comedy. The recurrent theme of involuntary, putative incest is especially well represented. No fewer than twenty-five plays written during the years 1630-1660 demonstrate this special form of interaction between the erotic and the political.[1]

Corneille's fascination with the dramatic use of identity confusion appears most strikingly in a group of plays from the middle period of his production. *Rodogune* (1644), *Héraclius* (1647), *Don Sanche* (1649), *Pertharite* (1652), and *OEdipe* (1659) have a close thematic resemblance. In each the identity of a lover or spouse is tied to the highest political imperatives. In three of the five, moreover, the *dénouement* depends on the avoidance of an incest, for even *OEdipe* is, because of an emphasized subplot, largely a drama of incest avoided. In *Héraclius* and *Don Sanche* Corneille bases the complex and unified plot on such an escape from a socially prohibited love and defines the heroes' identities in sexual and political terms. In so doing he engages the spectator in a variously ironic and suspenseful confrontation with the meaning of identity itself.

Many years before the action of *Héraclius*, the usurper Phocas had killed the emperor Maurice, his predecessor on the throne of Orient, the empress Constantine, and their five sons. Phocas spared only the emperor's daughter, Pulchérie. As the public knows, however, from the beginning of the second act, the governess Léontine while pretending to surrender the six-month old prince Héraclius substituted her own son Léonce. After murdering the supposed heir Phocas gave Léontine his son Martian to raise with hers. In a second switch Léontine raised Héraclius as Martian and the true Martian as Léonce. The pseudo-Martian knows from Léontine that he is son of Maurice while the real Martian believes that he is Léonce. Only Léontine's daughter Eudoxe, who is Héraclius's mistress, shares the secret of the true identities. Living almost as brothers, the two young men are very close, especially since Martian, the pseudo-Léonce, saved Héraclius's life in combat.

The crisis which precipitates the action of the play is Phocas's attempt to force Pulchérie to marry the pseudo-Martian in order to assure legitimacy for his dynasty. Pulchérie refuses this marriage, on the grounds that this would aid Phocas to continue his unlawful rule. She rejoices instead in a rumor that Héraclius is alive and about to topple Phocas, although she concedes that the pretender, whoever he is, could not be Maurice's dead son (I, i). Phocas's supposed son, the pseudo-Martian, also refuses this marriage. Phocas does not understand why. It becomes clear in the second act from a conversation between Léontine and Héraclius that for fear of incest and of the threatened alternative, Pulchérie's death, Maurice's son would reveal his identity and lead the people against their oppressor. Yet Léontine, for reasons of her own, restrains Héraclius. The hero does not know that Léontine's purpose is to use Martian's ardor for Pulchérie to spur him on to kill Phocas, thus committing an involuntary parricide: "Je ne l'ai conservé que pour ce parricide" (II, iii). Before Léontine can convince her daughter and confidante of the appropriateness of this punishment, the courtier Exupère enters with Martian, the pseudo-Léonce, and proclaims him the true Héraclius on the basis of a letter in which Maurice declared, "Sous le nom de Léonce Haraclius respire." Léontine accepts this testimony and falsely confirms Martian in his new identity, but she cannot reply satisfactorily to his questions about why she encouraged his love for the princess Pulchérie, his "sister." No longer trusting the advice of a mother anxious to see her daughter marry the apparent son of Phocas Martian as pseudo Héraclius leaves to seek counsel elsewhere. He intends to lead an army against Phocas (II, vii). Léontine, though not in control of the situation, is happy to see Phocas's son armed against his father. Her daughter Eudoxe, however, worries about the possible loss of the rights of the true Héraclius:

> Mais je m'étonne fort de voir à l'abandon
> Du prince Héraclius les droits avec le nom
> (761-62)

The lovers Pulchérie and Martian, confronted with their seeming kinship, seek in their troubled memory a true thread in the conflicting impulses they felt. As Pulchérie replies to the similarly confused Martian:

> Moi-même assez souvent j'ai senti dans mon âme
> Ma naissance en secret me reprocher ma flamme.
> Mais quoi! l'impératrice, à qui je dois le jour,
> Avait innocemment fait naître cet amour:
> . . .
> 'Mais prenez un époux des mains de Leontine . . . .'
> (783-86, 792)

They agree that she should marry Phocas's son in order to save him from the vengeance of the rebels loyal to Maurice's heir. But Phocas must be killed beforehand so that Pulchérie will not for one moment be the daughter-in-law of her family's murderer. Phocas, however, makes the pseudo-Héraclius a prisoner before he can carry out his plan of leading a rebellion. The courtier Exupère, now seeming loyal to the usurper, urges Phocas to execute the supposed Héraclius in public to show the rebel populace the death of its leader (III, iv). Meanwhile the true Héraclius, fearful for Martian, is furious with Léontine for giving away his own name:

> Confondre en Martian et mon nom et mon sort;
> Abuser d'un billet que le hasard lui donne;
> Attacher de sa main mes droits à sa personne . . . .
> (1138-40)

Héraclius cannot allow another to usurp his death, and he affirms his identity as the true Héraclius, a claim disputed at once by Martian, the supposed Héraclius, as pure *générosité.* Phocas is the true victim of the confusion. Believing that one of the two young men is his son and one the son of his dead predecessor, Phocas is paralyzed by the uncertainty of which to kill and which to crown. Neither prince is willing to decide for him, neither wishes to risk incest by marrying Pulchérie or accept the dishonoring name of Martian, son of Phocas the usurper. Héraclius has no way to convince the others of his identity. Pulchérie comes to believe that he is really Martian because of his hesitation to kill his putative father. Héraclius, on the other hand, argues that the supposed Héraclius's inflexibility is a sign of the heritage of his father's barbarity: "Il a le coeur plus dur étant fils d'un tyran" (1602). But none of these arguments can bring any of the three young principals to a decision. Neither of the princes is willing to undertake a *mariage blanc* with Pulchérie in order to save the lives of all three (V, v). Finally Phocas's oppression ends through the success of a conspiracy led by Exupère (V, vi-vii). Yet, the problem of the identification of Héraclius and the consequent resolution of the love story of the four young characters remains unsolved until within thirty verses of the end of the play. Since no one trusts Léontine or, for that matter, anyone else, the final testimony can come only from outside in the form of a letter from Constantine (1887-94). Before her death the empress wrote that Léontine had made a second exchange of children and that the true Héraclius is now the false Martian.

The suspense in which the characters are kept until the last scene emphasizes an aspect of identity which runs throughout the work. The names and thus the identities of the major male characters are separated from their persons and become abstractions, roles to be filled. Identity is defined as a relationship, in the world of *Héraclius*. The person who will fill the space assigned to Héraclius and the one who will take the space of Martian are missing, although the position of these spaces in the topology of the play (i.e., relations to Pulchérie, Phocas, Maurice, Eudoxe, the populace) is rigorously established. From the very first scene of the play, the power of the name Héraclius, independent of its possessor, should be clear even to Phocas, who hears from Crispe that the populace is near rebellion and than "Il nomme Héraclius celui qu'il ressuscite" (34). The usurper Phocas attributes the rumor of a living brother to Pulchérie, noting the distinction between the true Héraclius whom he has seen killed and "cette erreur populaire / D'un faux Héraclius qu'elle accept pour frère" (269-70). Because the effect of the name Héraclius is all-important for the people of Phocas's usurped empire, it is not enough to execute Maurice's son. The victim must proclaim his identity publicly before dying in order to destroy forever the place of Héraclius in the minds of the people; that is, in order to destroy an identity which might otherwise survive its bearer and appear again. In this sense Crispe, with every semblance of reason, counsels the public execution of Martian (thought to be Héraclius):

Mais le plus sûr pour vous est que sa mort éclate,
De peur qu'en l'ignorant le peuple ne se flatte,
N'attende encore ce prince, et n'ait quelque raison
De courir en aveugle à qui prendra son nom.
. . .
Et qu'il die, en mourant, à ce peuple confus:
"Peuple, n'en doute point, je suis Héraclius."
(1067-70, 1085-86)

Héraclius ("Martian") refers to the effect of the name on the people, "Au nom d'Héraclius à demi soulevé" (I, iii). While speaking to Pulchérie he accepts the notion that the name or role of Héraclius is more important than the proper assignment of the identity to a person:

J'irai pour l'empêcher jusqu'à la force ouverte;
Et puisse, si le ciel m'y voit rien épargner,
Un faux Héraclius à ma place régner!
(366-68)[2]

The hero, however, does not wish the separation to become irreversible. To Léontine he stresses the necessity of a timely revelation of identity, seeing a divine invitation to do so:

Que par un si grand bruit semé confusément,
Il dispose les coeurs à prendre un nouveau maître,
Et presse Héraclius de se faire connaître.
C'est à nous de repondre à ce qu'il en prétend:
Montrons Héraclius au peuple qui l'attend.
(472-76)

Héraclius is impelled to establish his identity for fear of seeing another person appropriate his name and turn its power against the name's rightful possessor.

Pulchérie's political outlook is based on the same possibility of using the identity "Héraclius" independently of any hope of finding the person Héraclius; for her the name is indeed an empty space in the system of relations necessary to restore her superiority to Phocas. The will to resemble Héraclius—in other words, to fulfill the people's and Pulchérie's hopes of rebellion—is the practical equivalent of being Maurice's son. She says to Phocas, of the rumor,

Je sais qu'il est faux; pour t'assurer ce rang
Ta rage eut trop de soin de verser tout mon sang,
Mais la soif de ta perte en cette conjoncture
Me fait aimer l'auteur d'une belle imposture.
Au seul nom de Maurice il te fera trembler:

Puisqu'il se dit son fils, il veut lui ressembler,
Et cette ressemblance où son courage aspire
Mérite mieux que toi de gouverner l'empire.
J'irai par mon suffrage affermir cette erreur,
L'avouer pour mon frère et pour mon empereur. . . .
                                                    (239-48)
In political terms it is the effect of the "guise" or disguise (verbal) on the people rather than the reality (biological) of the character's relation to the name he bears which is important.

Phocas shares this point of view in attempting to affirm his political control through the continuation of his family. For him the choice of a "Martian" is necessary for intellectual reasons, divorced from the questions of emotional attachment and natural sentiment. In choosing the real Héraclius as his son he makes an act of will designed to fill the gaps which remain in the system, even if the characters playing the roles assigned to them make no substantial claim to bear their proper names. Phocas's declaration, "Je t'adopte pour fils, accepte-moi pour père" (1676), is such an attempt to repair by artificial means the gap between social and natural identity. Although Phocas leans emotionally towards having Héraclius as Martian (through habit, or from the instinctive recognition of superiority?) he is willing to have either one, provided that the son fill this role willingly and completely. At this point in the play all of the characters seem to have accepted the principle of the independence of the identity from the human person. There remains a space or role to be filled by one of the interchangeable heroes. Phocas tells his adoptive son,

Fais vivre Héraclius sous l'un ou l'autre sort;
Pour moi, pour toi, pour lui, fais-toi ce peu d'effort.
                                                    (1677-78)
Héraclius and Martian themselves repeatedly distinguish their various identities (in the plural for both of them) from one another, creating a kind of pseudo-schizophrenic personality. Believing himself Héraclius, Martian says to Pulchérie,

Il n'est pas merveilleux si ce que je me crus
Mêle un peu de Léonce au coeur d'Héraclius.
A mes confus regrets soyez donc moins sévère:
C'est Léonce qui parle, et non pas votre frère.
                                                    (853-56)
Martian accepts Léontine's description of her sacrifice of Héraclius's name in place of his person:

J'allai pour vous sauver vous offrir à Phocas;
Mais j'offris votre nom, et ne vous donnai pas.
                                        (609-10)
Martian reproaches Héraclius for trying to deprive him of his identity
in order to save his life (1284). When Martian (as "Héraclius")
reminds Phocas that he owes the life of his son "Martian" to his own
efforts when he was called Léonce, Phocas replies by dividing his inter-
locutor into a number of distinct identities:
Tu prends pour me toucher un mauvais artifice:
Héraclius n'eut point de part à ce service.
J'en ai payé à qui seul était dû
L'inestimable honneur de me l'avoir rendu.
                                        (955-58)
Thus Martian is partitioned into his two recognized personalities of
"Léonce" and "Héraclius." In this way each of the major characters is
a human vehicle bearing several identities alternately and even
simultaneously. In those verses so satisfying to Corneille, Héraclius
refers to what seems at that moment of the play simple empathy;
presenting "Léonce" to Pulchérie he says:
Son bonheur est le mien, Madame; et je vous donne
Léonce et Martian en la même personne:
C'est Martian en lui que vous favorisez.
                                        (357-59)[3]
As Martian says towards the end of the play, it is he who has been
called upon to play the greatest number of roles and express the
greatest variety of sentiments in the effort to take the different places
assigned to him in the unchanging topography of the work:
. . .dans le cours d'une seule journée,
Je suis Héraclius, Léonce et Martian;
Je sors d'un empereur, d'un tribun, d'un tyran.
De tous trois ce désordre en un jour me fait naître,
Pour me faire mourir enfin sans me connaître.
                                        (1816-20)
The persistence, throughout the play, of the separation between the
identities Héraclius and Martian on one hand and the real, living
characters who must finally occupy them, justifies the view of identity
as an empty role, space, or word having its own effective significance.
Pulchérie can marry either young man but cannot marry "Héraclius." Phocas could place either of them on the throne but cannot
make an emperor of "Héraclius." In the same way the conspirators,

leading and at the same time urged on by the people, assassinate
Phocas in the name of Héraclius, not for any specific individual who
may claim that name. It is this emptiness which the second letter fills in
the last scene of the play, a scene which somehow ends as if it were a
beginning. The populace still awaits (as audience) the actor just
chosen to play Héraclius. As the hero says in the last verses of
Héraclius, in thanksgiving to an identity-giving divinity,

> Allons lui rendre hommage, et, d'un esprit content,
> Montrer Héraclius au peuple qui l'attend.

(1915-16)

The separation between man and his social identity which is
manifest in the dealings of one character with another is also shown as
plunging deep into the selfhood of the heroes, affecting their own
consciousness of their birth. The relation between nature—the
individual's physical characteristics, personal accomplishments,
générosité as manifest to others—and name, that final justification of
these outward signs by reference to an unchanging biological truth, is
made as tenuous as possible within the dramatic confines of cridiblity.
The characters not only demonstrate the multiplicity of functions
which they perform—son of emperor, son of usurper—but also the
impossibility of passing from the level of action and personal nature to
the level of knowledge in which this functional evidence is justified by
a definitive name. The dramatic from which is peculiar to *Héraclius* and
similar plays is constituted by the struggle outward from the
characters' actions toward the definitive name structure or hierarchy
of the tragedy or heroic comedy. The characters' experience and
emotion offer no resolution of the problem of the play. Only the
artificial—in the fullest dramatic sense of artifice—can impose the
heirarchy which the characters so desperately seek.

The deliberate distance which Corneille maintains between the
characters and their identity is exemplified by the peculiarly insistent
uses of the device of the *voix du sang*. Héraclius contains a startling
number of references to this presentiment of kinship. In contrast to his
predecessors, Corneille uses the device so that it no longer has "the
arbitrary, mechanical, and artifical superficiality which often
characterizes its use."[4] More remarkable is the way in which
Corneille, here more than in *Don Sanche*, plays on this convention of
earlier novels and theatre to undermine its credibility, using it as an
increasingly ironic reminder of the characters' impotence.

At the beginning of the play the spectator could, if he wished to refer the action to a framework characterizing, for example, Hardy (e.g., *La Belle Egyptienne*), interpret the motivations of the principal characters on the basis of a premonition of kinship.[5] Phocas's comment,

> Pulchérie et mon fils ne se montrent d'accord
> Qu'à fuir cet hyménée à l'egal de la mort,
> Et les aversions entre eux deux mutuelles
> Les font d'intelligence à se montrer rebelles
>   (71-75)

seems a possible foreshadowing of the ultimate kinship discovered. But this possibility of an instinctive resistance is revealed as specious by the ease with which the characters accept the new identifications attributed to them during the play. Pulchérie shows no more innate repulsion to marrying one than the other prince, provided that her husband not be the son of Phocas. Of "Martian" (in fact her brother Héraclius) she says,

> Ce fils si vertueux d'un père si coupable,
> S'il ne devait régner, me pourrait être aimable.
>   (217-18)

She would thus be able to marry him if her intelligence did not indicate the political folly of such a marriage. Her resistance therefore is not clearly instinctive. Héraclius's refusal of the marriage springs from a firm belief in his secret identity as son of Maurice, not instinctive but based on Léontine's information. His remarks on the subject of his birth are couched in an ironic form which again has only the appearance of referring to an instinctive repulsion to Phocas: "J'ai peine à reconnaitre encore un père en lui" (332). Thus in the first act each person who could be motivated by the true *voix du sang* is shown to have other reasons for acting as he does. In the second act Martian ("Léonce") is persuaded without difficulty that he is the son of Maurice. The only obstacle to his behaving as such comes from his frustrated love for Pulchérie, which he later interprets as being an instinctive fraternal affection. He also describes his hesitations before this love as based on presentiment of kinship rather than on learned social inhibitions. The *voix du sang* appears here already as what it will be at the very end of the play, a catchall retrospective justification for any feelings the characters have, or think they should have. Any emotion can be twisted into or explained by the conventional kinship instinct. Martian's love for Pulchérie seems to him in the third act to have been an indication of his fraternal attachment to her. Wondering how he could have been so bold as to love above his station, he says,

J'interrogeais ce coeur sur sa témérité,
Et dans ses mouvements, pour secrète réponse,
Je sentais quelque chose au-dessus de Léonce,
Dont, malgré ma raison, l'impérieux effort
Emportait mes désirs au delà de mon sort.
(778-82)
Pulchérie replies,
Moi-même assez souvent j'ai senti dans mon âme
Ma naissance en secret me reprocher ma flamme"
(783-84)

While the affirmations of both lovers may be viewed, judging from the conclusion of the play, as correct (in terms of a conflict between the bloods of Maurice and Phocas), such truths are only afterthoughts inserted into feelings which may have meant something else at the time of their appearance in the play. Even if they did feel a secret murmur, perhaps due as well to the actual inequality in rank emphasized by Martian, there was no way to convert this amorphous uneasiness into any real knowledge. Pulchérie and Martian demonstrate the unreliability of one's instincts of kinship by giving complete adherence to the half-revelation of Martian's identity.

When Phocas and Martian put the belief in a secret feeling of kinship to the test in the following act, they prove its uselessness and even nullity as an active means to reach a decision. Héraclius's claim to be son of Maurice (IV, iii) leads to reasonings by which Martian tries to show Héraclius's motivation for this "false" but generous claim. Phocas tries to weigh the evidence presented by each claimant, and soon encounters the total impossibility of resolving the problem by pure logic, typified by Exupère's presentation of equally possible alternatives in Léontine's actions: "Elle a pu l'abuser, et ne l'abuser pas" (1314). Héraclius and Martian soon reach a similar impasse in their discussion of Léontine's motivation for her statements to the two princes (1345-60). Reason, without more evidence, cannot solve the dilemma. The only apparent source of new information, moreover, is Léontine, whose statements are now more than ever suspect to Phocas. Martian had already begun to cast doubt on her affirmations at the end of the second act. Phocas then is left with the *voix du sang* as his only recourse. To be more precise, Phocas believes he should feel some instinctive sympathy but, in fact, he admits that he does not:

Que veux-tu donc, nature, et que prétends-tu faire?

Si je n'ai plus de fils, puis-je encore être père?
De quoi parle à mon coeur ton murmure imparfait?
Ne me dis rien du tout, ou parle tout à fait.
(1375-78)
What is Phocas's distress if not an admission that nature has no voice at all? If it has the slightest murmur it is only the principle, attributed to nature by society, that a man should not kill his son and, especially, imperial heir. Everything leads credence to the supposition that Phocas would hear the same *voix* even if neither of the young men were in fact his son. In the same way Martian feels as nature's urge the social dictate that one should avenge one's father. He learns later that this was not at all the call of blood. The artificiality of this alleged instinct appears acutely in the second scene of the last act, when Héraclius himself, knowing his identity from before the beginning of the play, begins to feel doubts about his birth:

Je ne sais qui je suis et crains de le savoir,
Je veux ce que je dois, et cherche mon devoir:
Je crains de le haïr, si j'en tiens la naissance,
Je le plains de m'aimer, si je m'en dois vengeance.
(1581-84)

He concludes, "Des deux côtés en vain j'écoute la nature" (1592). Pulchérie, in this case, tries without success to reconstitute hypothetically the instinct from what Héraclius and Martian say and do, presuming a certain cause for the effects she sees:

Et le sang, par un double et secret artifice,
Parle en vous pour Phocas, comme en lui pour Maurice.
(1599-1600)

Héraclius in reply argues that the inherited tendency exists but that Pulchérie reads it incorrectly,

A ces marques en lui connaissez Martian:
Il a le coeur plus dur étant fils d'un tyran.
(1601-02)

Not only does instinct fail those who should, like Martian, feel it, but it has become a notion undermining everyone's knowledge and action. The *généreux*, being most scrupulously observant of duty, is the most susceptible to the perversions and betrayals of nature by culture. In dramatic terms this appears as Héraclius's betrayal of his natural duty by his indecision while he attempts to hear the voice of nature. In Corneille's later play, *Don Sanche*, the hero protests vehemently against his true birth by trying to remain loyal to his "father."

Pulchérie's references in the third act to the *voix du sang* are based on its supposed capacity to warn against love of a prohibited nature—"Ma naissance en secret me reprochait ma flamme" (784)—but by the fifth act this monitory capacity has been exposed as empty. The princes and Pulchérie cannot afford the self-indulgence of Phocas, who wishes, in an act of will, to adopt Héraclius. Pulchérie, Héraclius, and Martian fear incest, that recurrent menace in identity plays. Its appearance here, in the fifth scene of the fifth act, is the result of the wearing down of the problem to its essence, its most schematic form. Even if Pulchérie would consent to marry the son of Phocas in order to guarantee her brother from death, even if one of the two princes could be brought to call himself Martian in order to save the other, they would soon reach the final barrier which they cannot cross by an act of will or an arbitrary choice:

Qui me le montrera, si je veux l'épouser?
Et dans cet hyménée à ma gloire funeste,
Qui me garantira des périls de l'inceste?

(1778-80)

The silence of the voice of nature is complete. Incest or the mere suspicion of it is a degradation far more severe than the already intolerable submission to the tyranny of Phocas. Caught between death and incest the heroes are left powerless to overcome the separation between the reality of their birth and the more real social hierarchy in which they must place themselves in order to act. It is precisely the lack of knowledge about their identities which leaves the heroes paralyzed.

The play ends, of course, without the heroes' having taken an active role in the resolution. Phocas's death is accomplished without their initiative, participation or knowledge. They are still trying to resolve the real problem of the play until the last scene, in which all hope of a definitive judgment seems gone. Their only witness, Léontine herself, says, "Je vous puis être encore suspecte d'artifice" (1879).

At this juncture Corneille reuses two forms of recognition from earlier in the work: the now discredited *voix du sang* and the letter. Martian's "Je ne sais quoi pourtant dans mon coeur en murmure" (1871) at the death of the usurper is accepted with the tentative "Peutêtre en vous par là s'explique la nature" (1872) of Héraclius. This last reminder of the convention of instinct is ambivalent. On one hand it is a juxtaposition of the variable and ineffective testimony of feeling with the more decisive proof in writing. Yet it is also an illustration of the retrospective and conciliatory nature of the *murmure* in Corneille's dramatic practice. The ambiguous promptings of feeling have no message of their own but simply conform to the view of reality imposed by other elements of the play. This instinct is a kind of floating causality with which the playwright smooths the plot resolution into a finality which does not seem totally arbitrary. Through it everything which happens is given both a past and a necessary connection with the nature underlying society (or supposed to do so). Thus the *voix du sang* is an imposition of the characters' sense of duty on their experience, part of the constant reinterpretation which the characters are obliged to perform for the purpose of reaching a coherent order. A final *tableau* must be created to signal the ending of the play in the form of theatrical convention. Martian, in this perspective, is suddenly brought to the position of the tragic mourner, the son of Phocas, yet speaks as if he had been living and feeling in the past what has lasted only a few seconds:

> Je ne m'oppose point à la commune joie,
> Mais souffrez des soupirs que la nature envoie.
> Quoique jamais Phocas n'ait mérité d'amour,
> Un fils ne peut moins rendre à qui l'a mis au jour:
> Ce n'est pas tout d'un coup qu'à ce titre on renonce.
> (1901-05)

Besides the fluid, inconstant experience of the characters there is the letter of the dead empress, a recognition device somewhat less common in plays of the period than the tale of an old witness, the birthmark, or the token. Even more significant here is the degree of formality of the letter. Written in a royal hand, as also in *Don Sanche*, it tends to take on a quasi-legal quality, as a command. It is as much more authoritative than the voice of Léontine, as her testimony was superior to the voice of unaided nature. The imperial letter is the highest form of articulation; the *murmure* is the absence of language, the indecipherable message. The letter organizes the heroes' feelings, gives them direction and provides the characters and their empire with a hierarchy. Constantine's words give Héraclius the *devoir* he has been seeking.

The second letter is dramatically necessary not only to provide an equilibrium with the first, but to fill the emptiness created by the gradually revealed degradation of the heroes' own means of acceding to the truth. Martian's actions are sometimes inferior, sometimes superior to those of Héraclius in Pulchérie's eyes (V, ii). When the

series of confrontations comes to its exasperated end in the last act, the
characters' emotional reactions to each other are clearly useless for
judgment. Léontine may lie. Certainty is restored by the written word,
the formal imposition of a name on a passive hero.[6]

Throughout this long search for identity the spectator remains
secure in his knowledge, while the characters are doubtful. In *Héraclius*
Corneille bases the continuous dramatic effect on an aesthetic of irony.
This tragedy places a maximum of distance between the spectator and
the character through the inequality of knowledge between them.
Such an effect is noticeable on the level of the most naïve first viewing
of the play since only Héraclius, of the major characters, knows as
much about his identity as the public does after the first scene of act II.
Thereafter the public remains convinced of the reality of this
identification, thanks to supplementary revelations of Léontine (II, iii)
which are not given to Héraclius, who would revolt against her tragic
design to have Phocas killed by his own son. Because of the viewer's
additional knowledge, he can watch from above and from a distance
the frantic searching for a provable identity carried on by Martian
and, at certain points by Héraclius, and the equal bewilderment of
Pulchérie and Phocas. The conclusion offers no surprise except
perhaps that, purely intellectual, in Georges May's terms, of the
particular means used to produce a final identification.[7]

Yet it is clear that to speak of a pure, naïve, or simply fresh first
viewing of a seventeenth century play is almost impossible. In many
cases, though not this one, the title suffices to recall the historical
episode on which the play is based or another play, ancient or modern,
using a similar plot. In other cases one assumes an unmeasurable
amount of information circulating generally among the public before
they come to the theatre. When we speak of the dramatic effect of a
particular work, we must therefore be constructing a sort of abstract
ideal view of the type apparently thought of by the abbé d'Aubignac
and by Corneille in his critical writing.[8]

For *Héraclius* Corneille supposes a very precise kind of spectator, the
retrospective or repeating one, whse accumulated knowledge makes
him, from the very beginning of the work, an ironic viewer. This is
particularly true for the first act, during which the audience is not
given any information which would undermine its belief in Phocas'
view of the situation: the children of the former emperor are all dead,
"Martian" (Héraclius) is Phocas's son and heir, "Léonce" (Martian)
is Léontine's son, lover of Pulchérie. However, full appreciation of the

scene is impossible without an understanding of the hidden names.
Héraclius says to Martian and Pulchérie ("Martian" to "Léonce"):

Que me dis-tu, Léonce, et qu'est-ce que tu veux?
Tu m'as sauvé la vie. . . .
. . .
Je te connais, Léonce, et mieux que tu ne crois:
Je sais ce que tu vaux, et ce que je te dois.
Son bonheur est le mien, Madame; et je vous donne
Léonce et Martian en la même personne:
C'est Martian en lui que vous favorisez.
(348-49, 355-59)

In the same vein Phocas's "son" had already refused Pulchérie's hand,
even as a means of assuring his succession, saying "Ma naissance suffit
pour régner après vous" (280). Corneille was proud of these *double-
entendres* but realized that they necessitate a special experience of the
play:

je n'ai pu avoir assez d'adresse pour faire entendre les
équivoques ingénieux dont est rempli tout ce que dit
Héraclius à la fin de ce premier acte; et on ne les peut
comprendre que par une réflexion après que la pièce est finie,
et qu'il est entièrement reconnu, ou dans une seconde repré-
sentation.[9]

What Corneille supposes, then, is a very knowing spectator indeed,
one who will see the play twice (appreciating it only during the second
performance) or will reflect in such detail that he can seize the shades
of meaning of the first act dialogue after the final curtain! On the other
hand, the ideal public must also attempt to read or to see the play with
the eyes of the uninformed and to know only what is parcelled out by
the playwright through his expository devices. Paradoxically
Corneille also implies that his reader must maintain this state of mind,
for how else coule he share the author's obvious delight in the way he
reveals the true identities to the public? Corneille writes in the *Examen*:

Surtout la manière dont Eudoxe fait connaître, au second
acte, le double échange que sa mère a fait
des deux princes, est une des choses les plus spirituelles qui
soient sorties de ma plume.

The retrospective and ironic aesthetic supposes a veritable
dialectical reading in which each element of the action has first one
meaning, then another during the process of the play and then
assumes a final and different meaning when seen "après que la pièce

est finie, et qu'il [Héraclius] est entièrement reconnu." Since the spectator is never the dupe of the vicissitudes as are the main characters, he sees the resultant devaluation and then revaluation of the characters' knowledge as the final highly conventional and formal imposition of stability on a represented world of instability and contradiction.

If the question of identity is the basis of a dramatic work, the problem of what happens is subsumed by the question of who knows what and when. In this regard Héraclius has a most interesting structure showing how successive phases of certainty prepare the confusion of the fifth act. In the first act all the characters present except Héraclius are certain of the false identifications of "Martian" and "Léonce," in other words four are mistaken and one knows the truth. The uninformed public is also mistaken. The act could be labeled, "Certainty: fallacy." The characters present (3) in the first half of the second act, scenes one to three, are aware of the true identities which the previously uninformed public now learns. The certainty of truth thus depicted is obscured again in the second half of the act by the certainty of a new fallacy contradictory to that presented in act one; Martian believes now that he is Héraclius and not Léonce. Two of the four characters of this half act believe this revised identification, the other two, knowing the truth, do nothing to discourage this belief. In the third act, all of the characters present in all of the scenes are fully duped by the claim that the ex-Léonce is Héraclius; again an act in which the certainty of a fallacy prevails.

The fourth act involves an introduction of the truth by the real Héraclius, resulting in a tripartite fragmentation of belief into a symmetrical pattern. In the first scene both characters know the truth; in the second, half of those present know the truth and the other half are convinced of the contrary. In scene 3, Héraclius is aware of the truth, Phocas and Exupère are thrown into confusion by his statement, and Martian is convinced of the false identity which he has borne since the end of act II. Scene 4 depicts an equal division into those confused about and those certain of the identities of the major characters, one knowing the truth, the other ignorant but using menaces to extract the information. The following act is filled with confusion of all the characters, even Héraclius. Léontine, who holds proof of the proper identities, appears only in the last scene. The final confusion is the result of beliefs canceling each other out and leaving nothing, rather than filtering out fallacies to leave substantial truth.

The scenic expression of this growing uncertainty through an increasing number of characters who are surprised and ignorant involves, in act IV, balancing the enlightened (and those who consider themselves so) with the frankly puzzled by putting the proper numbers of each on stage, including those who do not have speaking roles (e.g., Crispe in scene iv, Exupère in scene vii). Schematically this progression can be represented in diagram C.

Act	Scenes	Truth/	Number of characters aware of: Confusion		Fallacy
I	1-4	(1/)*		/4	Certainty:fallacy
II	1-3	3/			Certainty:truth
II	4-7	(2/)*		/2	Certainty:fallacy
III	1-6			/6	Certainty:fallacy
IV	1	2/			Certainty:truth
	2	2/		/2	Growing
	3	1/	2	/1	Confusion
	4	2/	3	/1	
	5	1/	1		
V	1-6	/	5		Confusion
	7	/	5		Confusion
	7	Resolution: final certainty			

*Numbers in parentheses indicate characters knowing truth but keeping it hidden.

Diagram C

The buildup of irony and increasing distance between the omniscient spectator and the confused characters and the way in which the final decision about Héraclius is made to resemble a *deus ex machina* tell a great deal about identity, especially political identity. The final decision about the imperial succession, the marriage of the heroes, the emperor-protagonist's final self-recognition—all of the puzzles finally resolved in the last scene—are clearly marked as theatrical. In a play which is ostensibly free from the bizarre and extravagant theatricality of the *Illusion comique*, in which the play designates its action (or a large part of its action) as pure *féerie*, Corneille reintroduces the drama as reference to drama. In *Héraclius* however the theatrical tends to adhere to the historical subject of the play, that is, the story of the imperial succession. The ironic public witnesses this apparent lack of internal necessity in the final designation of one of the characters as the true Héraclius. The gulf between nature and culture as determinants of individual identity and public rank grows as the gap between the spectators' knowledge and the characters' beliefs about identity widens. At the last verse of the play, when Héraclius announces his intention to present Héraclius "au peuple qui l'attend," the public not only recognizes the by now familiar distinction between Héraclius as person and as power symbol but may identify with the waiting *peuple*. The populace within the play, like the public of the Hôtel de Bourgogne, depends on the same theatrical convention which concludes the work. Politics is theatre.

This return to a heightened sense of the theatrical through the growth of an ironic consciousness or alienation of the public is in contrast with the use of surprise in *Don Sanche* two years later. At the beginning of the work all admire the bravery of the soldier Carlos, a man of unknown and presumably inferior birth. Dona Léonor, mother of Dona Elvire, heir to the throne of Aragon, worries because her daughter admires him more than any aristocrat:

Tout est illustre en lui, moi-même je l'avoue;
Mais son sang, que le ciel n'a formé que de boue
Et dont il cache exprès la source obstinément. . . .
(45-47)

Elvire's fascination with Carlos is especially serious since she must choose those who will accompany her to Aragon to reclaim her throne. Dona Isabelle, queen of Castille, at whose court they have stayed while a usurper occupied Aragon, must also make a choice. Her kingdom has selected three nobles from among whom she is to take a husband

and king. When the courtiers are gathered for this choice, Isabelle shows much favor to Carlos, permitting him to sit and conferring titles upon him to humiliate the three chosen suitors. Here the line is drawn between merit and birth. Carlos is a self-made man:

Se pare qui voudra des noms de ses aïeux,
Moi, je ne veux porter que moi-même en tous lieux;
Je ne veux rien devoir à ceux qui m'ont fait naître,
Et suis assez connu sans les faire connaître.
. . .
Ma valeur est ma race, et mon bras est mon père.

(247-50, 253)

The spectator knows no more than this and concludes with Don Lope, "Sans doute il n'est pas noble" (254). In spite of this low birth some fear, as does Don Manrique, one of the suitors, that Isabelle wishes to crown Carlos. Instead, she entrusts him with the choice of the most valiant of the three and promises to marry the one he chooses. Isabelle reveals to a confidante her love for Carlos in spite of his rank (II, i). This love, half confessed by Isabelle to Carlos, maintains the spectator in the hope of success. After all, Carlos's birth is not proven to be low. Yet the following scene, a soliloquy by Carlos, reveals his birth and dashes such hope:

. . . l'Aragon m'a vu naître.
O ciel! je m'en souviens, et j'ose encor paraître!
Et je puis, sous les noms de comte et de marquis,
D'un malheureux pêcheur reconnaître le fils!

(609-12)

From this scene forth the public enjoys an ironic superiority to the other characters through the certain knowledge of Carlo's birth. During the immediately succeeding scenes this distinction is not too important. The action instead concerns another pair of lovers, Elvire and Don Alvar. Alvar's love for Elvire can only find expression indirectly through his struggle to merit the hand of Isabelle in the combat proposed by Carlos. Then the question of Carlos's birth again comes to the fore. Manrique and Lope each refuse to give a sister's hand to Carlos as a condition, imposed by Isabelle, to marriage with her. Yet the two, earlier adamant about Carlos's inequality, now seem to soften their opposition. Manrique concludes the interview with Isabelle by saying that Carlos should judge his worthiness for such a marriage:

Nous vous obéirons, mais sans y consentir;
Et pour vous dire tout avant que de sortir,
Carlos est généreux, il connaît sa naissance;
Qu'il se juge en secret sur cette connaissance;
Et s'il trouve son rang digne d'un tel honneur,
Qu'il vienne, nous tiendrons l'alliance à bonheur.

(991-96)

Soon after, Isabelle's confidante announces the rumor that Elvire's brother, Don Sanche d'Aragon, is alive and will arrive shortly at the court. If this is so, says Isabelle, she will forget Carlos and the nobles since only the absence of a prince made her look to her subjects for a husband. These two scenes at the end of act III prepare a surprise for the beginning of act IV. Lope explains to Dona Léonor that, despite her belief that Don Sanche died in infancy, rumor holds that Sanche is none other than Carlos:

Nous avons méprisé sa naissance inconnue;
Mais à ce peu de jour nous recouvrons la vue.

(1177-78)

The public's knowledge of Carlo's birth here departs from the characters' wish. Carlos is only the son of a fisherman. Throughout the next four scenes Carlos defends himself against the honor done to him by those who suspect that he is Don Sanche. Submitted to a test of the *voix du sang* by a confrontation with Dona Léonor, Carlos insists that he knows his birth and denies that he is her son. Léonor replies:

Mon coeur vous en dédit; un secret mouvement,
Qui le penche vers vous, malgré moi vous dément;
Mais je ne puis juger quelle source l'anime,
Si c'est l'ardeur du sang, ou l'effort de l'estime;
Si la nature agit, ou si c'est le désir;
Si c'est vous reconnaître, ou si c'est vous choisir.

(1303-08)

This reply is a kind of summary of the various evaluations of the *voix du sang* as they appear in expanded and separated tirades in *Héraclius*. Once more the natural instinct of kinship which the characters suppose to exist is shown to be at best doubtful. Cultural standards for the choice of a king efface the "original" maternal feeling. Retrospectively the voice of "nature" will be correct. However at the moment when Léonor speaks her words simply point out the disparity between the character's blindness and the public's ironic knowledge. When Léonor commands, "Faites-vous connaître, ou n'aspirez à

rien" (1340) what she means is: accept the name Don Sanche. The
public knows with Carlos that the two identities cannot merge:

Qu'on ne confonde plus don Sanche avec Carlos;
C'est faire au nom d'un prince une trop longue injure.
(1356-57)

The name Don Sanche and its power exist independently of a
claimant. This distinction between name and person reappears when
Carlos confesses to Isabelle that he has another name, Sanche, and
that he was born in Aragon. But he is not Don Sanche. In order to be
happy Isabelle must either see the name and existence of Don Sanche
separated forever ("Mais non: pour fuir don Sanche, attendez qu'on le
voie; / Ce bruit peut être faux, et me rendre ma joie" [1445-46], or
find them joined in Carlos ("Que n'êtes-vous don Sanche! Ah! ciel!
qu'osé-je dire?" [1458]). The first three scenes of act V build suspense
concerning the possible identity of Carlos with Don Sanche in the
hopeful speculations of Elvire and Alvar (scene i), Léonor (scene ii),
and Isabelle (scene iii). The irony of the public's knowledge comes to
an end in the fourth scene when Blanche arrives with more
information for the three queens. Carlos's father has arrived and he is
nothing but a fisherman. At the point where this revelation occurs
three identities meet: Carlos, a name that is made of deeds without a
father in biological nature; Don Sanche, a name attributed to the hero
by a culture which knows what a king should be; and Sanche, the
name of a man whose birth and deeds are contradictory but known
and real. The hero wishes to remain "Carlos," but the two other
names force themselves upon him, finally destroying "Carlos":

En vain de ce faux bruit il se voulait défendre;
Votre cour, obstinée à lui changer de nom,
Murmurait tout autour: 'Don Sanche d'Aragon,'
Quand un chétif vieillard le saisit et l'embrasse.
Lui, qui le reconnaît frémit de sa disgrâce;
Puis, laissant la nature à ses pleins mouvements,
Répond avec tendresse à ses embrassements.
(1570-76)

Carlos's birth as Sanche is now fixed both for the characters and for the
public. Yet the inertia of the movement towards identification of
Carlos with Don Sanche is such that the very aristocrats who had
argued that merit could not repair the fault of birth now assume a
contradictory attitude. Manrique asks the queen to force Carlos to
maintain his *gloire*. "Tant de mérite," he says, "mérite une source plus

belle" (1626). Manrique, Lope, and the whole court are prepared to
defend the fiction of a noble Carlos through an *artifice* (1630) which
would perpetuate the natural hierarchy of their society: "le fils d'un
pêcheur ne parle point ainsi" (1660). For a moment the aristocracy is
ready to accept the *erreur* (1628) which would destroy it, the dissolution
of the temporal sequence birth-deeds. Carlos's life precedes his birth
(the apparition of his father) and Manrique for one refuses to see such a
glorious life end in such a humiliating birth:

> Nous avons pu souffrir qu'un bras qui tant de fois
> A fait trembler le Maure, et triompher nos rois,
> Reçût de sa naissance une tache éternelle.

(1623-25)

What is happening in this scene is a reversal of the public's ironic
position in regard to the characters. While they were uncertain about
Carlos's birth, the public knew that the protagonist was only a
fisherman's son. Now the characters seem to affirm something which
we as spectators do not know. Or rather, they wish to impose a fiction,
to triumph over the truth shared by Carlos and the public. This occurs
through an artifice generated by the actions of the play itself. Such a
moment, when the characters assume a kind of ironic superiority over
the public, does not exist in *Héraclius*. There the spectators clearly saw
the failure of the characters to find a name which they could accept,
either by will or by nature. In *Don Sanche* the spectator himself is dupe.
He sees the characters turn against the certain identity which is
established for Carlos in the spectator's eyes since the middle of the
second act. Then the fiction which the players (as characters as well as
actors) impose, the proof of a man's birth from his deeds, is confirmed
by the revelation that Sanche is indeed Don Sanche, only adopted by
the fisherman (act V). The hero's final identity is a surprise to him and
to the spectator, more a surprise than it is to the other characters. *Don
Sanche* in this way goes beyond the irony of *Héraclius* to make the
spectator the victim of the confusion which he watched in the earlier
play.

The two works have in common the *voix du sang* as a dramatic device
central to this ambivalent structure. Like any oracular device this
murmur of instinct takes its meaning from what follows. In this it
resembles Carlos's birth which derives from his deeds. But the *voix du
sang* pretends to have an unchanging truth, despite the contradiction
in its speech (e.g., to Sanche and to Léonor). Its truth belongs to
nature, which is the unchanging order of the conclusion of the play,

after the unnatural order maintained for more than four acts. The positions of Héraclius and of Sanche, rulers without provable paternity, without grounds on which to explain their *générosité* (etymologically derived from birth), is an unnatural one, belonging to a world which has lost its foundation. To bring this situation to a theatrical end, the *voix du sang* leads the play to the "verisimilar" conclusion that the truth was evident all along. This final unchanging truth belongs to the moment which abolishes the play. It restores the natural reality which is posited for the world outside the theatre.

Within the play itself the hero's identity and the very political system are thrown into a state of antinature, best exemplified by the unnatural love which may exist between brother and sister. This theme of incest, less explicitly developed than in *Héraclius*, is nonetheless present from the very first scene, when Léonor chides Elvire for her "secrète flamme" (41) for Carlos. Illicit because of the disparity in rank, this love would be even more criminal were its object fully known. It is typical of Corneille's political theatre to conjure away incest and the politically unnatural together. The love of Elvire and Sanche is not simply a potential sexual abberation but a failure of the political structure.

Identity, incest, politics are inextricably linked in these two texts. Is it true, as Doubrovsky asserts, that *Don Sanche* is more clearly political than *Héraclius* where "le sens politique était recouvert et en partie obscurci par l'angoisse métaphysique, et ne se manifestait qu'en 'filigrane,' comme une signification seconde, qui éclatait seulement dans toute sa force à la fin"?[10] Or does the search for identity and the risk of incest bear a political significance from the first moments of the work? Attending more closely to the complex connection between the three major sectors of these plots, one detects in them the interplay between man's freedom and the social context in which he lives. In both works the heroes are separated from the identities which society assigns. Their freedom is their captivity, for they wish to reintegrate themselves into the social pattern in which they can act with others. The "angoisse métaphysique" occurs because of the loss of direction experienced by the heroes as they attempt to follow the line which leads from *naissance* (birth, but also family identity) to marriage and power.

Beginning with birth this line leads in a circle back to generation through marriage, a sexual union of political importance. When the birth of an individual is unknown the entire circle risks becoing eccentric, the line of the hero's life may no longer pass through marriage but instead through incest and then political failure. Because of the inscription of his life in a certain ordained line, the hero, the *généreux*, fears to lose himself by losing his birth. When the young princes of *Héraclius* claim their names, or a name, they are attempting to find their way back into this circle of human society. They hope to replace themselves on the proper line leading backwards to birth and forward to marriage and a throne. And incest is a sign of the failure to pass from the confusion of their nameless individuality into the identity fixed for them by society. They must pass from nature to "Nature," as certified by a Natural marriage, according to the norms of society. Escaping from the solitary nature of his deeds—the socially unnatural—the hero enters the Nature of men. If Héraclius experiences a metaphysical anguish it results from his enforced solitude. Possessing within himself the need for social existence, he realizes that this existence is outside of himself and consists of a kind of role, conferred only by the sexual-political system of Orient. Again we encounter an insight of Doubrovsky: "L'enchevêtrement de l'intrigue, l'embrouillamini des situations visent à restituer à la condition humaine, à travers la *complexité dramatique*, qui brouille les traces et confond les pistes, le sens de *l'opacité originelle*, que les tragédies simplificatrices du choix avaient perdu . . . . Le choix, qui dans les tragédies précédentes, ne dépendait que de la décision d'une libre subjectivité, est soudain rendu impossible en vertu de circonstances purement extérieures."[11] While Héraclius encounters the limits of his subjective freedom, *Héraclius* shows how his existence depends on the hero's integration into the role which seems external to him. Héraclius strives to join his internal consciousness of identity with the complex social structure which gives and confirms identity.

By separating Héraclius as being and "Héraclius" (the emperor) as role within the imaginary society of the play, Corneille simply accentuates the dependence of the hero on the external. The characters are constantly pursuing the identity with which they must join in order to act. In *Don Sanche* the hero is not searching for a way to integrate himself in society by finding or proving an identity. Instead, by withholding information about his birth, Carlos attempts to create for himself what only society can give. Doubly separated from his birth, Carlos cannot relate to others either as a fisherman's son or as a self-created solitary, a soldier of fortune. Unlike the heroes of *Héraclius*, he attempts to remain in his individualistic, asocial position, but meets irresistible pressure to abandon this stance. The hero's claim to be born of his deeds, however compelling the evidence of his valor, creates an intolerable instability. It is the others who force upon him the identity of Don Sanche just as they had earlier proclaimed for him an ignoble origin. In both works the individual finds himself caught between his isolation and a rigid social order. Héraclius and Martian are constantly aware of the perils to which their namelessness exposes them. Carlos, attempting to ignore this social imperative, risks the same fate which they fear—the blindness of incest.

Sanche, finding in himself nothing but low birth, strives to lose this birth, his social being, through acts. His anguish at finding this birth return to destroy the fictive Carlos, when the fisherman comes to find his son Sanche, is the opposite of that experienced by the earlier heroes whose birth only too easily eludes them. Corneille's use of different expository methods in the two plays and the consequent difference in spectator's point of view is important in conveying the heroes' opposed attitudes towards their natural identity. In Héraclus we know since near the outset the correct names of each character. It is with a certain impatience that we wait to see this truth established. In *Don Sanche,* on the contrary, we the public know with the hero that the final revelation of his name will destroy him. Constant pressures to accept a definite identity therefore assault the spectator with the same unwelcome inevitability as they do Carlos. Yet when certain identification comes, we are as relieved as he. The public's closer participation in the hero's limited knowledge makes the public cling, as does Carlos, to his dangerous, impossible attempt at freedom. Only later do we see how this attempt at freedom led towards incest, while in Héraclius the pitfalls were evident all along.

This difference in point of view towards the same basic theme illustrates the ambivalence of all plays about identity. Rebel, Carlos defies his birth and the order which assigns him to a lowly station. If the play were to consist in this act alone it could justly be considered an attack against the whole basis of feudal society, a reflection of the decline of the older independent aristocracy of Corneille's day and the rise of a strong middle class. Some of the early public of *Don Sanche* appears to have seen the play in this way. An "illustre suffrage," perhaps finding Carlos a champion of the common man against aristocratic privilege, apparently was withdrawn.[12] But the text as a whole has a much more profound, more disturbing significance. For *Héraclius* and *Don Sanche* deal not with the relation between one character and his place in the social scale, but with the meaning of the social order in its entirety; with the line which divides society, in marriage, from its antithesis in incest; with the contact between a being and his corresponding identity in society. Whether the hero refuse, like Carlos, or, on the contrary, pursue anxiously the identity which the others rob him of, the play shows the dependence of the character on his name and the impossibility of a nameless existence.

This interaction between the loss of name and the sexual and political paralysis of the king is not simply part of Corneille's own imaginative world but forms part of the collective world vision of numerous playwrights of the period, and presumably therefore rises from and informs the imaginative world of the public. Although it is difficult to assess rapidly plays that consist exclusively of complications and misinformation, Corneille's work must be seen in the context of similar plays, often lacking his subtlety of language but equally revelatory of social preoccupations. When seen within this thematic pattern the tortuous plays of such neglected authors as Guérin de Bouscal appear more coherent and meaningful.

One of Guérin's most striking and bizarre works is based totally on the problem of royal namelessness and the danger of incest. In *Le Fils désadvoué* (1640), set in the Italy of the Ostrogoth Théodoric, Sinderic, a young Gothic officer, must prove his descent from the Roman monarchs in order to become himself a Roman king. He announces his birth after Théordoric's capture of Rome from Odoacre. When the king asks why he had hidden his race for so long, Sinderic replies,

> Seigneur je n'en avois aucune connoissance,
> Ce fut seulement hier qu'un de vos vieux soldats,
> Mortellement blessé dans nos derniers combats,
> Me dit que ma maison estoit dans l'Italie,
> Que j'avois pour parens, et l'Edipe [sic] et Julie,
> Que ma mère estoit veufve, et qu'il mouroit contant
> M'ayant peu descouvrir ce secret important.
>
>   (II, i)

Because the hero learns early in the play that he can no longer placidly accept his old identity, he must dedicate all of his action to acquiring fully a new name. This theme and revelation is prepared for the public by Julie's solitary lament, in the opening scene of the work, of the legitimate son she had been forced to give away in infancy. Sinderic however hears that Julie had no children by her hsuband Lepide. For fear of publishing his mother's shame, the hero hesitates to proclaim himself. Scarcely able to bear the state of namelessness, Sinderic cries,

Mais quoy puis-je souffrir qu'on trouve dans l'histoire,
Que Sinderic vescut sans parens, et sans nom?
Ah! c'est trop négliger l'honneur de ma maison!
(II, ii)

Finally he resolves to seek out Julie under a pretext in order to test her and himself. Before he arrives, however, the public learns from Julie's dialogue with her confidante that Lepide was never willing to accept paternity of his wife's unborn child. A secret birth, followed by the exile of the son into Gaul, kept the family honor intact (II, iv). When Sinderic visits Julie he tells the story of a banished infant as the plot of a play performed before Théodoric under the title of *le Fils désadvoué*. Sinderic thus carries out a form of disguise planned earlier:

Quand je l'entiendray de mes adversitéz,
Ce sera seulement soubs des noms empruntéz.
(II, ii)

Precariously perched astride two identities at once, Sinderic has his Gothic name and his fictive "noms empruntéz" of the play-within-the-play while he attempts to provoke the evidence of still a third and authentic name. Since he had earlier linked the need for parents and a name, only the mother's avowal can give him a true, that is, a socially acceptable identity, and the inner calm of an attachment to his own origin. The story he tells does provoke his mother's tears and her joyful confession that he is her son. Yet no sooner does he leave to tell Théodoric of his success than Julie changes her mind. She knows that Sinderic is her lost infant, but she is unwilling to recognize him publicly and lose the respect of her lover Maxime. The voice of nature is finally drowned by the joint demands of love and honor:

Nature taisez-vous, le conseil est pris.
Je veux résolument désadvouer mon fils.
(II, vi)

However, the escape from nature and the silence of its voice leads, as seen in the plays of the masked woman, to a directly opposite danger. Julie is soon trapped in the new role of Sinderic's mistress. Already in the eyes of Maxime, who accidentally saw the tender recognition of Julie and Sinderic, the young soldier is a rival (III, i). Maxime refuses to believe Julie's protestations that she loves the young "stranger" as she would a son (III, iii). Again the theatre presents the public with a kind of false incest, in which two close kin are joined, in the eyes of an ignorant third party, in an illicit sexual bond. The public perceives simultaneously the two points of view and by combining them recognizes the incongruity of the second because of social taboo.

Although the French were not the only people to find a fascination in the temporary fall of the king or prince into a state of namelessness, the frequency with which the theme appears makes it essential to any understanding of the collective imagination of Corneille's time. This demonstrable obsession of the literary mind with plots in which the prince avoids permanent degradation and separation from his role in society leads to many tantalizing problems of historical significance.[14] Can one for example postulate a special concern with royal legitimacy and the dangers of misidentification in the "collective consciousness" of the period? If so, such an anxiety certainly must not express itself only on the level of direct political discourse. *Héraclius* and *Don Sanche* may interest some critics, like Georges Couton, for their hypothetical resemblance with contemporaneous social events and anthologies of political *sententiae*.[15] This interpretation tends to emphasize the author's personal political interest at the expense of the sense of deeper elements of the text itself. Perhaps Don Sanche represents Mazarin and Isabelle, Anne d'Autriche, but this assumption proven or not, remains at the surface of the work.[16] Much more interesting, and largely neglected until Doubrovsky, is the recurrent structure of the fall into namelessness, loss of rank, risk of incest and final recovery of the original, natural order.[17]

More profound than Corneille's personal position during the Fronde, this thematic structure which, in a complex and probably subconscious way unites sexual and political anxieties, should be the starting point for an attempt to replace the work in its original context. Furthermore the true context of *Héraclius* is the active imagination of its time as it is accessible to us in texts. Undeniably the appearance of a group of plays like *Don Sanche*, *Rodogune*, and *Héraclius* in a time of political ferment is a striking fact. And with Couton one can agree that Corneille "exprime avec vigueur les sentiments de l'ancienne noblesse de race, et non ceux des couches nouvelles auxquelles il appartient."[18] Yet the deeper themes of identity belong not to a specific incident, date, or author, but betray a more generalized fascination with the social and sexual system—the family group, the name, the concept of birth and exogamous marriage—which underlies aristocratic and monarchic society.[19] Even an author like Guérin de Bouscal, whom Couton cites as an example of intellectual resistence to the natural rights of monarchs, wrote a play which adheres to the thematic of royal restoration and the conjuration of the unnatural.[20] Besides the conceivable gap between one's deep fears or fantasies and a conscious political stance, the author's role as purveyor to the public of themes which it demands may limit his individual freedom to abandon a successful *topos.* For these reasons the significance of the plot structure seems greater as a measure of the temper of the time than a few verses of political doctrine.

On this level of reading, *Héraclius, Don Sanche* and the other plays of identity are not so easily paraphrased as simple political declarations or allusions. Triumphant though the characters are over namelessness and incest, they do not necessarily embody the simple belief that the royal order is always just and naturally self-perpetuating. The return to the normal social order at the end of the work is a preparation for the real life into which the work and its public return. Yet the question remains as to how the spectator derives pleasure from drama and its reversal, in these plays, of the normal social order. Should we assume, for example, that the final recognition after prolonged tension is the primary source of pleasure? Or does the body of the play, the time during which the identity of the hero is lost and the social order reversed, possess some special fascination of its own, more or less independent of the conventional conclusion? Perhaps the twin themes of freedom from social identity and "happy" incest are both tempting and fear-provoking. The public would then be able to experience vicariously these dangerous possibilities, these lapses of reality, before the restoration of the reassuring rigidity of everyday life.

Footnotes

1. Among these plays are Baro's *Parthénie*, TC (1641), Dalibray's *Torrismon*, T (1635), Desfontaines' *Véritable Sémiramis*, T (1646), Du Ryer's *Alcimédon*, TC (1632), Du Ryer's *Bérénice*, TC (1644), Du Ryer's *Clithophon*, TC (1629), Du Ryer's *Cléomédon*, TC (1634), Gombauld's *Amaranthe*, P (1631?), Jacquelin's *Soliman*, T (1653), Mairet's *La Virginie*, TC (1633), Mareschal's *La Soeur valeureuse*, TC (1633?), Montauban's *Zénobie*, T (1652-1653), Montauban's *Les Charmes de Félicie*, P (1653), Montauban's *Le Comte de Hollande*, TC (1631-1632), Boisrobert's *Les Rivaux amis*, TC (1638), Boyer's *Tyridate*, T (1647), Guérin de Bouscal's *Le Fils désadvoüé*, TC (1640), L'Estoile's *La Belle Esclave*, TC (1642), Thomas Corneille's *Darius*, T (1658-59), Thomas Corneille's *Bérénice*, T (1657), and Thomas Corneille's *Pyrrhus* T (1663).

2. This verse is also important because of the use in it of double meanings. The "à ma place" could refer to Martian's place taken by a rebel or to Héraclius's place taken by a false Héraclius.

3. Verses full of "équivoques ingénieux" according to Corneille's *Examen* (in *Théâtre complet de Corneille*, ed. Maurice Rat; Paris: Classiques Garnier, n.d.), II, 461.

4. Clifton Cherpack, *The Call of Blood in French Classical Tragedy* (Baltimore: The Johns Hopkins Press, 1958), p. 53.

5. In Alexandre Hardy's play (published in 1628) a girl raised as a gypsy is recognized by her mother, the wife of a wealthy official, as a result of the functioning of a maternal instinct.

6. Although this seems to be the correct reading of the tragedy, one does not forget that one letter has already led to a fallacious identification:

Si ce billet fut vrai, Seigneur, il ne l'est plus:
J'étais Léonce alors, et j'ai cessé di l'être
Quand Maurice immolé n'en a pu rien connaître.

(1247-49)

But perhaps the chain of false names ends here and true identity is engendered by a conjunction of the male and female letters, giving a second birth to Héraclius.

7. Georges May, *Tragédie cornélienne, Tragédie racinienne* (Urbana: Illinois University Press, 1948), p. 92.

8. L'Abbé d'Aubignac in his *La Pratique du théâtre* (ed. Pierre Martino; Algiers: Jules Carbonel, 1927) hypothesizes a viewer who knows only what the dramatist tells him through the exposition and successive action on stage. His remarks about the introduction of unknown characters (p. 274) manifest this assumption that the ideal spectator comes to the theatre without any knowledge of the plot.

9. *Examen of Héraclius,* II, 461.

10. Serge Doubrovsky, *Corneille et la dialectique du héros* (Paris: Librarie Gallimard, 1963), p. 313.

11. *Ibid,* pp. 303, 304.

12. Ed. M. Rat, II, 605.

13. Doubrovsky, p. 309, observes that in Corneille incest is always between brother and sister, not between mother and son. In this Corneille simply reflects the general tendency of the time.

14. We here assume that both author and public are caught up in a complex circle of supply and demand in which the public's tastes influence the writer who lives by producing salable texts and are influenced in turn by the works which they are exposed to in the theatre and in reading.

15. Georges Couton, *Corneille et la Fronde* (Clermont: Publications de la Faculté des Lettres de l'Université de Clermont, fascicule 4, 1951).

16. *Ibid.,* p. 60.

17. Doubrovsky, pp. 313-316.

18. Couton, p. 51.

19. Couton suggests (p. 40) that the story of Tancrède de Rohan (1630-1649), recorded by Tallemant des Réaux *(Historiettes,* ed. Antoine Adam [Paris: la Pléiade, 1960], I, pp. 626-628, 641-647), may have directly inspired *Héraclius* and *Don Sanche.* But the story of this "long-lost child," while curious, is insignificant next to the great mass of texts which contain this theme. Perhaps Tancrède's adventure is interesting because it imitates literary convention.

20. Couton, p. 12.

Don Juan and the False Shepherd

A fundamental component of human identity, one that has been at least fleetingly evoked in all of the disguises we have studied, is social class. The aristocrat, the bourgeois, and the lower classes—urban workers, domestics, or peasants—exist in an identity spectrum that goes from the most highly individuated (there is only one true prince of Aragon) to the most completely indistinguishable, expendable, and interchangeable. The aristrocrat occupies the foreground of our consciousness in tragic and tragicomic theatre (tragicomedy being by definition in this period comic by its happy ending and tragic by its noble protagonist), the bourgeois in comic theatre, the peasant in farce. Yet in each of the two principal genres the identity of the upper classes cannot be seized without a background consciousness of the others. The noble is noble because of who he is and what he can do but also because of who he is not and what he cannot do. The theatre of identity with its confusions and disguises brings into focus this contrast, which in other plays remains peripheral and beneath our usual threshold of perception. In the plays of the unknown king, the movement of the protagonist is from a position of lesser individuation, from the background of the cast of characters, so to speak, towards a position of uniqueness and centrality. This is one of the principal schemas of tragedy and tragicomedy: the discovery of difference and an order in human relationships where only undifferenciation and disorder had been apparent.

But in a certain kind of plot the movement is reversed. The hero as noble or bourgeois sometimes flees the individuation of his social role by moving downward into the lower classes. This movement downward, one which is never fully achieved, is the basis for two sets of closely related themes in the baroque theatre, that of false shepherd and that of Don Juan. Both of these themes are based on disguises of class, both undertaken in the name of freedom from constraint and obligation. The first is more dependent on the exposure of the literary basis of identity and on its language; the second is more directly related to the historical movement of society towards a questioning of the justifiability of distinction in class.

No dramatic genre is more typical of the 1630's in France than the pastoral. Steadily enlarging its place in the theatrical repertory since the last decade of the preceding century, the pastoral reached its quantitative apogee between *Cléonice ou l'Amour téméraire* (1630) and *Les Advantures de Thyrsis* (1639), both anonymous *tragi-comédies pastorales*. From 1620 to 1629, twenty-six pastorals appeared; between 1630 and 1639, thirty-four. Then the genre quickly declined. The following decade witnessed the appearance of only a single pastoral, Mareschal's *Cour bergère* (1640).[1]

In addition to the many texts qualified as "pastoral" by their titles—*pastoralle, comédie pastoralle, bergerie en prose, tragi-comédie pastoralle*[2]—the themes and *personae* of pastoral appear under many other generic forms. Shepherds are frequent visitors to the stage in other plays not set entirely within the bucolic world. Du Vieuget's *Policandre et Basolie* (1632), a *tragédie*, Auvray's *Madonte* (1628) and *Dorinde* (1631), *tragi-comédies*, Grandchamp's *Avantures amoureuses d'Omphale* (1630), a *tragi-comédie*, and other plays contain episodes of shepherd life.[3] The way in which these works, not belonging to the pastoral genre, introduce shepherd episodes reveals the beginning of a transformation which may have contributed to the downfall of the pastoral itself. The pastoral state becomes explicitly the temporary hiding place for noble and middle-class characters. Pastoral identity has long been related to disguise. In the Virgilian tradition of pastoral poetry there is a constant tendency for the bucolic genre as a whole to become an extended series of disguised meanings or an allegory. Virgil's fourth *Eclogue* in which the poet sings the prophecy of the miraculous events to occur under the consular rule of Pollio is the conventional example of this poetic practice. Rapin, commenting on this eclogue,[4] notes its underlying metaphor of disguise. Political themes said to be contained in these poems "because they are accommodated to the Genius of Shepherds, may be the Subject of an *Eclogue*, for that sometimes will admit of Gods and Heroes, so they appear like, and are shrouded under the Persons of Shepherds . . . ."[5] Minturno had earlier defended this allegorical interpretation of Virgil's pastorals, seeing the shepherd as bearer of a hidden meaning.[6] Sebillet had also maintained this interpretation of pastoral as a disguised representation of the concerns of great men and public events. Shepherds, in the eclogue, are shown "traittans soubz propose et termes pastoraus, mortz de Princes, calamitéz de temps, mutations de Republiques . . . et téles choses ou pareilles soubz allégorie.''[7] George Puttenham, in 1589, thought that the pastoral was devised "not of purpose to counterfait or represent the rusticall manner of loves and communication: but *under the vaile of homely persons*, and in rude speeches to insinuate and glaunce at greater matters, and such as perchance had not bene safe to have disclosed in any other sort.''[8]

It is not a great leap from this use of the "vaile of homely persons" and the "termes pastoraus" as a disguise of heroic themes to the disguise of actual persons. Ronsard, for example, "disguised" Henri d'Orleans, François d'Anjou, and Henri de Navarre as Orléantin, Angelot, and Navarrin, respectively, in his *Bergerie* of 1563.[9] Given this tradition it is little wonder that readers of pastoral novels and plays of the seventeenth century use the term "disguise" repeatedly in their critical descriptions. Fontenelle wrote of the *Astrée* that its characters "paroissent des gens de Cour déguisez en Bergers, et qui n'en savent pas bien imiter les manières.''[10] H. C. Lancaster notes this disguise as the rule when describing the exception of Mairet's *Sylvie*, where he finds that "Except in their vocabulary, the shepherds are real shepherds rather than nobles *disguised as such*.''[11]

As the pastoral influence extends to plays which do not situate themselves fully in the dramatic pastoral genre and tradition (deriving from the *Aminta* and the *Pastor Fido*), the relation between the life of the shepherds and the life of the others—city folk or aristocrats—changes. The internal workings of rustic society are blurred, the bucolic life is surrounded by a world containing more evident hierarchies and conventions. As a result the shepherd life is depicted simply as the absence of the social pretentions of the other society. The shepherds no longer exist to celebrate or imitate princes. Instead of being an aristocratic society disguised or allegorized, the shepherds are a lower class refuge for individuals who wish to disguise themselves in order to flee an exalted and confining position.

Here the term "disguise" no long indicates a kind of allegorism. The characters, like those of Auvray's *Madonte*, are simply ordinary human beings whose private concerns lead them from one real society into another, deemed less complex and restrictive than the culture they flee. When Madonte and Thersandre disguise themselves as shepherdess and shepherd, they hope to avoid the persecution, slander, envy, and injustice inflicted on them earlier in the play. Similarly, in Le Hayer du Perron's *Les Heureuses Adventures* (1633), the

principal characters flee the court early in the play to live as
shepherds, far from the court of Sicily where they would have been
forced into unwanted marriages.

Such a flight into the country is not principally a spatial change but
rather a modification of the character's class identity. The "Arcadia"
into which the hero flees may be another country, across the sea from
his homeland, or simply the woodlands and meadows of his own
nation. In either case the value of his refuge is due not to its being
elsewhere but to its different social level. The hero escapes by traveling
a greater distance downward in the social hierarchy than he does in
any geographical direction. As a shepherd, the hero belongs to the
lowest level of society, composed of the most inconsequential persons.
Because of the little importance attached to their actions, the
shepherds are depicted as having few obligations and as being subject
to a minimum of restraints.[12] Since their loves and marriages are of no
importance and their actions of no consequence for the society of
masters far above them, the shepherds form the group in which a
character fleeing a higher class finds the most complete freedom. The
prince, becoming a shepherd, experiences a complete reversal in the
valuation of his social role. His actions, especially his marriage, had
been of grave consequence for the nation; now his loves are without
apparent significance for others.

The pastoral impulse is more complex than a simple abandonment
of aristocratic and middle class values. In fact it is the opposite of such
abandonment. Disguise is not a true transformation or reformation of
those who disguise themselves, but only a concealment of the traits
they wish to preserve unchanged. The portrayal of a world of
shepherds is a means of preserving the concerns and superiority of the
ruling classes by transposing those concerns into a world immune to
change and to the real workings of a society of class. By preempting the
life of the lowest class, the aristocracy transforms the world into a place
free of contestation from below, since there is nothing below, and from
above, since all that is above is outside Arcadia. Work, hunger, and all
that represents a lack of nobility and hence a threat to it from within
society, are removed by the creation of a world in which princes are
shepherds. One could describe the pastoral as a form of solipsism
which abolishes the other by assuming (and hence consuming) his
existence.

The hero of the pastoral is always in some ways a false shepherd, not
a shepherd. As the pastoral moves from the allegorical use of the

shepherd disguise towards a more individual and realist kind of disguise (not the kingdom disguised as Arcadia but the king himself disguised as an Arcadian) the paradox of the pastoral becomes more apparent. The value of the pastoral is that it is different from something else; the value of the pastoral disguise for the individual character is that it permits the freedom of the swain and the refinement of the courtier. The characters find themselves undermining the identity they have chosen, and they move back and forth from disguise to normalcy, from the literary model on which their disguise is based to an attempt to flee from the artifice required by such literary models and by disguise itself. The pastoral disguise thus ends in complete contradiction: the status of the shepherd is enviable because of its naturalness and lack of constraint but the disguise as shepherd is so constraining and artificial that the false shepherd is trapped in what had appeared to be freedom.

The exacerbated literary self-consciousness of the texts that use this theme in seventeenth-century theatre led to the creation of the burlesque pastoral—a genre which, even more than pastoral itself, exposes its literary and social presuppositions—of which the outstanding example is Thomas Corneille's *Le Berger Extravagant* (1653, based on Charles Sorel's novel of the same title).[13]

Corneille's play centers on Lysis, a Parisian who has come to Brie to live the Arcadian pastoral life with a young woman he considers his inamorat, Charite. We soon learn, from his cousin Adrian, that Lysis was driven mad by reading *L'Astrée* and other pastoral novels, apparently returned to normal when they went out of fashion, then went mad again when he saw, a hundred times, the dramatic pastoral *Amarillis*. For the duration of the play Lysis is led on by Charite and the other characters, except his cousin Adrian, who thinks him fit for the *petites maisons*. The others dress as shepherds and nymphs, speak in pastoral terms, and refer to earlier adventures in Arcadia before they came to Brie. There are, however, frequent interruptions of the shepherd illusion. When another pretended shepherd attempts to take away Charite, Lysis protests and is challenged to a duel but refuses to fight on the ground that the weapons proposed, swords rather than shepherd staves, violate pastoral usage and do not appear in any pastoral texts. Abandoned by Charite, Lysis goes off into the woods where he meets a man he takes to be a druid. As an alternative to Lysis's request to be made invisible, the "druid" persuades Lysis to disguise himself as a shepherdess and casts a spell to remove his beard.

Lysis presents himself to the women characters, tells the story of having been born "Célimène" but reduced by misfortune to disguise herself as the shepherdess "Amarillis." Accused of sexual misconduct by some satyrs, Lysis-Amarillis is about to be submitted to the test of fire when the supposed druid descends from above in a stage-machine chariot and carries off the false shepherdess. Lysis later finds Charite sleeping and wakes her by hitting her in the face to kill a fly that had settled there. When he reveals that he was the "Amarillis" of earlier, she berates him and leaves. Lysis climbs a tree to get a last glimpse of Charite's palace and falls into the trunk, thinks he is metamorphosed into a tree-god, and refuses to leave his trunk until night, when there are no humans around. Then he comes out to dance with the "nymphs," who are posted nearby. During his encounter with the young women disguised as tree-nymphs—with branches on which dried fruits are suspended—one of the other false shepherds takes his place in the trunk so that he cannot re-enter it. He is led off with the promise that he can live in a tree in the garden of the principal female character. During this succession of episodes involving Lysis and displaying his madness, there are interspersed discussions among the other characters who carry on their love affairs and comment on Lysis's extravagance while planning new tricks to further his delusions.

This plot can be described as taking place on three levels: Lysis's madness and the play-within-a-play that it occasions; the interruptions of this half-illusion by the other characters' discussions of his madness and of their activities humoring him; the love-story episodes of the other characters. The three levels are variously distributed throughout the acts, though all three are present in each act. They correspond roughly to the division in scenes, and all acts except the first end in Lysis's presence on stage and present the other two levels before arriving finally at Lysis. His displays of madness begin and end the play. The most obvious thing about these levels is the way in which they interrupt one another. Adrian's arrival (I, iii) provides the first explanation of the madness of Lysis and breaks the parodic pastoral of the first two scenes. The loves discussed by Anselme and Clarimond (I, iv) set the level of serious love maintained by the first scene of act II before the interruption of Angélique and Anselme, who talk about their pastoral imitation in preparation for the pranks on Lysis carried out in the following five scenes. There are thus two levels of love story carried out in pastoral dress, setting, and language—the parodic pastoral of Lysis and the earnest love of the other characters with the exception of Adrian. The third level, which is the critical level, appears when the causes of Lysis's madness are made explicit, particularly in reference to earlier texts. The distinction between the sequence of love scenes of the other characters and the scenes of Lysis is based on an absence of direct causal connection and on a contrast in the apparent style of the spoken parts.[14] Despite these evident differences, the level of the love passages of the other characters begins to take on a strong parallelism to the pastoral madness of Lysis. It is this ultimate relationship between the two apparently distinct and incompatible levels that makes the play more than parody.

Corneille's play is called a "burlesque" pastoral. This generic attribution is based primarily, is not exclusively, on what I have called the level of Lysis. Francis Bar, in his study of burlesque and in his introduction to *Le Berger Extravagant*, defines burlesque as the use of a particular style, of which the most striking feature is a mixed vocabulary, composed of words taken from various social levels of speech.[15] This is certainly part of the parodic nature of the scenes of Lysis. He speaks in a mixture of different registers and is also noticeably redundant. The stylistic parody of pastoral is thus an important element in the work, an element that can be explained without recourse to other critical concepts. This does not, however, account for the rest of the work, where such visibly anomalous language does not appear.

Another noticeable element of the parodic nature of Corneille's text, but one which ultimately becomes more than parody, is the reference to earlier works. The consciousness of genre and the popularity of pastoral texts was such that a pastoral was as immediately recognizable as science fiction or detective novel today. Every pastoral text is implicitly related to all of its antecedents and to all of its possible successors. The setting, the pastoral guise of the characters, the arrival of someone from outside Arcadia, the use of echo—all of these are components of pastoral. Combinations of them, perceived in the opening passages of a text, signal the genre. The complexity of *Le Berger Extravagant* is due to the explicitness of its relationship to previous texts. If the reference to other pastoral texts remained implicit, this reference would simply orient the audience's expectations, but since the reference is explicitly to specific texts, the genre begins to dissolve into the multiplicity of its historical realizations. The consequent self-consciousness makes of the present text, at the level of Lysis, a pastoral which fails to realize itself as pastoral but only as fragments of pastoral.

The number of explicit references to antecedent texts is large. Characters allude to, or quote, Ovid's *Metamorphoses*, d'Urfé's *Astrée*, Nicolas de Montreux's *Bergeries de Juliette*, Mairet's *Sylvie*, Tristan's *Amarillis*, Rotrou's *Célimène*, and Scarron's *Virgile Travesti*.[16] The ways in which the texts are noted convey not only the relationship between the *Berger Extravagant* and its textual basis but also recapitulate the relationships among the earlier texts. Lysis's way of talking is explained as the effect upon him of Scarron's *Virgile*: "depuis qu'il a leu *Virgile* en vers burlesques, / Il l'a toûjours farcy de cent termes grotesques" (473-74). The relationship between Tristan l'Hermite's *Amarillis* and its source, Rotrou's *Célimène*, is represented allegorically in Lysis's disguise as a shepherdess. In fact Tristan's text is little more than an adaptation, or disguise of Rotrou's work.

Lysis is the point within the play where these earlier texts meet. His speech comes largely from Scarron, his female disguise from *Astrée*. He figures in his personal history, as he tells it to the others, the literary history of *Amarillis / Célimène*. The temporal sequence of his madness figures the historical succession in the popularity of pastoral novel and theatre. Lysis undermines his own being by indicating that he is only a connotative figure (in the Hjelmslevian sense), a signifier created out of the form and content of other texts.

Within *Le Berger Extravagant* Lysis acts to reproduce this textual world of the pastoral and to draw all the other characters into his madness. It is as if Lysis were overflowing into the space around him, for his being is entirely composed of the residue of earlier pastorals, and his only activity is to fill the world with these pastoral signs. This appears in the first act in his haste to carve his name and that of his love, according to pastoral custom, on rocks and trees:

Il n'est arbre desja, ny rocher d'alentour
Où nos noms ne soient leus, pleins de chifres d'amour.
(I, ii)

The carving is pastoral, the haste (five or six days) is not. The world of the play is described by Lysis as without resistance, even in its rocks, to his passionate marking. Real being is sacrificed to the sign which covers it; Lysis's speech isolates the sign of the pastoral in anything he mentions. Conversation with him requires a similar attention to this sign. Speaking to Lysis, come to Brie to "vivre berger & porter la houlette" (to be a shepherd and to bear the sign of shepherdom),

Clarimond attempts to prove that he is not the god Pan by pointing out that he is "Ni fourchu par les pieds, ni cornu par la tête" (I, ii). Despite Clarimond's disclaimer of the signs of Pan, Lysis can interpret this appearance as a disguise, in itself characteristic of pastoral and godhood, "Sous cet habit mortel cachant l'être divin." The sign both reveals and conceals, and Lysis is able always to preserve his pastoral discourse by an interpretation that accepts appearance or refuses it. Lysis expounds the pastoral life to his cousin Adrian by emphasizing its non-natural, symbolic aspect, its concealment of something else, but he also displays madness by abolishing the separation between the concealing surface and the thing concealed. For example, the stars are not really stars but herds of sheep:

> Jadis, les plus grands Rois, que gloire m'est de suivre,
> Faisoient leurs fils Bergers pour leur apprendre à vivre.
> Les Dieux cent fois en terre en ont pris les habits,
> Apollon chez Admete a gardé les Brebis.
> Et mesme encore là haut ces Estoilles errantes
> Sont animaux paissans dans ces plaines luisantes
> Et qui les garderoit, si ce n'estoient les Dieux.
>
> (137-43)

Beginning with the disguise (or temporary assumption of the shepherd state) of princes, Lysis climbs the scale of dignities until he asserts the invisible pastoral nature of the stars (a metaphor interpreted non-figuratively) and then uses this assertion as the basis of the "inference" that such herds must be kept by the gods, returning thus to an analogue, on higher level, of the disguise of princes. Lysis frequently demonstrates this operation by which the pastoral nature of an object either appears on a surface truly indicative of content or is concealed by a surface which by its concealing power is only a different form of pastoral sign.

In the course of the play Lysis's finding of pastoral signs and his interpretation of such signs as reality becomes more and more in contradiction with the perception of the other characters and of the public. The druid's flying chariot (III, vii) is an illusionistic stage-device.[17] The young women wearing branches hung with dried fruits are not illusionistic. They are signs containing part of the thing represented—trees. They do not look like trees, however, and any possible similarity to an image of tree-nymphs (as distinct from trees) is reduced by the insistence of the text on the dried fruit. Only Lysis can see in the actresses *what* they represent, while the others can see only *how* (by what physical means, i.e. the combination of branches, women, and dried fruit) they represent them.

Despite the other characters' seeming clear-sightedness in regard to Lysis and his reading of everything as pastoral, they too are engaged in a discourse tainted with a pastoral illusion of the kind they mock. Corneille exposes their dependence on the possibility of a pastoral rhetoric of truth. When two of the normal couples—that is, those not visibly deranged by the saturating effect of literature—discuss the language of love, they find their discourse undermined by Lysis's madness and their own disguise. When Lucide and Monténor disguised as shepherds talk about love and the language in which it appears undisguised, they repeatedly find themselves in a parallel with Lysis and his absorption of earlier texts. Lucide tells her suitor,

> Un peu de complaisance & l'habit de Berger
> A ces propos d'amour semblent vous engager;
> Mais, de grace, avec moy mettez fin à la feinte,
> Ne vous imposez point cette dure contrainte
>
> (383-86)

She is, in other words, suggesting that Monténor has been trapped by the pastoral text as he undertook its representation for Lysis. The pastoral liberation from social constraints has become itself a constraint. When this happens the only escape from social determination (and with it a language prescribed and hence bearing no "information") is silence. An eloquent silence, to be sure, is what Lucide recommends, one which is itself a language marked by the "natural" superiority of transparency that pastoral pretended to bear over the language of the court:

> L'Amour, pour s'expliquer, a son langage à part:
> Il parle, il persuade en gardant le silence.
>
> (400-01).

The problem, then, is one of interpretation. As Monténor says, only a person ready to accept the message of love—someone already in love—can receive it:

> Et, quoy qu'un fol espoir en ose presumer,
> Des plus adroits soûpirs l'éloquence est muette
> Si le coeur n'est d'accord de sa propre défaite,
> Et leur intelligence a peine à subsister
> Quand l'amour n'ayde pas à les faire écouter.
>
> (412-16)

If Lucide does not possess this interpretive capacity, how can

Monténor make humself understood? In his desperation he turns to the language of pastoral, precisely the language which Lysis's pastoral mascarade and the conflict of texts has invalidated.

> J'en appelle à témoin les arbres de ces bois.
> Combien de fois, helas, cherchant leur solitude,
> Les ay-je entretenus de mon inquietude?
>
> (424-26)

says Monténor. Lucide replies, "Quand ils me le diront j'en croiray quelque chose" (430). The dialogue, which begins with the suspicion that the suitor is trapped in pastoral language, ends in his attempt to invoke that language, despite its status as disguise and convention, and hence its lack of persuasive power.

A similar exchange between Clarimond and Charite, as shepherd and shepherdess, exposes the emptiness of pastoral rhetoric. Clarimond opens the scene with a quotation of two verses from Mairet's *Sylvie*, immediately recognized by Charite, who replies to her *nouveau Filène* by reminding him of her right to speak in the role of a *Sylvie inhumaine*. Clarimond tries to separate himself from the character whose lines he had borrowed:

> . . . que de vous ces vers soient écoutez,
> Sans songer à celuy qui me les a prestez.
>
> (1353-54)

But how can he dissociate himself from the pastoral discourse once he has designated it as his own? How can he use *ces vers* without accepting the duplicity which they designate for him? The whole scene demonstrates the inability of the characters to return to an authentic language. Charite encourages her suitor with explicit references to *Sylvie* (205 of Mairet's play):

> Il n'est plus de rocher, & vos soins assidus
> Meritent son estime, & peut-estre un peu plus
>
> (1357-58)

but when he attempts to claim her words for himself, she separates Clarimond from Philiris, the shepherd role he plays for Lysis, "L'un est homme de Cour, l'autre simple Berger" (1370). Her hyperbolic praise of pastoral sincerity undermines any apparent belief in Clarimond. When shepherds bare their soul

> D'un air vraymentsincere ils sçavent l'exprimer,
> Ils ayment en effet, quand ils jurent d'aymer.
>
> (1377-78)

Hence if Philiris were to speak Charite would believe, she says.

Clarimond tries to use his false self, Philiris, as guarantor of the truth of his love:

> Souffrez que Philiris parle pour Clarimond;
> Car enfin, il tiendroit sa passion secrette
> Si Philiris n'osoit en estre l'interprete.
>
> (1390-92)

But the pretended sincerity of a love which can only be expressed by a theatrical entity (Philiris) which in turn borrows the words of another fictive being (the Filène of Mairet's play) is shown by Charite to be only the manifestation of his insincerity. Clarimond's mastery of pastoral discourse is the direct consequence of his courtliness. Charite says,

> Car enfin, Clarimond, je sçay trop qu'à la Cour
> C'est vertu que bien feindre en matiere d'amour.
>
> (1405-06)

Clarimond, like Monténor, keeps falling back into the pastoral discourse he had already exposed as pretense, and he attempts to use pretense as a proof of his authenticity. When he is exposed in his turn by Charite, Clarimond resorts to quotation, just as he had begun the scene by quotation. This time, however, he quotes himself, as if to create still another voice in which to assert a sincerity denied to him in all of his roles:

> Il est vray que, pour plaire à cent objets divers,
> On peut feindre des maux qu'on n'a jamais soufferts,
> Qu'il est aysé par tout de dire "je vous ayme";
> Mais sçachez qu'avec vous il n'en est pas de mesme,
> Et qu'il est impossible, en voyant vos appas,
> De dire 'je vous ayme', & ne vous aymer pas.
>
> (1421-26)

Clarimond's language is characterized by a desperate attempt to achieve that "difference" which pastoral rhetoric promises. Because he has already engaged in an elaborate parody of that rhetoric, Clarimond cannot resort to it to create a difference between his normal language and a more authentic one. He ends simply by setting off his own words, which he admits are often or usually said in pretense, and then affirming, without further demonstration, without hope of any proof, that his words, though identical to pretense, are true.

This entrapment of the other characters in the proliferation of empty signs moves the play from parody to a more general criticism of pastoral discourse. Lysis's attempt to achieve pastoral simplicity, a kind of discourse which would be different and more authentic than that of everyday life, is shown to be impossible and even comic. The conspiring and apparently lucid characters also need a way in which to engage in an authentic discourse, one different in some marked way from their normal one. But they have exposed the conventionality and pretense of pastoral rhetoric, and they have no other. The play as a whole, as a critical manifestation of pastoral, depends on a movement towards a closed world of aristocratic discourse in which the courtier can affirm his authenticity by obliterating the conventions of everyday life. By removing those distinctions, however, the pastoral encloses itself to such an extent that once the conventions of pastoral are exposed, there is no way out. Although the other characters' preoccupations and conversations maintain the problematic of authentic sharing and expression of love, typical of the French pastoral at least since *Astrée*, their attempts at a resolution of the problem are foredefeated by their own exposure of the madness of Lysis. The latter's madness bears an obvious resemblance to Don Quixote's. What Michel Foucault says of Cervantes' hero is true of Corneille's. Both engage in a proliferation of resemblances and of signs, a process which finally obliterates not only things (the visible world) but even the meaning of signs. Difference disappears in the madness of this *homosémantisme*.[18] But Lysis does not remain in the isolation foreseen for him by the other characters. His recognized madness, instead of being a purgation or conjuring away of a danger, is only a way of rendering more evident the unsoundness of the language of the others.

An unsoundness that afflicts all the others except Adrian. The infrequent presence of this practical and antiliterary Parisian (acts I, IV, V) permits an evaluative point of view totally outside pastoral and thus preserves the pastoral difference. But Adrian does not offer an alternative to pastoral discourse. He does not propose any language in which the concerns of the other characters could be discussed; he can only reject them *en bloc*. Just as Lysis's vision could be shared only by someone already deeply involved in the same texts as he, just as Monténor's silent language of love could be understood only by someone already in love, so the problem of the play as a whole can only be understandable to someone already engaged in the literary discourse which to Adrian is only a "chien de caquet." As spectators of Corneille's play or as readers, we are already devoting time to a literary enterprise, already sensitized to the problems of expression to which the practical Adrian remains deaf. The complicity between the audience and the pastoral characters of the play makes Adrian necessarily a relatively unsympathetic figure. *Le Berger Extravagant* offers, then, an elaborate criticism of pastoral, but retains, for pastoral, thanks to Adrian, a superiority—not of transparency and naturalness but of affective and aesthetic necessity. In so doing it preserves the discourse that it criticizes.

The other major form of class disguise in the thetre of the period requires the change of the hero's apparent identity but not that of the whole social milieu. Frequently the noble or bourgeois hero will seek, within his everyday social environment, the freedom offered by the simple lowering in social status. For instance, in Boyer's *Porus* (1646) King Porus pretends to be a member of his own embassy in order to visit his wife, captive of Alexander. The protagonist wishes to cancel his class identity while remaining within a certain category attached to his real identity as Porus, king of India. Two directions or axes of identity disguise are involved here—the vertical axis on which the different social ranks are aligned from emperor to pauper, and the horizontal axis of individualization within a given rank, the distance, for example, between two different princes. Porus's envoys are some distance below him on the vertical axis but they are very close indeed to Porus on the horizontal axis, hardly more than lower-class extensions of Porus himself. By taking the place of one of his own servants, the disguised king retains to some extent his name-identity or his political affiliation while passing below the barriers preventing the free movement of persons of his rank.

Combining Porus's descent into a non-noble extension of his true self with the theme of displacement of the lower classes from their own role, the master in many plays disguises himself as his personal servant. This disguise carries Porus's transformation into the realm of realistic and immediate class distinctions. At the same time the horizontal proximity of the two identities is made more apparent. Because the master is shown often as having a single personal servant or valet—a situation common in Roman comedy—the servant is very closely associated with his master's individuality. When the master chooses to assume himself the lower rank and the name of his servant, he makes a very minimal identity change except on the axis of class. With this close link between two persons of very different social class the dramatic world of class disguise reaches its narrowest point (after the broad separation between Arcadia and the court), the class distinctions become more evident, and the abdication of rank more violent. The best-known example of a hero who takes by force his servant's place is Don Juan. The sexual characteristics of Don Juan have passed into language in such a way that his perpetual flight from women in order to seek still more women to seduce—his claim, in the metaphor of Molière's Don Juan, to be the Alexander of love—seems to be his principal attribute. Yet this does not occupy the major part of Molière's text, nor is it what scandalized contemporary audiences about *Dom Juan* and its precursors. The hero's rejection of the constraints of his class, his refusal of any order temporal or religious, and his blasphemy are Don Juan's principal crimes. His final destruction is the consequence of this accumulated defiance, so that Don Juan's end, in Molière's work, like Alexander's is due to the smallness of the world. But for Don Juan the world is not too small to continue his conquests; it is too small to provide shelter from his pursuers. In both his amatory and his other adventures Don Juan's principal movement is escape. Disguise is the consequence of this flight, for it offers a kind of trap-door through which the noble character can fall when spatial movement no longer suffices.

Dorimont's tragicomedy *Le Festin de Pierre* (1658) and Villiers' play of the same title (1659) include two episodes of the Don Juan figure forcing an exchange of roles upon his servant. Don Juan first makes his valet dress as Don Juan in order to escape his enemies. (Dorimont II, v; Villiers I, v). Later the lord repeats this form of exchange by compelling a pilgrim to surrender his lowly habit (Dorimont III, ii, iv; Villiers III, iii, v). In return Don Juan promises him the rich clothing which neither he nor the pilgrim wants. The hero's protean nature is underlined in Villiers' play by the valet's stupefaction at his master's plan to seize the pilgrim's costume (announced brutally in the words, "Il faut avoir l'habit du Pelerin"). The servant exclaims,

Mais aussi tant d'habits, à quoy donc pensez-vous?
Je n'ay point encore veu de telles incartades,
Vous feriez bien vous seul cinq ou six mascarades;
L'habit d'un Pelerin, l'habit de son Valet,
Et tout cela pourquoy? pour aller au gibet.

(III, iii)

The servant disguise is for Don Juan a first bold refusal to pay for aristocratic privilege by accepting a corresponding limitation.

Shepherds and valets have few characteristics, for their superiors, except the absence of any individual merit and importance. This anonymity constitutes an advantage for the noble who assumes it, superficially, as a disguise without losing the skills and authority with which his hidden identity endows him. But the same anonymity is the chief danger faced by the true valet. He becomes a faceless being upon whom any identity can be discarded, and through whom any crime expiated. As Molière's Don Juan tells Sganarelle, "bien heureux est le valet qui peut avoir la gloire de mourir pour son maître" (II, v).

Don Juan's second disguise, his theft of the pilgrim's robes, combines the violation of the valet's class identity with a sacrilegious attack on the religious character. The pilgrim's habit signifies the total refusal of the distinctions between men imposed by the class system, wealth, and physical force. In taking this guise, Don Juan extends his first refusal of the social structure by concealing himself in an even deeper anonymity than that afforded by the servant's role.' The pilgrim is, essentially a nameless person, stripped of rank, family, vestimentary individuality, and physical characteristics (because of a concealing costume).

Don Juan's disguise differs from the peaceful masquerade of some of the pastoral and semi-pastoral plays by requiring a double disguise, the violent displacement of the original possessor of the identity which Don Juan seizes. While his conduct with women generally follows the pattern of seduction, Don Juan's assumption of his inferiors' identities is clearly a form of rape. The pilgrim is compelled at the point of a sword to surrender his identity to the profanation of Don Juan. The victim protests, in Villiers's play,

> Mon habit, quoy que fasse icy vostre industrie,
> Ne se dépouillera jamais qu'avec ma vie.

(III, iii)

Once he is disguised, Don Juan experiences contempt and immunity. Don Juan's enemy, Don Philippe, addresses him in the same terms of blind superiority: "Mon amy, pourriez-vous me montrer le chemin?" (III, v). Both the rustic and the religious disguise have in common this anonymous and pacific inferiority which makes the bearer no more than an object, like a road sign, for the aristocratic dupe.

In this non-aristocratic anonymity, Don Juan can indulge any whim, including cowardice and treachery. His two disguises of his class identity show the restless expansion of his will beyond the confines of the station to which he was born. The power of the hero's desire is such that any social constraint or obligation which stands in his way may be swept aside without hesitation or shame. These two increasingly violent disguises are steps in Don Juan's violation of the system of social roles. His hypocrisy—in the original sense of "playing a theatrical role"—grows in these apprenticeships for his final imposture. The hero's mastery and mockery of the social structure attain their ultimate perfection in Don Juan's incarnation of the false *dévot*. In this final transformation the aristocrat impersonates himself, or rather a better version of himself—the perfect Christian aristocrat, accepting all the constraints of his class and its religion. He appears, except to the spectator, to be the epitome of the forces which impose upon feudal Europe twin hierarchies, political and religious. But his disguise of the very class which he now proclaims has already illustrated the divorce between Don Juan's existence and these manifested identities.

Molière's *Dom Juan* (1665) belongs to a later period than most of the other plays we are studying, and its use of disguise is more subtle than in the earlier works. But it can profitably be read as belonging to the tradition of disguise of class. Molière more effectively than his predecessors emphasizes the obsessive flight from nobility that is at the heart of the Don Juan theme.

The ambiguity of Don Juan's relationship to his class identity is suggested in the first scene of Molière's work in the conversation of Don Juan's valet Sganarelle and Gusman, the domestic of Done Elvire, who is pursuing Don Juan. Sganarelle explains to the incredulous Gusman that his master has indeed abandoned the woman he has just married after persuading her to escape from her convent. Gusman appeals to Don Juan's rank, provoking thus the first indication of the hero's tenuous relationship to this kind of identity: "Un homme de sa qualité ferait une action si lâche?"—"Eh oui, sa qualité! La raison en est belle, et c'est par là qu'il s'empêcherait des choses" (I, i). The rest of Sganarelle's description of his master is filled with examples of Don Juan's unpredictable non-nobility. He is interested in any kind of woman and will marry any kind—"Dame, demoiselle, bourgeoise, paysanne . . ." He is, in brief, a "grand seigneur méchant homme," and the coupling of the two terms in this apposition is perhaps the most revealing of Sganarelle's remarks about his master. Don Juan is noble in all his prerogatives and when it suits him, but he is simply a wicked man when his aristocratic status becomes a burden. Sganarelle returns to the power of Don Juan's aristocracy in the first of numerous lectures he delivers to his master on right and wrong. "Pensez-vous que pour être de qualité . . ." he begins, attempting to show that even aristocrats are not permitted every freedom. When Done Elvire appears in the third scene she too brings up Don Juan's apparent lack of nobility, a lack in her eyes that goes to the point of his not being able to deceive in a noble way! "Ah! que vous savez mal vous défendre," she says, "pour un homme de cour, et qui doit être accoutumé à ces sortes de choses! J'ai pitié de vous voir la confusion que vous avez. Que ne vous armez-vous le front d'une noble effronterie . . . ." (I, iii). Of course such judgment of Don Juan's actions (reminiscent of Florante's lesson of virility for Filandre in *Célimène*) is made according to a scale of values that is not applicable, as far as he is concerned, for Don Juan is as indifferent to this diatribe as he is, in the fourth act, to his father's reproaches for dishonoring the family and its class.

The various suggestions of the hero's escape from responsibility in the first act are rendered in more spectacular terms in the following acts. As Jacques Guicharnaud has said, *Dom Juan* is the story of a fall and degradation from ancient ideals of noble conduct and obligations.[19] Scenically this degradation appears in the change of object of Don Juan's courtship in act II. He puts his romanesque adventure with Done Elvire behind him as he attempts to seduce two peasant women in scenes that are more farce than comedy. In act III Don Juan's treatment of Elvire's brothers, who are pursuing him, introduces the hero's reductive attitude towards aristocratic honor. As Guicharnaud says, "Le code compliqué et souvent douloureux de l'honneur est ramené à une médiocre vendetta; l'obligation morale du code aristocratique, au plaisir élémentaire de rendre le mal pour le mal."[20] In act IV Don Juan abases himself to flattering his bourgeois creditor Monsieur Dimanche, treating him as an equal in order to avoid having to pay his debts. In act V his most outrageous fall from nobility, the last step in what many spectators found Don Juan's intolerable blasphemy is his pretending to be a convert to a strict religious life, a posture which offers an apparently flawless protection against the claims of his earthly pursuers, but not, of course, against heaven.[21]

Disguise is not externalized in the same way in *Dom Juan* as it is in the other plays on this theme. The hero disguises himself in costume only during the third act, where he passes as a nobleman but is not recognizable as Don Juan. But the possibility of disguise is in some ways more provocative and tension-creating for its latent status. Guicharnaud's study of the play emphasizes the resolution of thematic problems in Molière's theatre by an appeal to formal and specifically theatrical means. The signal of the completion of the adventures of Don Juan is thus, according to Guicharnaud, the hero's assumption of a typically theatrical posture in the last act, the hypocrisy that can be described as a kind of disguise. When Don Juan becomes a *personnage de théâtre*, says Guicharnaud, "la comédie de la pièce est enfin complète."[22]

We can add to Guicharnaud's masterful analysis of this complex work some understanding of why this final transformation is satisfying as a signal of completion, for any signal supposes a code in which it can be understood and hence the inscription of that code in some earlier moment of the text to prepare the reader-spectator for its eventual utilization. There are reasons to see this final disguise as the realization of the last step in a series, and they are not fully compatible with the impression that "Dom Juan a cessé d'être la force impressionnante par son caractère unique et sans faille, il éclate en un masque et une nature: lui qui était monstrueusement authentique, le voici devenu de la fausse monnaie.[23] What prepares us for this disguise is precisely the latent but clearly suggested disguise of Don Juan, a project for which the spectator waits with all the more suspense in that it is not fully carried out, as we expect, until the last act. Our knowledge that the hero has at his disposal, from the very beginning of the play, such alternative identities is what makes the comedy complete when Don Juan uses the theatrical means at hand. In the last scene of act II, for instance, Don Juan announced that he would give his clothes to Sganarelle. By the beginning of the following act, however, Sganarelle managed to persuade his master not to force on him the deadly identity. Don Juan's identity is thus always ready to be sloughed off.

Although few protagonists are as protean as Don Juan in the outward transformation of their class identity, there are many variations of the same basic impulse. The hero's disguise may involve a complete reversal and exchange of identities, as it does when Don Juan both seizes his valet's identity and rejects upon the servant his own aristocratic one. Or the hero may leave this pattern incomplete and utilize only one half of the possible identity reversal. This happens when the master displaces the lower class individual without offering an alternative identity to the victim. Such a situation arises in the plays about Jupiter's disguise as the mortal Amphitryon. The two mortal victims of Jupiter and Mercury's disguises in Rotrou's *Les Sosies* (1637) lose their rightful identities but do not receive the place of gods in exchange for their names and places. The situation is especially ironic in that it is a human master, not simply a servant, who is evicted from his place by the god who desires Amphitryon's wife. Both the husband and his "valet" Sosie are left without any identities in which to clothe their existences.

This aristocratic restlessness with the confines of rank (even after the collapse of the pastoral tradition) affects the image of the middle class as it appears in the theatre. While Don Juan was manifesting the explosion of the aristocratic identity, another hero of Villiers, Léandre in the farcical one-act *Les Ramonneurs* (1659-1660), was escaping temporarily from the *bourgeoisie*. Both Léandre and his mistress disguise themselves as chimney sweeps to elude her brother, Captain Scanderbec. In another one-act play of the same year, Montfleury carried this middle class impatience with social distinctions to a kind of absolute negation of this kind of identity. In his *Le Mariage de Rien*, Montfleury depicts the plight of a suitor rejected by the girl's father. The "docteur" refuses each suitor in turn because each profession presents some drawback and each suitor some special incompetence. After trying various disguises, Lisandre returns to the father and claims to be *rien*. Since the father is not prepared with any objections to that particular social state and has no way of imposing judgments of value on it, Lisandre succeeds in his courtship. By pretending to be Nothing, the hero has escaped the boundaries of class and profession.

The *Mariage de Rien* and the Don Juan theme which flourishes at the same moment mark the distance which the theatre has come from the use of pastoral as the primary disguise of class. Henceforth the theatre will not resort to such vague and remote refuges from class but will depict the real society which surrounds the theatre while at the same time negating the social categories of that society.

The importance of the real or feigned changes in class identity in the works of Molière and his successors is evident. The *Médecin volant* (1650-1658), *L'Etourdi* (1655), *Les Précieuses ridicules* (1659), *Dom Juan* (1665), *Le Bourgeois gentilhomme* (1670) are in large part concerned with class disguise, as in Regnard's *Légataire universel* (1708). The significance of the themes of class disguise changes, however, in a direction which is already discernible in the earlier transformation of the pastoral. From having been a dream-like and unreal outlet for aristocratic and, to a lesser extent, middle-class impatience with social restriction, especially in love, the disguise of class becomes a sharply focused contrast between the qualities and conditions of the different classes. The aristocracy is still the source of social rank—M. Jourdain owes his farcical elevation to the rank of *mamamouchi* to a noble—but the direction of the change is different. Defending itself against a rising bourgeoisie, the aristocracy is not shown anxious to plunge into the lower or middle class in the same carefree pursuit of love.

The continued rise of an urban civilization, which already changed the rustic disguise into the domestic one, made the middle class a source for the aristocracy, not of temporary freedom, but of money. In this climate the nobility no longer wishes to surrender its title but to use it as a means of barter, as in Dancourt's *Chevalier à la mode* (1687). There the *chevalier* can still attempt to procure for himself a wealthy marriage by using his title as bait. The noble Vanderk family of Sedaine's *Le Philosophe sans le savoir* (1765), however, is reduced to complete abdication of its title and position in favor of the material advantages of the mercantile middle class. Meanwhile the servant has become much more mobile and no longer serves simply as an extension of the master during his disguise. Le Sage's *Crispin rival de son maître* (1707) or his *Turcaret* (1709) are examples of the importance acquired by the servant as a being capable of his own transformation, not simply an *alter ego* of his master. Furthermore, the outward changes in characters' social position, like Turcaret's are not simply disguises. Social mobility is now a real change, not only a momentary departure from reality.

Footnotes

1. See the bibliography of the French dramatic pastoral established by Jules Marsan in *La Pastorale dramatique en France à la fin du XVIe siècle* (Paris: Hachette, 1905), pp. 504-517.

2. These genres are represented by plays like La Morelle's *Philine, ou l'amour contraire*, P (1630), de Coste's *Lizimène*, CP (1632), and J. B. Croisilles' *Chasteté invincible* (1633), a "bergerie en prose." See Marsan, *loc. cit.*

3. Among these plays are Le Hayer du Perron's *Les Heureuses Adventures*, TC (1633), Mareschal's *Lizidor ou la Cour bergère*, TC (1638), Pichou's *Folies de Cardénio*, TC (pub. 1634), Quinault's *Mariage de Cambise*, TC (1658), Beys' *Céline*, TC (1633).

4. René Rapin, *Dissertatio de Carmine pastorali* (1672). I have used Creech's translation: *Discourse upon Pastorals* (London: E. Curill, 1713).

5. *Ibid.*, p. 21.

6. Antonio Sebastian Minturno, *De Poeta* (Venice: Francescus Rampazetus, 1559), pp. 162-163.

7. Thomas Sebillet, *L'Art poétique françois*, ed. F. Gaiffe (Paris: STFM, 1910), p. 159.

8. George Puttenham, *The Arte of English Poesie* (1589), in *Ancient Critical Essays upon English Poets and Poësy*, ed. Joseph Haslewood (London: Robert Triphook, 1811), pp. 30-31 (we underline).

9. Pierre Ronsard, *Oeuvres complètes*, ed. G. Cohen (1950; rpt. Paris: Gallimard, Bibliothèque de la Pléiade, 1966), I, 917-947.

10. Bernard Le Bovier de Fontenelle, *Discours sur la nature de l'églogue* (Paris: M. Brunet, 1715), p. 176.

11. H. C. Lancaster, *A History of French Dramatic Literature in the Seventeenth Century*, I, 242 (we underline).

12. Fontenelle (p. 162) alludes to the advantage of the rustic world over the urban one because of the "peu de soins dont on y [in the shepherd world] est chargé . . . l'oisiveté dont on y jouït."

13. I have used the critical edition of Francis Bar (Genève: Droz, 1960). I treat Corneille's text without consideration of its source in Charles Sorel's novel of the same title (1627-1628). For a study of

Sorel's work see Burt Kay, "A Writer Turns Against Literature: Charles Sorel's *Le Berger Extravagant*," *Revue de l'Université d'Ottawa*, 43 (1973), 277-291.

14. Bar observes, with disarming understatement, in his introduction to Corneille's play, "C'est à propos de l'unité d'action que l'on peut faire des réserves. Elle n'existe guère en ce qui concerne Lysis, qui paraît, comme nous l'avons dit, dans une suite de tableaux peu liés entre eux. D'autre part, les amours des autres personnages n'ont avec lui que des rapports bien indirects, puisqu'il les ignore" (p. 27).

15. "Un ensemble de procédés artificiels, qui consiste à utiliser, suivant un dosage variable, un vocabulaire composite: ce vocabulaire mélange tous les tons du langage familier, jusqu'au plus 'bas'; il puise aux langues techniques comme aux idiomes étrangers et pratique largement l'archaïsme." Introduction to *Le Berger Extravagant*, p. 64. See also Bar's *Le Genre burlesque en France au XVII*ᵉ *siècle: étude de style.* Paris: D'Artrey, 1960.

16. See Bar's detailed annotation of sources.

17. This constitutes a supplementary exposure of the play as play since the scene in Brie is fused with the theatre in which such machines are available.

18. Michel Foucault, *Les Mots et les choses* (Paris: Gallimard, "Bibliothèque des sciences humaines," 1966), p. 63.

19. *Molière: une aventure théâtrale* (Paris: Gallimard, "Bibliothèque des Idées," 1963), p. 282.

20. *Ibid.*, p. 264.

21. Antoine Adam, *Histoire de la littérature française au XVII*ᵉ *siècle* (Paris: del Duca, 1962), III, 333-335.

22. Guicharnaud, pp. 298-299.

23. *Ibid.*, p. 334.

Conclusion

Prior to the work of Jean Rousset it was common to think of the early seventeenth-century text as a particularly misshapen, over-ornamented, and obscure version of what would later flower, after the linguistic pruning of Malherbe, into French classicism. Rousset's studies, along with those of several disciples, did much to demonstrate the wholeness of the baroque. Its literary form is justified by the general world-view that it expresses. Rather than attempting to set forth in an inappropriate form the world-view of the later decades of the century—a notion implicit in terms like "preclassicism"—the literature of the early 1600's conveys the world-view of a transitional period in aesthetics, logic, science, and social organization. The more recent and broader studies of Michel Foucault, tracing the general epistemological conditions of the period in *L'Histoire de la folie à l'âge classique* and in *Les Mots et les choses*, have argued that the apparently bizarre patterns of some seventeenth-century texts are the result of the survival or resurgence of an *epistémé* that had become obsolete.

Les Mots et les choses reveals in particular the passage from an epistemology of resemblance to an epistemology of difference and sameness. Where medieval and renaissance man had seen a world of almost unlimited similarity—in almost everything there was something that could be interpreted as recalling, calling to, or imitating everything else in the world—modern man looks for difference. With the advent of a nominalist and mathematically oriented world-view, the structure of the world became fixed in categories available to manipulation and calculation. Complex things could be decomposed into their constituent elements, and then these elements, rather than the wholes, compared. These elements could be shown individually to be either identical—hence, interchangeable—or different. The comparison of the wholes would be made only as a result of the comparison of the elements, one of the basic methodological tenets of Descartes.

The literary text can serve as an intermediary to facilitate passage between conflicting world-views. It is not bound to the norms of rationalism and can seek an aesthetic union of contradictory perceptions. The well-known preoccupation with madness in the theatre of the period can be explained in part at least as the survival of a world in which madness was not yet institutionalized. The theatre indulges the fascination of obsolete conducts—madness—while enclosing them in a framework of normalcy. The creation of hospitals under Louis XIV (edict of 1656) similarly provided a social structure into which the poor and the mad could be placed. Foucault has also shown that the madman is he who sees resemblance everywhere (*cf.* the Lysis of Thomas Corneille's *Berger Extravagant* in our Chapter V). There is thus a link between the thematics of resemblance, and the rhetoric of resemblance, best exemplified by the metaphor, source of one of the major literary quarrels of the second third of the seventeenth century.

The disguise or confusion of identity is in some ways an overflow of resemblance into social conduct and hence into plot structure. Not restricted to the mad, ignorance of exact identity creates or recreates situations preventing classification into rigid orders of identity and difference. In a sense disguise permits protagonists to act in a way that would otherwise be considered mad, and it draws into this aberrant conduct the other characters of the dramatic world. It is not surprising that the themes of identity confusion and madness should flourish at the same period and so frequently be side by side in a single work.

But madness and disguise both have their method. The study of disguise in the theatre of the early seventeenth century shows that the drama does more than adopt at random or with mechanical regularity and indifference this plot element. The theatre does systematize the possibility of confusion of identity within the social system of the period in an exhaustive way, that is, it uses all of the given identity elements of its time and combines them in all of the conceivable ways—the woman as man, the man as woman, the king as commoner, the commoner as king, and so on. But within each of these disguises there is a specific pattern of conduct, such as the triadic relationships in woman's disguise and the dyadic ones in man's disguise, that seems to represent certain patterns of fantasy available to the period.

The particular enthusiasm with which the authors and public of 1630-1660 greeted the theatre of disguise could be seen as the expression of conflicts between changing orders of identity that resulted from the gradual degradation of the nobility both *d'épée* and *de robe*, consequent changes in sexual roles, and the need to retrace continuously the outlines of what constituted each of the forms of identity. The social function of art in transitional periods such as the early seventeenth century is in this sense a highly serious one, but a difficult one for later generations to perceive or accept in aesthetic terms. When the problems posed by social and intellectual movements change, what had been the aesthetic and emotive core of texts of one period becomes ornamentation (almost always described in pejorative terms) to another.

This social function is politically ambivalent, as we can see by comparing the theme of the valet's disguise as master with the depiction of the valet become master in a real social transformation. The regularity of the appearance of this theme of disguise promotes it to the level of a mythic tale. Seen in this light it shows suggestive analogies to the myth as described by Roland Barthes in the concluding remarks of *Mythologies*. Myth for Barthes is reactionary. It is a de-politicized language which arises when the contact with the world is that of the spectator, not that of the producer. The servant (as also in their turn the master, the woman, the man) is placed in this situation of spectatorship. His possible active modication of his state has been replaced by an illusory role and by the involuntary spectatorship of his own identity, assumed by his master. The result of the fictive transformation of identity, in the plays of the servant's disguise as in the others we have studied, is the final restoration of the established order. The final discovery serves to underline the inescapability of orthodox society and sexuality. The structures of works like *Célimène*, *Le Festin de Pierre*, and the *Berger extravagant* demonstrate the control exercised over the whole project of disguise by the male, the aristocrat, and the middle classes. The eighteenth-century theatre will demonstrate in even more direct ways (e.g. the recognitions of the *comédie larmoyante*) the conservative value of the reintegration of the unknown into middle-class identity.

Rotrou's *Célimène* opens this study in large part because of its attention to the fundamental codes by which identity is communicated. The theme of the false shepherd concludes our survey because it is this disguise that leads towards new preoccupations in the following century. In the form of the disguise of Don Juan, the disguise of rank had already shown a more explicit connection with the world of social reality than do the other disguises. In the Don Juan plays the social background is no longer a vague and conventional Arcadia, the exotic kingdoms of Argénis, the schematized great city of the masked woman.

The major revival of disguise plots in the eighteenth century in the work of Marivaux, Lesage, Voltaire, and their contemporaries is based on a reworking of the disguise of master and servant in the context of the real social transformation of the servant into master through the rise of the bourgeoisie. The use of disguise is thus more directly mimetic in the eighteenth century than it is in the early seventeenth century, where it constituted an imaginative creation of patterns of conduct which departed from the everyday workings of identity.

But for the generation of Rotrou and Corneille, and for the audiences of the early years of Molière, the theatre functioned not as an exposition of a verisimilar transformation of the social order, but, on the contrary, as a place where the unlikely and impossible were contained and exposed. Here Jean Rousset's comparisons between baroque literature and fine arts are especially enlightening. Like the architectural and scenic perspectives in *trompe l'oeil* and the ubiquitous mirror imagery of the period, the disguises of the theatre are framed in various ways and thus tamed. The characteristic lack of *vraisemblance* that was much criticized later in the century assures a necessary separation between theatre and life, thus permitting the extravagance of the theatre of disguise.

Bibliography

The publishing dates given are those of the editions I have used.

I. Plays Containing Episodes of Disguise

Anonymous. *Le Capitan*, C. Paris: A. Courbé, 1639.

————. *Les Adventures de Thyrsis*, TCP. Rouen: J. Cailloüé, 1639.

————. *La Juste Vengeance*, TC. Paris: A. Courbé, 1641.

————. *Persélide*, TC. Paris: A. Courbé, 1646.

————. *L'Amour combatuë*, poème dramatique. Lyons: P. Compagnon, 1652.

————. *La Fille généreuse*, TC. (1650?) Manuscript, Bibliothèque Nationale, fonds français no. 25489.

Auvray, Jean. *Dorinde*, TC. Paris: A. de Sommaville and A. Soubron, 1631.

————. *Madonte*, TC. Paris: A. de Sommaville, 1631.

Baro, Joseph. *Célinde*, poème héroïque. Paris: F. Pomeray, 1629.

————. *Parthénie*, TC. Paris: A. de Sommaville and A. Courbé, 1642.

————. *Clarimonde*, TC. Paris: A. de Sommaville and A. Courbé, 1643.

————. *Le Prince fugitif*, poème dramatique. Paris: A. de Sommaville, 1649.

————. *Cariste*, poème dramatique. Paris: A. de Sommaville, 1651.

Bazire d'Amblainville. *Arlette*, P. Paris: Roulet Boutonné, 1638.

Bénésin. *Luciane*, TCP. Poitiers: A Mourin, 1634.

Benserade, Isaac de. *Iphis et Iante*, C. Paris: A. de Sommaville, 1637.

————. *Gustaphe ou l'heureuse ambition*, TC. Paris: A. de Sommaville, 1637.

Beys, Charles. *L'Hospital des foux*, TC. Paris: T. Quinet, 1636.

————. *Céline ou les frères rivaux*, TC. Paris: T. Quinet, 1637.

Boisrobert, François Le Métel, abbé de. *Pyrandre et Lisimène*, TC. Paris: T. Quinet, 1633.

————. *Les Rivaux amis*, TC. Paris: A. Courbé, 1639.

—————. *Les Deux Alcandres,* TC. Paris: A. de Sommaville and T. Quinet, 1640.

—————. *La Vraye Didon ou la Didon chaste,* T. Paris: T. Quinet, 1643.

—————. *La Jalouse d'elle-mesme,* C. Paris: A. Courbé, 1650.

—————. *Les Trois Orontes,* C. Paris: A. Courbé, 1653.

—————. *La Folle Gageure,* C. Paris: A. Courbé, 1653.

—————. *Cassandre,* TC. Paris: A. Courbé, 1654.

—————. *L'Inconnue,* C. Paris: G. de Luyne, 1655.

—————. *Les Apparences trompeuses,* C. Paris: G. de Luyne, 1656.

—————. *Les Coups d'amour et de fortune,* TC. Paris: G. de Luyne, 1656.

—————. *La Belle Invisible,* C. Paris: G. de Luyne, 1656.

Boursault, Edme. *Les Cadenats,* C. Paris: Guignard, 1662.

de Bourzac. *L'Esclave couronnée,* TC. Paris: A. de Sommaville, 1638.

Boyer, Claude. *La Soeur généreuse,* TC. Paris: A. Courbé, 1647.

—————. *Porus,* T. Paris: T Quinet, 1648.

—————. *Aristodème,* T. Paris: T. Quinet, 1649.

—————. *Tyridate,* T. Paris: T. Quinet, 1649.

—————. *Fédéric,* TC. Paris: C. de Sercy, 1660.

Bridard. *Uranie,* TCP. Paris: J. Martin, 1631.

Brosse (the elder). *Les Innocens coupables,* C. Paris: A. de Sommaville, A. Courbé, T. Quinet, and N. de Sercy, 1645.

—————. *Les Songes des hommes esveillez,* C. Paris: N. de Sercy, 1646.

—————. *Le Turne de Virgile,* T. Paris: Vve N. de Sercy, 1647.

—————. *L'Aveugle clairvoyant,* C. Paris: T. Quinet, 1650.

Chabrol, Claude. *Orizelle ou les Extrêmes mouvements d'amour,* TC. Paris: M. Colombel, 1633.

Chappuzeau, Samuel. *Damon et Pythias,* TC. Amsterdam: J. Ravesteyn, 1657.

—————. *Armetzar,* TC. Leyden: J. Elsevier, 1658.

—————. *Le Cercle des femmes,* Entretiens comiques. Lyons: Duhan, 1656.

Chevreau, Urbain. *L'Avocat duppé,* C. Paris: T. Quinet, 1637.

les Cinq Auteurs. *La Comédie des Tuileries,* C. Paris: A. Courbé, 1638.

—————. *L'Aveugle de Smyrne,* TC. Paris: A. Courbé, 1638.

Corneille, Pierre. *Théâtre complet,* ed. Maurice Rat. Paris: Classiques Garnier, n.d.

Corneille, Thomas. *L'Amour à la Mode,* C. Rouen: L. Maurry; Paris: G. de Luyne, 1653.

—————. *Le Berger extravagant,* C. Paris: A. de Sommaville, 1656.

————. *Le Geôlier de soi-même*, C. Rouen: L. Maurry pour A. Courbé, 1656.

————. *Les Engagements du hasard*, C. Rouen: L. Maurry; Paris: G. de Luyne, 1657.

————. *Timocrate*, T. Rouen and Paris: A. Courbé and G. de Luyne, 1658.

————. *Le Charme de la voix*, C. Rouen and Paris: A. Courbé and G. de Luyne, 1658.

————. *Bérénice*, T. Rouen and Paris: A. Courbé and G. de Luyne, 1659.

————. *Darius*, T. Paris: A. Courbé and G. de Luyne, 1659.

————. *Le Galant doublé*, C. Rouen and Paris: A. Courbé and G. de Luyne, 1660.

————. *Pyrrhus, roi d'Epire*, T. Paris: G. Quinet, 1665.

Croisac, de. *Méliane*, P (1653-1654?). MS in Bibliothèque Nationale, fonds français No. 25497.

D'Alibray, Vion. *Aminte*, P. Paris: P. Rocolet, 1632.

————. *Le Torrismon*, T. Paris: D. Houssaye, 1636.

————. *Soliman*, TC. Paris: T. Quinet, 1637.

Desaci (le jeune). *Les Travaux amoureux du marquis de la Rotonde, gentilhomme de la nouvelle fabrique*, C. Amsterdam: 1660.

Desfontaines, Nicolas-Marc. *Eurimédon ou l'illustre corsaire*, TC. Paris: A. de Sommaville, 1637.

————. *Orphise ou la Beauté persécutée*, TC. Paris: A. de Sommaville, 1638.

————. *Hermogène*, TC. Paris: T. Quinet, 1639.

————. *Bélisaire*, TC. Paris: A. Courbé, 1641.

————. *Le Martyr de Saint Eustache*, T. Paris: T. Quinet and N. de Sercy, 1643.

————. *Alcidiane ou les quatre rivaux*, TC. Paris: T. Quinet and N. de Sercy, 1644.

————. *La Véritable Sémiramis*, T. Paris: P. Lamy, 1647.

————. *L'Illustre Olympie ou le Saint Alexis*, T. Paris: P. Lamy, 1648.

Desmarets de Saint Sorlin, Jean. *Mirame*, TC. H. le Gras, 1641.

————. *Erigone*, TC. Paris: H. le Gras, 1642.

————. *Scipion*, TC. Paris: H. le Gras, 1647.

Dorimond, (Nicolas Drouin). *La Rosélie*, C. Paris: J. Ribou, 1661.

————. *L'Inconstance punie*, C. Paris: G. Quinet, 1661.

————. *La Femme industrieuse*, C. Paris: G. Quinet, 1661.

————. *L'Amant de sa femme*, C. Paris: G. Quinet, 1661.

————. *Le Festin de Pierre*, TC. Paris: E. Loyson, 1665.

d'Ouville, Antoine Le Métel, sieur. *L'Esprit folet*, C. Paris: T. Quinet, 1642.

————. *Les Fausses Véritéz*, C. Paris: T. Quinet, 1643.

————. *La Dame suivante*, C. Paris: T. Quinet, 1645.

————. *Les Morts vivants*, TC. Paris: C. Besongne, 1646.

————. *La Coiffeuse à la mode*, C. Paris: T. Quinet, 1647.

————. *Aymer sans sçavoir qui*, C. Paris: C. Besongne, 1647.

Du Cros, Simon. *Fillis de Scire*, P. Paris: A. Courbé, 1630.

Du Fayot. *La Nouvelle Stratonice*, C. Paris: C. de Sercy, 1657.

Du Rocher, R.-M. *L'Indienne amoureuse ou l'heureux naufrage*, TC. 1631; rpt. Paris: J. Corrozet, 1635.

————. *La Mélize ou les Princes reconnus*, PC. 1634; rpt. Paris: J. Corrozet, 1639.

Durval, I. J. *Agarite*, TC. Paris: F. Targa, 1636.

————. *Panthée*, T. Paris: C. Besongne, 1639.

Du Ryer, Pierre. *Argénis et Poliarque ou Théocrine*, TC. Paris: N. Bessin, 1630.

————. *Argénis, deuxième journée*, TC. Paris: Vve N. Bessin, 1631.

————. *Lisandre et Caliste*, TC. Paris: P. David, 1632.

————. *Alcimédon*, TC. Paris: A. de Sommaville, 1635.

————. *Cléomédon*, TC. Paris: A. de Sommaville, 1636.

————. *Clarigène*, TC. Paris: A. de Sommaville, 1639.

————.. *Bérénice*, TC. Paris: A. de Sommaville and A. Courbé, 1645.

————. *Clitophon*, TC. MS in Bibliothèque Nationale, fonds français 25496.

Du Vieuget. *Policandre et Basolie*, T. Paris: P. Billaine, 1632.

Frénicle, Nicolas. *La Fidelle bergère*, CP. Paris: J. Dugast, 1634.

Gilbert, Gabriel. *Marquerite de France*, TC. Paris: A. Courbé, 1641.

————. *Téléphonte*, TC. Paris: T. Quinet, 1642.

————. *Chresphonte*, TC. Paris: G. de Luyne, 1659.

Gillet de la Tessonerie. *Francion*, C. Paris: T. Quinet, 1642.

————. *Le Campagnard*, C. Rouen: G. de Luyne, 1657.

Gombauld. *Amaranthe*, P. Paris: F. Pomeray, 1631.

Gougenot. *La Fidelle tromperie*, TC. Paris: A. de Sommaville, 1633.

————. *Comédie des comédiens*, TC. Paris: P. David, 1633.

Grandchamp. *Les Avantures amoureuses d'Omphale*, TC. Paris: Vve P. Chevalier, 1630.

Guérin de Bouscal, Guyon. *Doranise*, TCP. Paris: C. Cramoisy, 1634.

————. *Dom Quixote de la Manche*, C. Paris: T. Quinet, 1640.

————. *Le Fils désadvoüé*, TC. Paris: A. de Sommaville, 1642.

Jacquelin. *Soliman ou l'Esclave généreuse*, T. Paris: C. de Sercy, 1653.

La Barre, de. *Clénide*, TCP. Paris: T. Quinet, 1634.

La Calprenède, Gautier de Costes de. *Bradamante*, TC. Paris: A. de Sommaville, 1637.

La Caze. *Cammane*, T. Paris: A. de Sommaville, 1641.

La Fontaine, Jean de. *L'Eunuque*, C. *Oeuvres diverses*, ed. Pierre Clarac; Paris: Gallimard, Bibliothèque de la Pléiade, 1958.

Lambert. *La Magie sans magie*, C. Paris: C. de Sercy, 1661.

————. *Les Soeurs jalouses ou l'escharpe et le brasselet*, C. Paris: C. de Sercy, 1661.

La Mesnardière, Hippolyte Pilet de. *Alinde*, T. Paris: A. de Sommaville, 1642.

La Morelle. *Philine ou l'amour contraire*, P. Paris: M. Collet, 1630.

La Serre, Puget de. *Pandoste*, T. Paris: Pierre Billaine, 1631. ‹

————. *Climène*, TC. Paris: A. de Sommaville and A. Courbé, 1643.

————. *Thésée ou le Prince reconnu*, TC. Paris: A. de Sommaville, A. Courbé, T. Quinet, and C. de Sercy, 1644.

La Tour, de. *Isolite*, TC. (1630?) Manuscript, Arsenal, MS3087.

Le Hayer du Perron. *Heureuses adventures*, TC. Paris: A. de Sommaville, 1633.

L'Estoile, François de. *La Belle esclave*, TC. Paris: P. Moreau, 1643.

Le Vert. *Le Docteur amoureux*, C. Paris: A. Courbé, 1638.

————. *Aricidie ou le mariage de Tite*, TC. Rouen and Paris: T. Quinet, 1646.

Magnon, Jean. *Josaphat*, TC. Paris: T. Quinet, 1647.

————. *Le Grand Tamerlan et Bajazet*, T. Paris: T. Quinet, 1648.

————. *Tite*, TC. Paris (no publisher given): 1660.

Mairet, Jean. *Chryséide et Arimand*, TC. Paris: J. Besongne, 1630.

————. *La Virginie*, TC. Paris: P. Rocolet, 1635.

————. *Les Galanteries du duc d'Ossonne*, C. Paris: P. Rocolet, 1636.

————. *Marc-Antoine*, T. Paris: A. de Sommaville, 1637.

————. *Solyman ou la Mort de Mustapha*, T. Paris: A. Courbé, 1639.

————. *L'Illustre corsaire*, TC. Paris: A. Courbé, 1640.

————. *Sidonie*, TC héroïque. Paris: A. de Sommaville and A. Courbé, 1643.

Marcassus, Pierre. *L'Eromène*, P. Paris: P. Rocolet, 1633.

————. *Les Pescheurs illustres* (no genre given). Paris: G. Sassier, 1648.

Mareschal, André. *La Généreuse allemande*, TC. Paris: P. Rocolet, 1631.

――――. *La Soeur valeureuse ou l'Aveugle amante*, TC. Paris: A. de Sommaville, 1634.

――――. *L'Inconstance d'Hylas*, TCP. Paris: F. Targa, 1635.

――――. *Le Véritable capitan Matamore*, C. Paris: T. Quinet, 1640.

――――. *Lizidor ou la Cour bergère*, TC. Paris: T. Quinet, 1640.

――――. *Le Jugement équitable de Charles le Hardy*, T. Paris: T. Quinet, 1645.

Molière (Jean Baptiste Poquelin). *Oeuvres complètes*, ed. Maurice Rat. Paris: Gallimard, Bibliothèque de la Pléiade, 1956.

Montauban, Jacques Pousset de. *Zénobie*, T. Paris: G. de Luyne, 1653.

――――. *Le Comte de Hollande*, TC. Paris: G. de Luyne, 1654.

――――. *Les Charmes de Félicie*, P. Paris: G. de Luyne, 1654.

Montfleury (Zacharie Jacob). *Le Mariage de Rien*, C. Paris: G. de Luyne, 1660.

Montgaudier. *Natalie* (no genre given). Paris: C. Calleville, 1654.

Nicole, Claude. *Le Phantosme*, C. Paris: C. de Sercy, 1656.

Pascal, Françoise. *Amoureux extravagant*, C. Lyons: S. Matheret, 1657.

――――. *Sésostris*, TC. Lyons: A. Offray, 1661.

P. B. (Passard?) *Cléonice ou l'amour téméraire*, TCP. Paris: N. Rousset and J. Martin, 1630.

Pichou, Claude. *L'Infidèle confidante*, TC. Paris: F. Targa, 1631.

――――. *La Filis de Scire*, CP. Paris: F. Targa, 1631.

――――. *Les Folies de Cardénio*, TC. Paris: C. Marette, 1634.

Prades, Jean le Royer de. *Annibal*, TC. Paris: P. Targa, 1649.

Provais. *L'Innocent exilé*, TC. Paris: A. de Sommaville, 1640.

Quenel, Léon. *Sélidore*, TCP. Rouen: R. Malassis, 1639.

Quinault, Philippe. *Les Coups de l'Amour et de la Fortune*, TC. Paris: G. de Luyne, 1655.

――――. *La Généreuse ingratitude*, TCP. Paris: T. Quinet, 1657.

――――. *La Comédie sans comédie*, C. Paris: G. de Luyne, 1657.

――――. *Le Feint Alcibiade*, TC. 1658; rpt. Amsterdam: 1660.

――――. *Le Fantôme amoureux*, TC. 1657; rpt. "Suivant la copie imprimée à Paris," 1662.

――――. *Le Mariage de Cambise*, TC. 1659; rpt. "Suivant la copie imprimée à Paris," 1662.

――――. *Les Rivales*, C. "Suivant la copie imprimée à Paris," 1662.

――――. *L'Amant indiscret ou le Maistre estourdi*, C. Amsterdam: A. Schelte, 1696.

Rampale, N. *Bélinde*, TC. Lyons: Pierre Drobet, 1630.

Rayssiguier. *Les Amours d'Astrée qui se déguise en berger*, TCP. Paris: N. Bessin, 1630.

————. *Aminte*, TCP. Paris: A. Courbé, 1632.

————. *La Bourgeoise*, TC. Paris: P. Billaine, 1633.

————. *La Célidée sous le nom de Calirie*, TC. Paris: T. Quinet, 1635.

Richemont-Banchereau. *Les Passions égarées ou le Roman du temps*, TC. Paris: C. Collet, 1632.

Rotrou, Jean. *Oeuvres*, ed. Viollet-le-Duc. Paris: Th. Desoer, 1820.

Sallebray. *L'Amante ennemie*, TC. Paris: A. de Sommaville and A. Courbé, 1642.

————. *La Belle Egyptienne*, TC. Paris: A. de Sommaville and A. Courbé, 1642.

Scarron, Paul. *Jodelet ou le Maître-valet*, C. Paris: T. Quinet, 1646.

————. *Les Trois Dorothées ou Jodelet souffleté*, C. Paris: T. Quinet, 1650.

————. *L'Héritier ridicule*, C. Paris: T. Quinet, 1650.

————. *Dom Japhet d'Arménie*, C. Paris: A. Courbé, 1654.

————. *Escolier de Salamanque*, TC. Amsterdam: R. Smith, 1656.

————. *La Fausse Apparence*, C. Paris: G. de Luyne, 1663.

————. *Le Marquis ridicule ou la Comtesse faite à la haste*, C. Paris: J. P. Loyson, 1670.

————. Le Gardien de soi-même, C. Paris: G. de Luyne, 1688.

————. *Prince Corsaire*, TC. Paris: M. David, 1696. Scudéry, Georges de. *Ligdamon et Lidias, ou la ressemblance*, TC. Paris: F. Targa, 1631.

————. *Le Prince déguisé*, TC. 1636. ed. B. Matulka. New York: Institute of French Studies, Columbia University, 1929.

————. *Le Vassal généreux*, TC. Paris: A. Courbé, 1636.

————. *Le Fils supposé*, C. Paris: A. Courbé, 1636.

————. *Amour tyrannique*, TC. Paris: A. Courbé, 1639.

————. *Eudoxe*, TC. Paris: A. Courbé, 1641.

————. *Orante*, TC. Paris: A. Courbé, 1659 (sur l'imprimé).

Somaize, A. Baudeau de. *Véritables prétieuses*, C. Paris: J. Ribou, 1660.

————. *Procèz des Prétieuses*, C. Paris: E. Loyson, 1660.

————. *Prétieuses ridicules*, C. Paris: E. Loyson, 1661.

Tristan L'Hermite, François. *Amaryllis (de Rotrou)*, P. Paris: A. de Sommaville and A. Courbé, 1653.

————. *Le Parasite*, C. Paris: A. Courbé, 1654.

Vallée. *La Fidelle Esclave*, C. Paris: P. Rocolet, 1659.

Verronneau. *L'Impuissance*, TCP. Paris: T. Quinet, 1634.

II. Critical, Historical, and Theoretical Works

Aristotle. *Poetics.* Trans. Gerald F. Else. Ann Arbor: University of Michigan Press, 1967.

Artaud, Antonin. *Le Théâtre et son double.* 1938; rpt. Paris: Gallimard, Collection des Idées, 1964.

Aubignac, François Hédelin, abbé d'. *La Pratique du théâtre* (1657). Ed. Pierre Martino. Algiers: Jules Carbonel, 1927.

Bar, Francis. *Le Berger extravagant* of Thomas Corneille, critical edition with introduction. Geneva: Droz, 1960.

————. *Le Genre burlesque en France au XVIIe siècle. Etude de style.* Paris: d'Artrey, 1960.

Barthes, Roland, *Mythologies.* Paris: Le Seuil, 1957.

————. *S/Z.* Paris: Le Seuil, 1970.

————. *Le Plaisir du texte.* Paris: Le Seuil, 1973.

Blin, Georges. "Notes pour une Erotique du Rire." *Cahiers de la Pléiade,* Spring 1950, pp. 129-135.

Boorsch, Jean. "Remarques sur la technique dramatique de Corneille." *Studies by Members of the French Department of Yale University.* Yale Romanic Studies, XVIII (1941), 101-162.

————. "L'Invention chez Corneille: comment Corneille ajoute à ses sources." *Essays in Honor of Albert Feuillerat.* Yale Romanic Studies, XXII (1943), 115-128.

Boussuet, Jacques-Bénigne. *Maximes et réflexions sur la comédie.* Ed. Ch. Urbain et E. Levesque, *L'Eglise et le Théâtre.* Paris: Grasset, 1930.

Bowen, Barbara C. *Les Caractéristiques essentielles de la farce française et leur survivance dans les années 1550-1620.* Illinois Studies in Language and Literature, 53. Urbana: University of Illinois Press, 1964.

Brasillach, Robert. *Corneille.* Paris: Arthème Fayard, 1938.

Bravo-Villasante, Carmen. *La Mujer vestida de hombre en el teatro español (siglos XVI-XVII).* Madrid: Revista de Occidente, 1955.

Bullough, Edward. "'Psychical Distance' as a factor in Art and an Aesthetic Principle," *British Journal of Psychology,* V (part 2, June 1912), 85-118.

Castelvetro, Ludovico. *Poetica d'Aristotele vulgarizzata e sposta.* Second edition. Bâle: Pierre de Sédabon, 1576.

Cherpack, Clifton. *The Call of Blood in French Classical Tragedy.* Baltimore: The Johns Hopkins Press, 1958.

Couton, Georges. *Corneille et la Fronde.* Publications de la Faculté des Lettres de l'Université de Clermont, fascicule 4. Clermont, 1951.

Culler, Jonathan. *Structuralist Poetics.* Ithaca, New York: Cornell University Press, 1975.

Dars, Emile, and Benoit, Jean-Claude. *L'Expression scénique.* Paris: Editions Sociales Françaises, 1964.

Deierkauf-Holsboer, S. Wilma. *L'Histoire de la mise en scène dans le théâtre français de 1600 à 1657.* Paris: Droz, 1933.

Delcourt, Marie. *La Tradition des comiques anciens en France avant Molière.* Bibliothèque de la Faculté de Philosophie et des Lettres de l'University de Liège, fascicule LIX. Paris: Droz, 1934.

Doubrovsky, Serge. *Corneille et la dialectique du héros.* Paris: Gallimard, 1963.

Duvignaud, Jean. *L'Acteur, esquisse d'une sociologie du comédien.* Paris: Gallimard, 1965.

—————. *Sociologie du théâtre: Essai sur les ombres collectives.* Paris: Presses Universitaires de France, 1965.

Ehrmann, Jacques. *Un Paradis désespéré: l'amour et l'illusion dans l'Astrée.* Paris: Institut d'Etudes françaises de Yale, 1963.

Ellis, John M. *The Theory of Literary Criticism: A Logical Analysis.* Berkeley: University of California Press, 1974.

Empson, William. *Some Versions of Pastoral.* London: Chatto and Windus, 1935.

Fagniez, Gustave. *La Femme et la Société française dans la première moitié du XVIIᵉ siècle.* Paris: J. Gamber, 1929.

Faguet, Emile. *En lisant Corneille.* Paris: Hachette, 1913.

Fontenelle, Bernard Le Bovier de. *Discours sur la nature de l'églogue.* Paris: M. Brunet, 1715.

Frazer, Sir James George. *The Golden Bough.* Abridged edition, 1940; rpt. New York: The Macmillan Company, 1963.

Freud, Sigmund. *Jokes and Their Relation to the Unconscious.* Trans. James Strachey. New York: W. W. Norton, 1963.

Genette, Gérard. *Figures* II. Paris: Le Seuil, 1969.

Gerhardt, Mia I. *Essai d'analyse littéraire de la pastorale.* Assen: Van Gorcum, 1950.

Girard, René. *Mensonge romantique et vérité romanesque.* Paris: Bernard Grasset, 1961.

Goldman, Lucien. *Le Dieu caché.* 1959; rpt. Paris: Gallimard, 1967.

Guichardnaud, Jacques. *Molière, une aventure théâtrale.* 1963; rpt. Paris: Gallimard, 1968.

Hubert, J. D. "Le réel et l'illusoire dans le théâtre de Corneille et dans celui de Rotrou." *Revue des Sciences Humaines,* XCV (JulySeptember, 1958), 333-350.

Jarry, Jules. *Essai sur les oeuvres dramatiques de Jean Rotrou.* Lille: L. Quarré, n.d.

Jeffery, Brian. *French Renaissance Comedy, 1552-1630.* Oxford: Clarendon Press, 1969.

Jones, Ernest. *Hamlet and Œdipus.* 1949; rpt. New York; Anchor Books, 1954.

Knutson, Harold C. *The Ironic Game: A Study of Rotrou's Comic Theater.* University of California Publications in Modern Philology, 79. Berkeley and Los Angeles: University of California Press, 1966.

————. "Le dénouement heureux dans la tragédie française du XVII ͤ siècle." *Zeitschrift fur Fransösiche Sprache und Literatur,* 77 (1967), 338-346.

Kris, Ernst. *Psychoanalytic Explorations in Art.* New York: International Universities Press, 1952.

La Mesnardière, Jules de. *La Poétique.* Paris: Antoine de Sommaville, 1639.

Lancaster, Henry Carrington. *A History of French Dramatic Literature in the Seventeenth Century.* 9 vols. Baltimore: The Johns Hopkins Press, 1929-1942.

Lanson, Gustave. *Esquisse d'une histoire de la tragédie française.* 2nd edition. Paris: H. Champion, 1927.

Lough, John. *Paris Theatre Audiences in the Seventeenth and Eighteenth Centuries.* London: Oxford University Press, 1957.

McKendrick, Malvina. *Woman and Society in the Spanish Drama of the Golden Age: A Study of the Mujer Varonil.* Cambridge: Cambridge University Press, 1974.

Marsan, Jules. *La Pastorale dramatique en France à la fin du XVI ᵉ et au commencement du XVII ᵉ siècle.* Paris: Hachette, 1905.

Matejka, Ladislav and Titunik, Irwin R., eds. *Semoitics of Art: Prague School Contributions.* Cambridge, Massachusetts: MIT Press, 1976.

Mauron, Charles. *Des Métaphores obsédantes au mythe personnel.* 1962; rpt. Paris: Corti, 1964.

————. *Psychocritique du genre comique.* Paris: Corti, 1964.

May, Georges. *Tragédie cornélienne, Tragédie racinienne.* Illinois studies in language and literature, v. 32, no. 4. Urbana: University of Illinois Press, 1948.

Minturno, Antonio Sebastiano. *De Poeta.* Venice: Franciscus Rampazetus, 1559.

Moore, Will G. *The Classical Drama of France.* Oxford: Oxford University Press, 1971.

Morel, Jacques, *Jean Rotrou, dramaturge de l'ambiguité.* Paris: Armand Colin, 1968.

Morissette, Bruce, "Structures de la sensibilité baroque dans le roman préclassique." *Cahiers de l'Association Internationale des Etudes françaises,* no. 11 (May 1959), 86-103.

Nelson, Robert J. *Corneille, his heroes and their worlds.* Philadephia: University of Pennsylvania Press, 1963.

————. *Immanence and Transcendence: The Theater of Jean Rotrou, 1609-1650.* Columbus: Ohio State University Press, 1969. Orlando, Francesco. *Rotrou: Dalla Tragicommedia alla Tragedia.* Torino: Bottega d'Erasmo, 1963.

Plato. *The Republic.* Trans. H. D. P. Lee. 1955; rpt. Baltimore: Penguin Books, 1968.

Puttenham, George. *The Arte of English Poesie* (1589) in *Ancient Critical Essays upon English Poets and Poësy.* Ed. Joseph Haslewood. London: Robert Triphook, 1811.

Rank, Otto. *Une Etude sur le double.* Trans. S. Lautman. Paris: Denoël et Steele, 1932.

Rapin, René. *Discourse upon Pastorals.* Trans. Creech. London: E. Curill, 1713.

Reiss, T. J. *Toward Dramatic Illusion: Theatrical Technique and Meaning from Hardy to Horace.* New Haven: Yale University Press, 1971.

Riddle, Lawrence M. *The Genesis and Sources of Pierre Corneille's Tragedies from Medée to Pertharite.* Baltimore: The Johns Hopkins Press, 1926.

Rousset, Jean. *La Littérature de l'âge baroque en France. Circé et le paon.* 1954; rpt. Paris: Corti, 1965.

————. *L'Intérieur et l'extérieur.* Paris: Corti, 1968.

Sakharoff, Micheline. *Le Héros, sa liberté et son efficacité de Garnier à Rotrou.* Paris: Nizet, 1967.

Schérer, Jacques. *La Dramaturgie Classique en France.* Paris: Nizet, 1950.

————. "Pour une sociologie des obstacles au mariage dans le théâtre français du XVII siècle," in *Dramaturgie et Société, XVI e et XVII e siècles,"* ed. Jean Jacquot. Paris: Publications du Centre National de Recherche Scientifique, 1968, I, 297-302.

Sebillet, Thomas. *L'Art poétique françois.* Ed. Félix Gaiffe. Paris: Société des Textes français modernes, 1910.

Souriau, Etienne. *Les Deux cent mille situations dramatiques.* Paris: Flammarion, 1950.

————. *Les Grands problèmes de l'esthétique théâtrale.* Paris: Centre de Documentation Universitaire, 1960.

Tallemant des Réaux, Gédéon. *Historiettes.* Ed. A. Adam. Paris: Editions de la Pléiade, 1960.

Tanquerey, F.-J. "Le Romanesque dans le théâtre de Corneille." *Revue des Cours et Conférences,* 1 ere série, XL (1938-1939), 57-68, 263-79, 373-82, 456-72, 625-46.

Van Baelen, Jacqueline. *Rotrou, le héros tragique et la révolte.* Paris: Nizet, 1965.